THE FOURTH R
FOR THE THIRD MILLENNIUM

Education in Religion and Values
for the Global Future

Edited by Leslie J. Francis, Jeff Astley
and Mandy Robbins

on behalf of

The International Seminar on Religious Education
and Values (ISREV)

LINDISFARNE
BOOKS

Published 2001 by
Lindisfarne Books
7/8 Lower Abbey Street
Dublin 1

Availble in the UK from:
Veritas Company (UK) Ltd
Lower Avenue
Leamington Spa
Warwickshire CV31 3NP

Lindisfarne Books is an imprint of Veritas Publications.

ISBN 1 85390 507 0

British Library Cataloguing
in Publication Data.
A catalogue record for
this book is available
from the British Library.

Cover design by Bill Bolger
Printed in the Republic of Ireland by
The Leinster Leader, Naas, County Kildare

Veritas books are printed on paper made from the wood pulp of
managed forests. For every tree felled, at least one tree is planted,
thereby renewing natural resources.

CONTENTS

PREFACE

It was a privilege to host the 1998 meeting of the International Seminar on Religious Education and Values in Wales. Nearly one hundred eminent researchers in the fields of religious education and values education met over a period of five days to debate and to shape the place of education in religion and values education for the global future of the third millennium.

When the participants returned to their various homes across the globe, the editors took up the challenge of selecting and developing ten key contributions from the seminar. We are grateful to the ten authors who have worked with us to bring this enterprise to fruition and to the many other contributors to the seminar who helped to shape thinking on these themes. We also wish to acknowledge our gratitude to those colleagues who worked so hard with us to make the seminar such a productive forum for the interchange of ideas: Ros Fane, Mike Fearn, Jane Lankshear, Clare Lankshear, Gareth Longden, Anne Rees and Mandy Williams-Potter. Mike Fearn has also worked with us on shaping the text and preparing the indexes. We would like to express our thanks to the staff of Veritas for their perceptive and professional guidance.

This volume represents the well-established collaboration that exists between the Welsh National Centre for Religious Education and the North of England Institute for Christian Education, two church-related foundations committed to research and development in religious education in schools and churches.

Leslie J. Francis
Jeff Astley
Mandy Robbins
September 2000

5

FOREWORD

John M. Hull

The International Seminar on Religious Education and Values (ISREV) is a group of researching and publishing religious educators who maintain regular contact in order to share ideas and to participate in joint projects. The seminar was formed in 1977 and met for the first time at the University of Birmingham School of Education in 1978. Since then the seminar has met in Schenectady, New York (1980), Eindhoven, Netherlands (1982), Kemptville, Ontario (1984), Dublin, Ireland (1986), Stoney Point, New York (1988), Humlebaek, Denmark (1990), Bamf, Alberta (1992), Gosla, Germany (1994), Los Angeles, California (1996), Carmarthen, Wales (1998) and Kiryat Anavim, Israel (2000). Originally the seminar consisted of about thirty-five persons. Now the seminar has grown to a membership of ninety-two, and has expanded from its original British/North American base to include scholars from twenty-five countries.

The meetings of the seminar provide a unique opportunity to examine trends in religious education worldwide, whether it be the new world religions syllabus of Norway, the developments in Hong Kong since incorporation into the Republic of China, or the curriculum in Namibia. The purpose of the seminar is to raise the quality of research into religious education, whether it be provided by the state or by religious communities, and to seek to influence the development of the subject in the various countries represented.

As we enter the third millennium, with boundless wealth for a few and increasing poverty for the many, with growth of co-operation between religions and at the same time continuing rivalry between religions, the role of religious education as a carrier of critical values and as a vital contributor to spirituality becomes still more important. The committee was therefore delighted when three members of the seminar, Leslie J. Francis, Jeff Astley and Mandy Robbins, offered to prepare for publication a selection of papers on the theme of the 1998 seminar. The present volume is the result of their work. I am proud to offer this volume to the religious education community, to teachers and administrators of the subject, to ministers of religion, to parents, and to all those who seek through an improved religious education to help build a world of justice and peace.

THE FOURTH R FOR
THE THIRD MILLENNIUM:
AN OVERVIEW

Jeff Astley

In England the basic educational curriculum has often been described as 'the three Rs', representing reading, (w)riting and (a)rithmetic. In this vein, both practical religious educators and scholarly students of the subject have referred to their own field as 'the fourth R', implying that religious education should have no less a priority in a young person's education than these other three fundamental foci of teaching and learning. Some three decades ago an influential report on religious education, produced by a Commission set up by the Church of England Board of Education and the National Society, was published under the title *The Fourth R*. In his preface Bishop Ian Ramsey (1970: xii), the Chairman of the Commission, wrote of his hope that the report would point the way forward to a view of religious education as:

> an activity which is sound in its intellectual basis, creative in its actual practice, and effective in its concern for maturity and fulfilment; an education which combines openness and commitment, exploration and conviction.

This ideal would be widely endorsed by the authors whose work has been selected for this volume. In publishing these chapters under the title *The Fourth R for the Third Millennium,* the editors intend to express the sense that religious education today can and should play a significant role in the education of children and youth, whether through the state's educational provision or through the work of the faith communities.

The contributors to the present collection operate in a wide variety of contexts, illustrating perspectives on religious education from

Britain, continental Europe, Australia and the United States of America. They do not always agree in their analyses of the educational issues at stake, nor in their proposals of how best to meet the needs of students while being true to the insights of religious tradition and experience. But they do all share our conviction that religious education can make a positive and much-needed contribution to education in this new millennium.

Jeff Astley's chapter proposes a particular view of the connection between religious education and scientific understanding. Although conflict has often marked the relationship between science and religion in the past, there are plausible arguments for holding that science is not ultimately opposed to religious spirituality or belief. Astley suggests ways in which education in religion may have a positive effect on students' attitudes towards, and understanding of, the values, conclusions, methodology and logic of the natural sciences. In particular, learning certain spiritual values can help pupils identify and respond to the undergirding values of the scientist, and some appreciation of the complex epistemological structure and social setting of religious belief-systems can alert the learner to similar phenomena in the philosophy and phenomenology of science. Where conflicts between science and religion do arise, a good religious education can help students to tread their way through the warring factions to a perspective that offers a more peaceful synthesis, or at least a truce that will allow the possibility of dialogue. It may even aid the development of a holistic understanding that incorporates science while drawing on religious spirituality, so that the world of nature that is explained by science 'may become again a home where our hearts may rest'.

Leslie J. Francis adopts an empirical perspective on the significance of religious education in his chapter, in challenging the sociological assumption that religion itself has been privatised and marginalised in the modern world. His own work on adolescents shows, to the contrary, that religion persists as an important predictor of adolescent values. Drawing on studies that stress the importance of self-assigned religious affiliation, Francis examines the views of thirty thousand adolescents in British schools, so as to test the hypothesis that religious affiliation can help to explain individual differences in social attitudes.

Focusing attention on a number of personal, family and social values, ranging from a sense of purpose in life to a concern for the environment, Francis presents data that reveal a number of statistically significant differences, not only between the views of those who belong to a faith group and those who do not, but also between adolescents from Christian and non-Christian faith groups, and within those faith groupings themselves. He concludes that religion remains a significant social influence in the modern world, even among young people. This claim is of considerable interest for discussions of the context and consequences of religious education.

J. Mark Halstead draws our attention to the long and contentious debate over the legal requirement for a daily act of collective worship in schools in England and Wales. He first reviews the strong arguments, based on the assumptions of a liberal education, against this practice and the counter-arguments they have generated. He then turns for illumination to the work of the French postmodernist social theorist, Jean Baudrillard, particularly his understanding of 'simulation' as removing the difference between the real and the imaginary. From a postmodernist perspective, Halstead argues that collective worship may most appropriately be reconceptualised as 'simulated worship': 'it no longer involves a conscious imitation of the public worship that goes on in churches, but has taken on a life of its own'. While such an understanding can more readily resist the liberal arguments arraigned against school worship, it does face other criticisms, including the claim that this sort of worship no longer has any reference to any reality outside itself. Halstead concludes with some reflections from a Baudrillardian perspective on possible new approaches to school worship and the difficulties they face.

Brian V. Hill explores the relevance of religious education for modern youth, for whom social reality is largely constructed by the commercial media and the Internet, 'a youth cohort the like of which has never been seen before'. He addresses the widening credibility gap between contemporary youth and religious educators and reviews some revisionist attempts to close the gap, for example, by an emphasis on global ethics or intuitions of transcendence, or by rewriting 'the fourth R' in terms of the 'S' of spirituality. While acknowledging some positive aspects in these proposals, Hill argues that such attempts fail to connect at anything more than a superficial level with the consciousness of modern youth. They also ignore recent resurgent trends in world religions, particularly those marked by more moderate, non-fundamentalist 'renewalists'. Hill concludes by suggesting some ways to re-establish connections between religious education and young people by focusing on their own religious life-worlds, helping them to interrogate their cultural conditioning, and engaging them in dialogue and values negotiation, seeking always to transcend self-centredness for the sake of society and the environment. Christian educators should also overhaul the worship and governing structures of their churches if they want 'to meet an egalitarian and electronic generation on its own ground'.

Mary Elizabeth Mullino Moore argues that educational theory and practice need to be informed by, and to engage people with, the rich diversity of the world, for 'the very richness of creation is a source of revelation and guidance for educational practice'. She rehearses the 'cries of pain' emanating from our neglected planet and some of its neglected people, before drawing on personal experience of a particular situation in which both organised and spontaneous diversity led to a positive, unifying outcome and revealed a world where respect is possible. Interpreting respect epistemologically and educationally, Moore argues the educational case for respect for particularity, respect for nature and its delicately balanced eco-systems, and 'respect for the value of every being to the whole'. To these ends, a number of educational approaches are commended: 'dancing with difference', 'diving into conflict' (by facing together into differences), seeking convergence (rather than just resolving conflict or relying on processes of enculturation or assimilation), building communities and encouraging meaningful action.

Eleanor Nesbitt's contribution is concerned with the way in which faith traditions are represented in religious education. Taking the example of the characterisation of Sikhism in syllabuses and curricular materials in Britain, Nesbitt traces the divergence between, on the one hand, the curriculum writers' understanding both of key terms from the tradition and of the nature of Sikh identity, and, on the other, the insights provided by her own ethnographic studies. She discusses the role of Sikhs themselves in influencing educational material and some of the problems of translation and linguistic usage, recognising that such factors raise questions of relevance to those who teach about the religion. Nesbitt continues by widening her discussion to challenge the popular understanding of 'world faiths' as discrete, reified religions. Ethnographic research, by contrast, lends weight to a deconstruction of religious boundaries, particularly as we move into the third millennium. She concludes with an analysis of the different ways in which ethnography can contribute to the articulation of faith traditions in religious education for a multifaith society.

Friedrich Schweitzer's chapter confronts the challenges posed by supranational and global developments. 'Globalisation', understood as a cultural rather than merely an economic phenomenon, and exemplified by the worldwide dimension of modern consumer culture, transport and the mass media, implies a new situation for religious education. Although globalisation itself has religious roots, its main effects have been a relativisation of religion (with religious traditions appearing increasingly arbitrary and losing their status and authority), the sequestration of experience (as abstract systems develop that leave no space for moral and existential experience), and the consequent privatisation of religion. Fundamentalism is often the religious response, but Schweitzer draws on accounts of an alternative future for religion in which it may still play a public role, and describes religious, theological, moral and societal visions that seek to provide a more adequate response to the problems of globalisation. After exploring European unification, as a concrete example of supranational development that presents both challenges and possibilities for the development of religious education theory and practice, Schweitzer details what globalisation means for religious education. His analysis includes an underscoring of the centrality of its ecumenical and interreligious dimensions; the need for confessional religious education to incorporate dialogue with other religious traditions and truth claims; and the recognition both of the importance of a public role for religion and of the challenge of religious fundamentalism (described as 'a misguided response to globalisation . . . based on understandable motives'). Religious education research and reflection must themselves become more international and more political in order to respond to the challenge.

Heinz Streib concentrated on the issue of religious fundamentalism in his research project on Christian fundamentalist converts and deconverts. The project employed qualitative research, reconstructing the biographies of subjects from the data provided by narrative interviews. Streib's chapter here presents two cases from this research: that of the twenty-one-year-old female deconvert (Sarah), and the example of a forty-eight-year-old male (Thomas) for whom conversion is 'a repeated experience of getting deeply involved'. The research project as a whole showed that, while there was no single typical 'sect biography', three main types of fundamentalist careers may be identified, including 'accumulative heretics' such as Thomas 'whose biographies are a tour through different religious orientations'. Such people develop more easily into progressive transformation than do those born into a fundamentalist grouping. Streib then seeks to explore fundamentalism from the standpoint both of modernity and of cognitive developmental psychology. Describing religious development in terms of a cumulative sequence of styles rather than of stages, he identifies one style (the 'reciprocal instrumental') as characteristic of fundamentalism. The chapter concludes with some pastoral and educational reflections on appropriately sensitive forms of religious education for the fundamentalist student, including the promotion of 'playful ease', 'acquaintance with diversity' and 'aesthetic adventure'.

Andrew Wright is concerned to explore the contribution of liberal religious education to the well-being of liberal society. He begins by sketching the contours of liberalism through an analysis of its core values, which he traces back to John Locke: individual liberty, equality of respect, consistent rationality and 'intolerance-of-intolerance'. This leads to an account of how religious education has developed in the context of modern liberal society, both with regard to its exclusion from public education (as an expression of freedom of belief) in some states and its inclusion in others. The latter situation often demands that religious education take a non-confessional form, as a 'neutral presentation of religion' tempered with the cultivation of an openness to spiritual experience. This is taken to express public tolerance of religious pluralism and an endorsement of personal freedom, along with 'the liberal commitment to reason through the development of public religious literacy'. However, there are difficulties with liberal religious education, in particular its tendency to bypass questions of theological truth, with a consequent undermining of the distinctive claims not only of religious traditions but also of their secular critiques. Wright argues that the 'liberal expression of exclusive non-liberal truth claims' does not allow non-liberal religious representations a fair hearing, and 'paradoxically ignores the liberal commitment to reasoned debate and instead moves prematurely towards a process of repression and censorship'. Drawing on an alternative soft pragmatic version of liberalism (as an interim political ethic or procedural virtue, rather than a comprehensive, substantive worldview), Wright maintains that we should highlight the principle of rational debate, 'turning to the repression of intolerance only as a final resort'. He believes that in this way religious education can best serve liberal democracy, by developing a religiously literate society in which the value of reason takes precedence over an opposition to religious intolerance through censorship.

Hans-Georg Ziebertz begins his chapter with a survey of some of the social, political and educational implications of immigration in Germany, tracing the ways in which the dominant conceptualisation shifted from assimilation and integration to multicultural education. Drawing on the analysis of pluralism provided by Wolfgang Welsch, especially his claim that in our postmodern age unity may only be conceived within the framework of multiplicity, Ziebertz then explores two possible reactions to cultural pluralism and their consequences for intercultural learning. The first is fundamentalism, which he describes as the public face of religious exclusivism. While we inevitably define ourselves in relation to others, he argues that education should properly intervene if this leads to such exclusivism and dominance. Relativism poses different problems. If diversity is the highest value, and harmony is bought at the expense of the claim that everything is equally valid, 'we find ourselves in a dubious educational situation'. Ziebertz advocates a third way in which unity is something to be worked for within diversity, by means of a dialogue with strangers whom we both understand and allow to be different. This demands an appropriate form of discourse that 'would free communication from the compulsion to attain universal consensus or endure total heterogeneity'. Intercultural learning should also help students to practise new ways of changing their perspectives. Ziebertz concludes by reviewing four ways of responding to the foreign: as counter-image, as a sounding-board for one's own tradition, as an amplification of it, or as something complementary to it. He argues that all four of these may be used in schools providing that their limitations are faced, but the complementarity mode, within which 'native and foreign are equally respected', can best provide the framework for a dialogue-orientated religious education.

Reference

Ramsey, I.T. (1970), *The Fourth R: report of the commission on religious education in schools* (The Durham Report), London, National Society and SPCK.

1

FROM RELIGION TO SCIENCE: RELIGIOUS EDUCATION AND SCIENTIFIC UNDERSTANDING

Jeff Astley

Science, religion and education

The conventional account of the fundamental relationship between science and religion as being in a state of 'conflict' (e.g. White, 1922) has been challenged by many historians of science and most recent writers on science and religion (e.g. Berkhof, 1968; Butterfield, 1973; Brooke, 1991: chapter 1; Habgood, 1972; Polkinghorne, 1986; Barbour, 1990: chapter 1; Watts, 1996; Ward, 1996a; McGrath, 1998: chapter 1). Greek philosophers, through their search for a wisdom of explanation, may be said to have initiated a reflection on nature that developed into science, and it was the 'rediscovery of Greek learning during the Renaissance that we generally recognise as the starting-point of science in the modern sense of the word' (Hutten, 1962: 13). But Greek science lacked a truly empirical as well as an experimental element. This was a dimension that the doctrine of a voluntary, and therefore contingent, and relatively independent creation demanded, for 'the contingent is knowable only by sensuous experience' (Foster, 1973: 311; cf. Hooykaas, 1972: chapters 1 and 4; Torrance, 1985: 6-8). The rise of science, at least in the West, was thus partly motivated or at least nurtured by theological considerations, including, paradoxically, the banishing of mystery from nature in seventeenth-century and eighteenth-century science (Midgley, 1992).

Science is not ultimately opposed to religious spirituality or belief. Indeed, some have written of a complementarity or 'consonance' between the two, even a 'cousinly relationship', on the grounds that science and theology at least are 'intellectual cousins under the skin'

(Polkinghorne, 1994: 47; cf. 1995: 59). It is this interpretation that I wish to develop in the present chapter. Nevertheless, educational institutions often embody a distrust between those who teach or research in the two subject areas, and students frequently express their own position in terms of some version of the conflict thesis.

Empirical background: attitudes towards science and religion

According to Leslie Francis, a positive interest in science and science lessons is shown by approximately two-thirds of twelve- to sixteen-year-olds, whereas a positive interest in religion, and towards 'finding out' about Christianity and other world religions, is displayed by only one third. Females show significantly more interest in religion and religious education than males, whereas males show more interest in science and science education than females (Francis, 1992). Older pupils show significantly less interest in both religion and learning about religion, and significantly more interest in science and science lessons than do younger pupils. Francis' data also reveal that about half of school pupils of this age are uncertain where they stand on the 'science and religion conflict'. Being male and being older positively correlates with viewing science as having demonstrated the inadequacy of religious and biblical interpretations of creation and history. The gender differences are addressed in more detail by William Kay (1996), whose research shows that the claim that 'science has disproved religion' is endorsed by over 21% of boys, but less than 11% of girls, in a population mainly aged between twelve and fifteen years.

Helmut Reich has argued for a stage theory to account for the way young people deal with these apparently competing explanatory theories (cf. Greer, 1972). While children below eleven years are unable to regard them both as true, about a third of eleven- to fourteen-year-olds, and over three-quarters of fifteen- to twenty-year-olds, can engage in 'complementarity thinking' or 'relational and contextual reasoning' that treats both theories as necessary for an adequate description of reality (Oser and Reich, 1987; Reich, 1989; Reich, 1994). A similar, though perhaps more mature perspective, would be adopted by those (usually older) subjects who are at Stage 5 of Fowler's faith development scheme. People who are in this more dialectic and inclusive style of faith refuse to collapse tensions between multiple perspectives and are willing and able to hold together paradoxical claims (Fowler, 1987: 72; Moseley, Jarvis and Fowler, 1993: 61). Such cognitive perspectives are adopted where each claim proves to be useful 'for providing deeper understanding in particular situations and under particular circumstances' (Reich, 1994: 82), and where both are needed for a proper explanation that neither alone can supply 'in a mutual movement toward the real and the true' (Fowler, 1981: 187).

According to Reich, 'complementarity reasoning is crucial to religious development' (Reich, 1991: 88). He contends that, in order to reduce students' cognitive dissonance over science and religion, we should (a) avoid suggesting that religion is in competition with science when providing explanations of natural occurrences, (b) help learners to appreciate the different kinds of truth and different levels of symbolic meaning and transcendence in the two domains, and (c) encourage them to accept 'the apparent conflicts caused by complementarity in thinking as being the reflection of a complex reality in our limited mind' (Reich, 1989: 66; cf. MacKay, 1974).

Much of the empirical work on children and adolescents that relates to science and religion concentrates on the extreme positions of 'scientism' (the view that absolute truth is obtainable through science, and through science alone) and 'creationism' (which advocates a literal interpretation of the Genesis stories, bolstered by a 'creation science' that strives to support this interpretation using scientific data). These issues are discussed further by Kay and Francis (1996: chapter 8) and by Fulljames (1996). The data from these studies show that the pupils who adopt the perspective of scientism are those most likely to think of Christianity as involving creationism, and that those who believe that creationism is an essential part of Christianity are also less likely to show an interest in science. Unsurprisingly, those who adopt scientism are less likely to be favourably disposed to Christianity, and this is particularly the case if they are strongly interested in science. Those who think that Christianity necessarily involves creationism tend to have a more negative attitude to Christianity, after individual differences in creationist belief have been taken into account. It is significant that the adoption of scientism is found to be independent of an interest in science, as this supports the interpretation that scientism is an ideological stance unrelated to the scientific quest. Interest in science neither suppresses nor encourages a favourable attitude to Christianity, but adopting a creationist position is detrimental to an interest in science. Kay and Francis correctly argue that complementarity is impossible between scientism and creationism for logical reasons (Kay and Francis, 1996: 110).

Data such as these lend support to the recommendation that religious education curricula should include topics in science and religion, the nature of science and theological interpretations of the biblical creation stories (cf. Dieterich, 1990; Poole, 1990a, 1992, 1995; Fulljames, 1996). Michael Poole (1990b: 72) writes of education in this area:

> More help needs to be given to students to enable them to discuss where beliefs and values are located, how to spot where they follow from the subject matter or were imported at the beginning, what are the available options among them and . . . appropriate criteria for testing their truth-claims.

Although there is some evidence that university students of science tend to show more religious behaviour than do arts students (Rees, 1967), it is often said that adolescents discard religious belief because they believe it to be incompatible with a scientific worldview (Tobacyk, Miller and James, 1984; Greer, 1988). Glock and Stark claimed that 'at the level of human behavior, religion and scientific scholarship are infrequently found together' (Glock and Stark, 1965: 286). However, De Vaus has found evidence that it is the most religious students, measured in terms of their religious belief and practice, who most value a 'scientific orientation', expressed in terms of testing the truth of new ideas against evidence (De Vaus, 1981). He argued from his own data that sixteen- to eighteen-year-olds do not undergo religious change because they adopt a more scientific viewpoint, or indeed because of anything else they have learned through their formal education. On his view, it is social rather than intellectual factors that are 'fundamental in the process of religious change' (De Vaus, 1981: 43; cf. De Vaus, 1980; Kay and Francis, 1996: 144).

The objectives of this chapter

There is clearly much still to play for in the empirical exploration of these issues. In this chapter I assume only that there may be sufficient transfer of learning between religious education and science education to make it worthwhile to discuss the likely influence of the one on the other. Leaving aside the question as to whether studying science should help or hinder an appreciative understanding of religion, I want to ask *whether a proper education in religion may assist the learner in his or her understanding of the nature of the scientific enterprise.* I do not pretend to propose here anything more than suggestions, which are themselves predicated on particular ways of engaging in the enterprise of religious education, and particular ways of understanding the nature of religion. I must leave it to others to explore their empirical and practical implications.

I mention here three preliminary points of clarification. First, the present chapter is offered both as additional ammunition for those who seek to justify religious education in public educational systems, and to help combat the claim that learning religion in a religious community is necessarily anti-educational. I therefore have in mind not only the sort of education in religion that may properly be undertaken in 'secular' or 'common' schools and institutions of higher education, but also the educative induction of people *into* religion which overlaps it, and is often designated as religious 'nurture' or 'formation'. My concerns will primarily relate to religious education focused on those monotheistic religious traditions that identify God as creator of the universe, in particular the western prophetic traditions of Judaism, Christianity and Islam.

Second, 'scientific understanding' is, of course, an ambiguous term and I should acknowledge at the outset that I do not claim that understanding religion can lead to scientific understanding in the sense of the understanding delivered by the disciplines and fields of knowledge of the sciences. Religious education will not help us do physics. But where it might help is in the *understanding of* science, in the sense of our understanding the nature of the scientific enterprise and the 'theory of science' (Laura and McCarthy, 1985: 5) that underlies these disciplines and fields.

Third, it would make my task a great deal simpler if I were to focus on the social sciences in this discussion. Patently, the study of religion is the study of a social phenomenon, and reflection on some of the processes involved in the study of religion may therefore illuminate other work in the social sciences. I am attempting here to justify a more difficult thesis: that education in religion assists our understanding of the values, dynamics, methods and logic of the *natural sciences*.

Learning attitudes and values

There are, of course, enormous differences between science and religion, but among the parallels that can be traced are some features of the affective as well as the cognitive domain. There are many reasons for claiming both religion and science as great 'creations of the human spirit'. Both religion and science are human explorations of, and claim to be appropriate responses to the Other, whether that be construed as wholly natural or as both natural and divine, and activities of this kind inevitably display an evaluative orientation. Evidently, religion is the more obviously 'spiritual' of the two subjects, in the sense of expressing and evoking attitudes, values, beliefs and practices by which people live and through which they reach out to whatever is beyond. Indeed, one major theological criticism that could be brought against the thesis of this paper is that religion itself is not to be understood in explanatory or cognitive terms at all, and is, therefore, in no way analogous to science (e.g. Bultmann, 1958; Phillips, 1976). Although I have more sympathy than most with this position, I believe that interpreting religion as at least including a set of cognitive beliefs is more true to the received understanding of religion and more appropriate in an educational context (cf. Astley, 1994b: chapter 6; Astley, 1996). Yet religion is *primarily* a powerhouse for attitudes, and this may be its most useful contribution to a scientific education.

Attitudes to the world

Religious believers have sometimes thought of nature as a sort of book: a book of God's works that is in some sense parallel to the book of God's words. Both have the same author and both may reveal God's mind (cf. Peacocke, 1979: chapter 1). Although this perspective may not actually explain anything within nature, it is likely to change our attitude toward nature.

If nature is viewed as a gift from God's hand, and evaluated as 'very good' (Genesis 1:31), attitudes of gratitude, esteem and respect may be evoked as an appropriate response. By endorsing their significance, the material world and the physical body are honoured. Judaism has been enthusiastic in this regard, but Christianity has all too often sought to eschew such vulgarity, coughing in embarrassment. Some blame for this situation must lie with the fact that Christianity was influenced early in its history by dualist or separatist accounts of reality, such as Platonism, Gnosticism and Manicheism, that celebrated only the Spirit, the Mind or the eternal Forms, and disparaged the earth, the body, animals, sex and *life*. Similar attitudes have had their political and social consequences down the centuries. Industry is often still seen as a grubby business and manual work as suitable solely for menials. 'Let us seek only the things that are above', false religion implores: armchair reflection perhaps, or, failing that, commodity stockbroking. True religion and true religious education, however, like true science and true life, get their hands dirty. Both consider the lilies of the field and the fowls of the air; they rejoice in them and learn from them. They both recognise that all human existence is an in-the-world existence and that we are ourselves a part of nature. The best religion acknowledges that we are embodied selves and were created and intended as such. We are not angels who have got stuck in the mud by accident.

The creationists' rejection of the theory of evolution (see Kitcher, 1983) expresses their concern to maintain a radical distinction between *homo sapiens* and other animals. In the nineteenth century, Darwin's theory was treated with most repugnance over this issue, for evolution put at risk the dignity that the doctrine of special creation had conferred on the human creation. Bishop Samuel Wilberforce's sour joke during the notorious debate with T. H. Huxley on 30 June 1860 was about whether the latter had an ape as his grandfather (or, even more horrid thought to the Victorians, his grandmother!).

Religious education should teach that the biblical view of the dignity of human beings is deeply paradoxical. In Genesis, humankind (*Adam*) is made from the dust of the earth (*adhamah*); yet it is also described as but a 'little less than God' (Psalm 8:5). Our human dignity, as God's trustees and the bearers of God's image, is therefore not incompatible with our more earthy origins.

In any case, what is so wrong about being an animal? Mary Midgley reminds us that it is mainly humans who kill without being hungry, and inflict physical pain and mental suffering on others who are no threat to their own survival. Although this is human behaviour, we speak of it as acting like an animal – being 'brutal', 'bestial', 'beastly'. To allow our kinship with other animals is to see ourselves in them and them in us. In Midgley's words, 'Our dignity arises *within* nature, not against it' (Midgley, 1980: 196). Why are we as we are? It is surely partly because of evolution, from and through these other beasts. Our feelings and instincts, our bodies and behaviour, have evolved, as theirs have, for our survival and reproduction. That does not mean that we are nothing more than animal instincts, but it does mean that we are those things as well. We need not feel ashamed to be animals or to feel close to other animals; as we study them through the sciences we should expect to learn more about ourselves.

Religious education can help us to develop such attitudes to the world. These attitudes are in any case 'natural' to us, in the sense of life-enhancing and salvific. Religious education may help us to recognise this also. But can the development of these attitudes help us in our approach to science? It can help to place the necessary 'objectivity' of science within an affective value framework, and that might prevent the callous manipulation of nature that mars the work of some scientists. It might also discourage a destructive dualism of fact and value. Keith Ward (1996b: 120) writes:

> Perhaps the sciences adopt an objective set of attitudes to the world, seeking to describe its observable features dispassionately and neutrally. Religious discourse may express a reactive response to the world, as emotionally responded to and affectively engaged with. But it is the same world to which these attitudes are being directed.

On the whole scientists treat nature with respect and often, according to Richard Dawkins, with 'a poetic sense of wonder'. He contends that the spirit of wonder that inspired the poets 'is the very same spirit that moves great scientists' (Dawkins, 1998: xii, 27). Einstein went much further, in characterising every 'true searcher' of nature as having 'a kind of religious reverence' for its masterly order and harmony (Polkinghorne, 1986: 63). Such wonder and reverence have an ethical dimension, and the majority of scientists appreciate their responsibility towards nature as well as their place within it. When scientists (or religious believers) behave otherwise, it is because we are all finite, blinkered sinners. Perhaps religious education may, in this context, appropriately raise our consciousness of sin.

Ecological values

The picture presented by earlier scientific thinking, of a wholly determined, mechanistic universe, was fuelled by a rigid Cartesian dualism, whose effects were often brutal. Today, most scientists operate with a very different portrait of nature, as more open, unified, emergent and hierarchical (Peacocke, 1979, 1986, 1993; O'Hear, 1989; Ward, 1990). Biology has uncovered in considerable detail the interconnectedness and vulnerability of life on earth. According to Peter Hodgson, ecology is simply one aspect of a holistic, relational view of nature, a view that may even be described as an 'ecological cosmology' (Hodgson, 1994: 92). Nevertheless, there is no guarantee that the study of science on its own will generate environmental values. Perhaps religious education may serve as a more potent source, in exposing students to a spirituality and doctrine of creation that demands an ecological ethic, a duty of care for the world.

It is true that these values present themselves most clearly in some other religious traditions, especially Taoism and Zen; and it is also true that Christianity's attitude to nature has often been exploitative (White, 1967: 1205). Yet Christian theology can exemplify this ecological thrust in a marked way. Certainly, sacramental theology can effectively engender a deep respect for nature, as can the less traditional options of process theology, ecofeminism and radically immanentist creation-spirituality (cf. Fox, 1991; Barbour, 1992: chapter 3; Clark, 1993; Bouma-Prediger, 1995; Pannenberg, 1994: 204; Page, 1996).

Religious education for attitude change?

Is religious education justified in promoting this sort of attitude change? *Formative* religious education (religious nurture) will of course have among its objectives the development of a range of religious attitudes and values, but what about non-confessional religious education in the common school? In Britain at least, school religious education has been taken to include the development of certain affective states that may be categorised as 'implicitly religious' or 'quasi-religious', and I have argued elsewhere that developing an empathic understanding of religion is dependent, to some degree, on the development of similar attitudes and emotions in the learner (Astley, 1994a). If these claims can be justified, religious education may be allowed to promote some 'creation values', even in secular education.

Intelligibility and other 'scientific values'

Religious attitudes towards nature, as infused with meaning (as in the 'two books' account) or charged with God's presence and power (as in religious experience), are often transposed into another key in the interests of religious apologetic, with the help of the Design Argument (cf. Crowder, 1993, 1994). Richard Swinburne has defended a version of this argument 'from the temporal order of the world' that highlights the significance of the orderliness of nature and its 'regularity of succession', as these features are captured in laws of nature that describe the universal powers of things. Because of its 'intrinsic improbability', Swinburne argues, this orderliness cries out for an explanation in terms of a supernatural agent's intention. This is a 'personal explanation' with a vengeance, and transcends the scientific explanations that operate simply by referring to the framework of natural laws (Swinburne, 1979, 1983).

The structure of Swinburne's inductive argument includes the claim that God, 'in virtue of his postulated character . . . [would have] very good, apparently overriding, reasons for making an orderly universe' (Swinburne, 1979: 147). This suggests that theistic belief may itself be one, perhaps strong, reason for adopting a view of the orderliness of nature, which is one of the (necessarily non-evidential) fundamental presuppositions of science. The idea of a creator may thus 'give confidence to those undertaking a scientific investigation' (Trigg, 1998: 83). An analysis of this kind may strengthen my claim that religious education can bear fruit in terms of scientific understanding, in this case when it encourages belief in – or at least belief in the plausibility of – the existence of a creator God.

The orderliness of nature is presupposed by the existence of ordered human reasoning about nature (cf. Trigg, 1993: 148). The scientific attitude to the world includes a trust in this order, in nature's intelligibility and in its regularity, hence science's scepticism about miracles, which it shares with history. Science insists that the universe makes sense; it is intelligible to human minds (cf. Torrance, 1984: 196; 1985: chapter 1). This 'scientific faith' relates also to the remarkable unity and simplicity, even beauty, of scientific theorising. These features are all regarded as scientific virtues in themselves. Such a vision of the human mind 'attuned to nature in its essence, and expressing its love for nature in doing science' (O'Hear, 1989: 227) is surely in the end a spiritual perspective, and one that religious education might well encourage.

Other values have been identified as internal to scientific study, and indeed to all enquiry. These more directly educational values include loyalty to the truth, co-operation in the creation of agreed knowledge, honesty, disinterested learning, rationality, freedom of thought, and an openness to evidence and willingness to rethink beliefs that has been called 'organised scepticism' (cf. Barbour, 1992: 28-29). Some of these are spiritual values that religious learning can help to form (cf. Astley, 1998) and that are also expressed in the study of religion (Habgood, 1972: chapter 16). We may note that Simone Weil writes of *attention*, which is a feature of an open waiting upon truth, as something that underlies both academic study and prayer (Weil, 1959: 66-76).

It is perhaps worth mentioning a further, slightly more recondite, epistemological virtue that is shared both by religion and by science. This is the disposition not to be trapped in a 'common sense' account of reality. Despite the claims of some teachers, and indeed of T. H. Huxley, science is not glorified, 'trained and organised' common sense. To the contrary, science is often highly surprising and counter-intuitive, as quantum theory, relativity and much of biology reveal (Wolpert, 1992). At the very least, science shows us that our commonsense views of reality do not apply at the extremes of the scale of magnitude. Neither the very small nor the very large (nor the very fast) make that sort of ordinary 'sense'. As Neils Bohr famously put it, 'Anyone who is not shocked by quantum theory has not understood it'. Religious education may anticipate this, by provoking reflection that goes beyond the superficialities of ordinary thought. The sense of awe in religion may then serve as a prolegomenon to science's recognition of the mystery of nature.

Learning about grammar and method

Can learning something of the methodology, 'logical grammar' and epistemological structure of religion also function as a useful introduction to understanding these dimensions of the sciences? Parallels between the logic and patterns of justification of the two areas of discourse (e.g. Rolston, 1987: chapter 1; Barbour, 1990: chapter 2; Banner, 1990) might suggest that this is so.

Undergirding principles

Donald Hudson has argued that all education is education *in* a subject, in the sense of initiating students into 'the principle of procedure on which that whole discipline depends' (Hudson, 1982: 26). In natural science this is the principle of natural causation (the uniformity of nature). In (theistic) religion it is the existence of God. Learning to think religiously, according to this view, is learning to explain and respond to what goes on in terms of God's existence. Even 'secular religious education' would then be a matter of teaching people *how* to think and act religiously, but without persuading them actually to do so (Hudson, 1987).

Although this is a contentious position, there may be merit in viewing some elements of religious education as teaching people how to think theologically: that is, how to understand what it means to think theologically. Discerning the 'logic' of religion in this way demands a certain sophistication. But how else can students really understand religious believing and thinking? Perhaps a religious education of this kind will help them to a clearer view of the logic of science, by encouraging them to identify *its* assumptions and structure. Laura and McCarthy have identified certain additional factors among the 'constitutive concepts' or 'epistemic primitives' of science, including our trust in the reliability of our senses and in our memory. These serve as foundations of science, not in the sense that they are the ultimate pillars of evidence, but rather by determining what we count as evidence (Laura and McCarthy, 1985: 8). Recognising the non-evidential nature of these principles should help scientists avoid the pitfalls of scientism.

Intuition and reason
The role of creative and imaginative intuition in scientific discovery, both in identifying analogies and implications and in thinking up hypotheses and experiments, has been emphasised by many scientists (Medawar, 1969). The scientific 'conjectures' on which Karl Popper lays such store (Popper, 1974: chapter 1) often arise as highly creative acts of the human imagination. Developing this theme, Derek Stanesby writes that 'science is a superb example of the exploration of the human imaginative spirit. In that sense it is a spiritual enterprise' (Stanesby, 1994). Religion places even more significance on intuition, and Christian education at least has been articulated in terms of the development of the imagination (Harris, 1987). In most religious traditions this is usually balanced by the employment of elucidatory, synthetic and corrective reason. Again, an understanding of how religious reflection works may assist students to perceive similar patterns within the sciences.

Getting the level right
If the explanations generated by science and those offered by the doctrines and revelations of religion are taken to be operating at the same level, conflict will often result, as between a belief in the evolution of species over billions of years and belief in the special separate creation of every species over several days. Theology can often solve such problems, but only by shifting the level at which it operates (Astley, 2000: chapter 5). Properly interpreted, theism can accommodate almost any science, for the doctrine of creation is about that which lies below and beyond the physical and biological accounts of natural origins, at a '*meta*physical' level. Hence, whenever science proposes an account of the development of the universe, the believer can always add 'and God sustains all this'.

A religious education that helps students perceive the metaphysical status of central religious claims could assist science education by clearing the ground so that these unnecessary conflicts are avoided from the outset.

Justifying beliefs

Thomas Kuhn sought to identify explanatory and methodological frameworks that rule in 'normal science'. He claimed that these 'paradigms' or 'disciplinary matrices' are resistant to falsification; examples include Newtonian physics and evolutionary biology. According to Kuhn, different paradigms are incommensurable because they contain their own criteria of evaluation. Shifts in these paradigms may arise in scientific revolutions (or 'conversions') for arational, particularly social and psychological, reasons (Kuhn, 1970). Karl Popper, by contrast, argued that scientific, as opposed to ideological, revolutions are rational and that scientific theories are falsifiable and held with considerable tentativeness (Popper, 1974, 1975). Imre Lakatos (1970, 1981) espoused a mediating position in terms of scientific 'research programmes' which supersede one another in the history of science. These programmes include a central 'hard core' of ideas that are highly resistant to falsification, along with 'auxiliary hypotheses' that are created, change and die more easily. A similar structure of central and peripheral beliefs is apparent in religious thinking (Barbour, 1974; 1990: chapters 2 and 3), indeed this epistemological structure is much more obvious in religion. Such reflections enhance the sense of a 'cousinly' resemblance between science and faith.

When drawing parallels between the methods of science and those of theology, however, apologists for religion are sometimes tempted to pass over the *differences* too lightly. The main contrast between science and religion still lies in their differential openness to falsification and the testability of their predictions. We must grant that a wide-ranging scientific theory such as the theory of evolution is not open to simple falsification (cf. Vollmer, 1987) and that it does not possess high predictive power (cf. Ward, 1998: 129). But the 'God-hypothesis' that God loves us, despite the conflicting evidence, seems even more remote from falsifiable experiences than these most general theories of the scientists.

There is a spectrum of falsifiability in science, from small-scale (readily falsifiable) hypotheses, through theories of varying degrees of generality, to research programmes, and beyond to the metaphysical assumptions of science[1] (which are most highly resistant to falsification). At this far end of the spectrum we do find something similar to metaphysical or religious belief-systems that attempt to explain *everything*. Such systems are judged mainly by the formal criteria of simplicity, comprehensiveness and coherence, and by more personal criteria of intellectual satisfaction, and only partly by their loose 'empirical fit' to the world. The logic of systems of this nature is that the wider their cover, that is, the more they take into account, the less notice is taken of the 'lack of fit' revealed by the apparent exceptions to them. Metaphysical claims that purport to explain 'everything' have already taken into account all possible evidence, including evidence that counts against them (Astley, 1994b: 50-55).

Bearing in mind these similarities, we might argue that giving students some experience of religious doctrines, their resistance to empirical refutation and the criteria that are used in assessing them, might help them to a better understanding of the nature of science as well, without blurring the distinctions between the two subjects.

Learning about community: co-operation and interdependence

One of the fundamental points of distinction between scientific and religious (if not second-order *theological*) assertions is often taken to be the different extents to which they involve a personal element. Thus, Donald Evans has contrasted the 'self-involving' nature of religious commitments with the 'logically neutral' status of the assertions of science, and argued that the latter are comprehensible 'impersonally' in the sense that their comprehensibility is 'not directly dependent on profoundly personal conditions' such as revelatory depth-experiences (Evans, 1968: 117; cf. Evans, 1963; Ward, 1996b: 120).

On the other hand, Michael Polanyi presents convincing arguments that the scientist's personal and passionate participation in the discovery and validation of science is an essential part of his science, that knowledge is always personal and that knowing is always an art. 'The excitement of the scientist making a discovery is an *intellectual* passion', he writes, 'telling that something is *intellectually* precious and, more particularly, that it is precious to science. And this affirmation forms part of science' (Polanyi, 1962: 134-135). Evans would surely agree that the image of the dispassionate, computer-brained scientist is highly misleading. The scientist is a person, and his or her (often tacit) skills are learned in an apprenticeship within a community of other scientists. Personal involvement, interpretation and judgement (which is not 'private', for objectivity is here ensured by 'personal involvement in community') should be acknowledged in any proper account of scientific achievement. A good education in religion should alert students to an appreciation of this role of personal involvement in human knowing. According to Ian Barbour, in religion this differs in 'degree and form . . . [but] not in any absolute contrast' (Barbour, 1966: 183, 228) from that of science. In particular, religious education can help students to identify the normative role of the community in forging and testing new truth-claims (Peacocke, 1971: chapter 1). The picture of the independent, autonomous genius making a lonely contribution to knowledge is a fantasy in most spheres of life and thought.

Learning about language
No religious education worthy of the name should neglect to induct students into an appreciation of the diverse uses of language in religion. The employment of analogical and metaphorical language by religionists, in an attempt to be articulate about divine mystery while preserving a representative function for religious language, has often been noted (e.g. Ramsey, 1957; Soskice, 1985). The significance of systematically articulated and developed metaphors ('models') needs to be at the forefront of any account of how theology works, and a recognition of this is essential to any attempt by students to do theology for themselves. (A linguistically sophisticated interpretation of the Genesis stories may have a positive effect on students' interest in science, as we have seen.)

Religious education about religious language might help to alert students to the 'use of analogies as instruments of persuasion' in much scientific rhetoric (Poole, 1995: 49 and chapter 3 *passim*; Poole, 1996). It should also assist them in understanding the more positive employment of model language, particularly of complementary models, in scientific theory (e.g. Ramsey, 1964; Austin, 1967; Ferré, 1969; Barbour, 1974; McGrath, 1998: chapter 5; cf. Astley, 1984). For example, the believer contends that God is both a 'father' and a 'rock', while the scientist contends that, within quantum mechanics, electrons behave both like waves (undulations of energy) and like particles of matter. Mystery that beggars the imagination is thus an aspect of the creation, as well as of any putative creator. It is possible that reflecting on models and mystery in religion may encourage in students a willingness to acknowledge their central position elsewhere. Where else in our increasingly literal-minded educational systems will that happen?

Most accounts of the use of models assume a critical realism about the referents of 'transcending concepts' (whether subatomic particles or supernatural beings). Critical realism interprets the models as proper representations, but not literal descriptions, of reality (cf. Hesse, 1954: 150-151; Barbour, 1966: 172). The alternative instrumentalist account in the philosophy of science views its concepts and theories merely as useful instruments for predicting observations.[2] Theories of religious language that treat it solely as expressive of attitudes and commitments, or as a useful device for evoking religious experience, may similarly be described as instrumentalist (Austin, 1976: chapter 13). A religious education that has reflected on the status of religious doctrines will already have opened up this distinction to students (cf. Hobson and Edwards, 1999: chapter 4). It may note how instrumentalism construes religious language as non-cognitive and therefore non-refutable. 'Instrumentalism leaves no room for describing a theory as true or false, since a theory describes nothing' (Theobald, 1968: 37). It is this feature that led Popper to dismiss instrumentalism in the scientific area as incapable of accounting for scientific progress (Popper, 1974: 113).[3] But scientific progress may also be said to depend on 'the ability of scientists to work out analogies or construct models' and 'to see the unfamiliar as an example of the familiar' (Theobald, 1968: 135-136), and these are skills that can be learned by using language outside science, for example, in exploring religion.

Learning about learning

In his magisterial four-volume *Science in History*, J.D. Bernal distinguished science and religion partly on the grounds that religion is concerned with the preservation of an 'eternal truth', while science strives to change accepted truth (Bernal, 1969: 43, 1029). As we have seen, however, others have argued for a greater similarity between these two spheres with regard to their balancing of commitment and tentativeness, or tradition and experience. Thus, the pattern of a tradition-based 'normal' science, occasionally being overthrown by innovative scientific revolutions, has been compared to a similar scenario in a person's religious biography (Hull, 1990); and a parallel pattern has been debated by scholars reflecting on the history of Christian theology (Küng and Tracy, 1989).

In educational terms, this may be interpreted as an issue about the balance between forming the learner in a tradition and teaching him or her to be critical of received truth (Mitchell, 1994; Astley, 1994b: chapter 5). Despite the rhetoric of some educationalists, science teaching in the classroom often leaves little room for *self-critical science*. As Trevor Cooling has pointed out, this contrasts markedly with religious education, at least in the secular school, which positively provokes an intellectual critique (Cooling, 1990)! Perhaps students' reactions to religious education may be used to illuminate for them the role of prejudice and prejudgement in resisting, and indeed in enabling (Gadamer, 1982: 235-274), our understanding of alien beliefs in general. In this way reflection on religious education might help students to have more of a feel for the history of ideas, including the development of scientific ideas.

Conclusion: religious education for a scientific millennium?

Einstein is often quoted as saying that science without religion is 'lame' (Tilby, 1992: 6). One sense in which this may prove true is when science pretends to offer a presuppositionless, value-free, untouched-by-human-hand form of knowledge. Another example is when science limps off on its own and seeks to replace all other forms of human knowledge and perception by some abstractive, murdered-to-dissect analysis of reality, especially of the reality of human nature.[4]

Avoiding scientism and synthesising meaning

Fraser Watts has argued that reductionist 'nothing-buttery' ideas in science, such as eliminative materialism, are metaphysical assumptions that are probably originally derived from 'religious ideas that have taken an atheist turn'. One aim of the theological study of science, and I would add of a proper religious education, is 'to bring all this out into the open, so it is seen for what it is' (Watts, 1996: 17). Avoiding scientism is a good educational objective in itself: good for science as well as for society (Kay and Francis, 1996: 155). A good religious education may help us in this quest, but note that qualifier 'good'. I am *not* arguing that any old religious education will deliver this particular educational holy grail.

Science and religion make compatible, if sometimes uneasy, bedfellows for several reasons, as we have seen. One further educational reason is that both analytic and synthetic thinking are natural to us and needed by us. The analytic, 'taking apart and relabelling' form of understanding is at the heart of the scientific method. It is enormously powerful and absolutely essential. Its efforts are presumed by the equally valuable synthetic, 'putting things together and finding new combinations', mode of understanding (Melchert, 1981) which is more characteristic of cognitive understanding within religion. Science is often over-analytic, especially when it degenerates into scientism. Education in religion may redress the balance.

'Reading the mind of God' and reading the 'story of nature'?

John Polkinghorne has made a different point. He notes how a distinction between 'explanation' and 'understanding' may be made in both science and theology. Understanding is a deep experience of 'intellectual contentment with the picture being entertained' (Polkinghorne, 1994: 36). It can run before or lag behind explanation, which in science is a function of the predictive power as well as the simplicity of its theories, but in theology is rather more of a speculative matter. We know more than we can tell in both (Polanyi, 1962), but theology is perhaps more concerned with this 'intellectual contentment'.

Stephen Hawking famously concluded his very secular *A Brief History of Time* with the hope that if we were to discover an understandable and complete unified theory in physics we should 'all be able to take part in the discussion of the question of why it is that we and the universe exist'. This would be 'the ultimate triumph of human reason – for then we would know the mind of God' (Hawking, 1988: 175). I wonder if science could ever give us that (cf. Midgley, 1992: 8). Science is about causation. To find *meaning* in it is to treat it as history or story, particularly as a story with a moral. In this sense at least, 'nature has no history' (Collingwood, 1946: 114). We can read it as a narrative – we may adopt that particular, very human attitude toward it; but science itself does not force any such interpretation on us. 'Scientific rationality is a tool for discovering general and increasingly abstract truths about nature, rather than about how things appear to us and affect us' (O'Hear, 1989: 231).

Some have written of their hope for a *transformation* of science into interpretative story or 'meaning-laden history' (Rolston, 1987: 338), a transformation that would render nature truly 'understandable'. It has been further argued that religious cognition has similarities with 'reading a work of art', in that both are personal responses of interpretation that are only partly constrained by the work itself (Watts and Williams, 1988: 70). An education that emphasises the role of narrative meaning-making in religion might help in this evolution of cool, technical scientific education into something more human and accessible – in a word, more 'meaningful'. It would be the development of an holistic understanding that *incorporated* science, but also drew on the affective power of religious spirituality so that the world of nature that our scientific minds seek to explain may become again a home where our hearts may rest.

Such a goal would provide a worthwhile, if ulterior, motive for promoting religious education in our scientific millennium.

Notes

1. Metaphysics ('ontology'), it has been said, is 'developed by reflection upon what must be the case for science to be possible, and this is independent of any actual scientific knowledge' (Bhaskar, 1978: 39).

2. Chalmers professes a mediating position between a descriptive objective realism, in which scientific theories describe the world as it really is, and a relativist instrumentalism, in which theories are simply useful predictive devices. Theories are social products that 'successfully come to grips' with the world of nature, yet are subject to revolutionary change (Chalmers, 1982: chapter 14). Many accounts of critical realism offer just such a compromise position.

3. Experimentalism has been said to provide compelling grounds for realism in science (Hacking, 1983). Religious education may ask whether there is any equivalent practice that demands this interpretation of the status of religious concepts.

4. Anthony O'Hear describes 'the belief that science and scientific method (and they alone) can provide us with complete and satisfactory explanation of all phenomena' as the 'mythology of science' (O'Hear, 1989: 206).

References

Astley, J. (1984), Paradox and christology, *King's Theological Review*, 7 (1), 9-13.

Astley, J. (1994a), The place of understanding in Christian education and education about Christianity, *British Journal of Religious Education*, 16 (2), 90-101.

Astley, J. (1994b), *The Philosophy of Christian Religious Education*, Birmingham, Alabama, Religious Education Press.

Astley, J. (1996), Theology for the untheological? Theology, philosophy and the classroom, in J. Astley and L.J. Francis (eds), *Christian Theology and Religious Education: connections and contradictions*, pp 60-77, London, SPCK.

Astley, J. (1998), The Christian vocation of teaching and learning, *Tufton Review*, 2, 57-72.

Astley, J. (2000), *God's World*, London, Darton, Longman and Todd.

Austin, W.H. (1967), Waves, particles and paradoxes, *Rice University Studies*, 53 (2), 1-103.

Austin, W.H. (1976), *The Relevance of Natural Science to Theology*, London, Macmillan.

Banner, M.C. (1990), *The Justification of Science and the Rationality of Religious Belief*, Oxford, Clarendon.

Barbour, I.G. (1966), *Issues in Science and Religion*, London, SCM.

Barbour, I.G. (1974), *Myths, Models and Paradigms*, London, SCM.

Barbour, I.G. (1990), *Religion in an Age of Science*, London, SCM.

Barbour, I.G. (1992), *Ethics in an Age of Technology*, London, SCM.

Berkhof, H. (1968), Science and the biblical world-view, in I.G. Barbour (ed.), *Science and Religion: new perspectives on the dialogue*, pp 43-53, London, SCM. First published 1965.

Bernal, J.D. (1969), *Science in History*, Harmondsworth, Penguin.

Bhaskar, R. (1978), *A Realist Theory of Science*, Hassocks, Harvester.

Bouma-Prediger, S. (1995), *The Greening of Theology: the ecological models of Rosemary Radford Ruether, Joseph Sittler, and Jürgen Moltmann*, Atlanta, Georgia, Scholars Press.

Brooke, J.H. (1991), *Science and Religion: some historical perspectives*, Cambridge, Cambridge University Press.

Bultmann, R. (1958), *Jesus Christ and Mythology*, London, SCM.

Butterfield, H. (1973), *The Origins of Modern Science, 1300-1800*, London, Bell.

Chalmers, A.F. (1982), *What is This Thing Called Science?* Milton Keynes, Open University Press.

Clark, S.R.L. (1993), *How to Think about the Earth: philosophical and theological models for ecology*, London, Mowbray.

Collingwood, R.G. (1946), *The Idea of History*, Oxford, Clarendon.

Cooling, T. (1990), Science and religious education: conflict or co-operation, *British Journal of Religious Education*, 13 (1), 35-42.

Crowder, C. (1993), The design argument, *Dialogue*, 1, 3-8.

Crowder, C. (1994), The design argument part 2: why it fails, *Dialogue*, 2, 11-19.

Dawkins, R. (1998), *Unweaving the Rainbow: science, delusion and the appetite for wonder*, London, Penguin.

De Vaus, D.A. (1980), Education and religious change among senior adolescents, I: questioning some common research assumptions, *Journal of Christian Education*, 69, 13-24.

De Vaus, D.A. (1981), Education and religious change among senior adolescents, II: findings of an enquiry, *Journal of Christian Education*, 70, 33-45.

Dieterich, V.-J. (1990), Science and theology in religious education, *Journal of Empirical Theology*, 3 (1), 47-57.

Evans, D.D. (1963), *The Logic of Self-Involvement*, London, SCM.

Evans, D.D. (1968), Differences between scientific and religious assertions, in I.G. Barbour (ed.), *Science and Religion: new perspectives on the dialogue*, pp 101-133, London, SCM.

Ferré, F. (1969), Mapping the logic of models in science and theology, in D.M. High (ed.), *New Essays in Religious Language*, pp 54-96, New York, Oxford University Press. Originally published 1963.

Foster, M.B. (1973), The Christian doctrine of creation and the rise of modern science, reprinted in C.A. Russell (ed.), *Science and Religious Belief*, pp 294-315, London, London University Press. Originally published 1934.

Fowler, J.W. (1981), *Stages of Faith: the psychology of human development and the quest for meaning*, San Francisco, California, Harper and Row.

Fowler, J.W. (1987), *Faith Development and Pastoral Care*, Philadelphia, Pennsylvania, Fortress.

Fox, M. (1991), *Creation Spirituality: liberating gifts for the people of the earth*, San Francisco, California, HarperSanFrancisco.

Francis, L.J. (1992), Christianity today: the teenage experience, in J. Astley and D. Day (eds), *The Contours of Christian Education*, pp 340-368, Great Wakering, McCrimmons.

Fulljames, P. (1996), Science, creation and Christianity: a further look, in L.J. Francis, W.K. Kay and W.S. Campbell (eds), *Research in Religious Education*, pp 257-266, Leominster, Gracewing Fowler Wright.

Gadamer, H.-G. (1982), *Truth and Method*, New York, Crossroad.

Glock, C.Y. and Stark, R. (1965), *Religion and Society in Tension*, Chicago, Illinois, Rand McNally.

Greer, J.E. (1972), The child's understanding of creation, *Educational Review*, 24, 94-110.

Greer, J.E. (1988), *Hardest to Accept*, Coleraine, University of Ulster.

Habgood, J. (1972), *Religion and Science*, London, Hodder and Stoughton.

Hacking, I. (1983), *Representing and Intervening*, Cambridge, Cambridge University Press.

Harris, M. (1987), *Teaching and Religious Imagination*, New York, Harper Collins.

Hawking, S.W. (1988), *A Brief History of Time*, London, Bantam.

Hesse, M. (1954), *Science and the Human Imagination*, London, SCM.

Hobson, P.R. and Edwards, J.S. (1999), *Religious Education in a Pluralist Society: the key philosophical issues*, London, Woburn Press.

Hodgson, P.C. (1994), *Winds of the Spirit*, London, SCM.

Hooykaas, R. (1972), *Religion and the Rise of Modern Science*, Edinburgh, Scottish Academic Press.

Hudson, D. (1982), The loneliness of the religious educator, in J.G. Priestley (ed.), *Religion, Spirituality and Schools*, pp 23-36, Exeter, University of Exeter Press.

Hudson, D. (1987), Two questions about religious education, in R. Straughan and J. Wilson (eds), *Philosophers on Education*, pp 109-126, London, Macmillan.

Hull, J.M. (1990), Religious education and science: a problem of meaning, *British Journal of Religious Education*, 13 (1), 1-3.

Hutten, E.H. (1962), *The Origins of Science: an inquiry into the foundations of western thought*, London, Allen and Unwin.

Kay, W.K. (1996), Male and female conceptualisations of science at the interface with religious education, in J. Astley and L.J. Francis (eds), *Christian Theology and Religious Education: connections and contradictions*, pp 247-270, London, SPCK.

Kay, W.K. and Francis, L.J. (1996), *Drift from the Churches: attitude toward Christianity during childhood and adolescence*, Cardiff, University of Wales Press.

Kitcher, P. (1983), *Abusing Science: the case against creationism*, Milton Keynes, Open University Press.

Kuhn, T.S. (1970), *The Structure of Scientific Revolutions*, Chicago, Illinois, Chicago University Press.

Küng, H. and Tracy, D. (eds) (1989), *Paradigm Change in Theology*, Edinburgh, T. and T. Clark.

Lakatos, I. (1970), Falsification and the methodology of scientific research programmes, in I. Lakatos and A. Musgrave (eds), *Criticism and the Growth of Knowledge*, pp 91-196, Cambridge, Cambridge University Press.

Lakatos, I. (1981), History of science and its rational reconstructions, in I. Hacking (ed.), *Scientific Revolutions*, pp 107-127, Oxford, Oxford University Press. Originally published 1970.

Laura, R.S. and McCarthy, D. (1985), Religious education versus science education: on taking the dogma out of dogmas, *Educational Research and Perspectives*, 12, 3-9.

MacKay, D.M. (1974), 'Complementarity' in scientific and theological thinking, *Zygon*, 9, 225-244.

McGrath, A.E. (1998), *The Foundations of Dialogue in Science and Religion*, Oxford, Blackwell.

Medawar, P.B. (1969), *Induction and Intuition in Scientific Thought*, London, Methuen.

Melchert, C.F. (1981), 'Understanding' as a purpose of religious education, *Religious Education*, 76, 178-186.

Midgley, M. (1980), *Beast and Man*, London, Methuen.

Midgley, M. (1992), *Science as Salvation*, London, Routledge.

Mitchell, B. (1994), *Faith and Criticism*, Oxford, Oxford University Press.

Moseley, R.M., Jarvis, D. and Fowler, J.W. (1993), *Manual for Faith Development Research*, Atlanta, Georgia, Emory University.

O'Hear, A. (1989), *An Introduction to the Philosophy of Science*, Oxford, Clarendon.

Oser, F.K. and Reich, K.H. (1987), The challenge of competing explanations: the development of thinking in terms of complementary 'theories', *Human Development*, 30, 178-186.

Page, R. (1996), *God and the Web of Creation*, London, SCM.

Pannenberg, W. (1994), *Systematic Theology*, Vol. II, Edinburgh, T. and T. Clark.

Peacocke, A.R. (1971), *Science and the Christian Experiment*, London, Oxford University Press.

Peacocke, A.R. (1979), *Creation and the World of Science*, Oxford, Clarendon.

Peacocke, A.R. (1986), *God and the New Biology,* London, Dent.

Peacocke, A.R. (1993), *Theology for a Scientific Age,* London, SCM.

Phillips, D.Z. (1976), *Religion Without Explanation,* Oxford, Blackwell.

Polanyi, M. (1962), *Personal Knowledge: towards a post-critical philosophy,* London, Routledge and Kegan Paul.

Polkinghorne, J. (1986), *One World: the interaction of science and theology,* London, SPCK.

Polkinghorne, J. (1994), *Science and Christian Belief,* London, SPCK.

Polkinghorne, J. (1995), *Serious Talk: science and religion in dialogue,* London, SCM.

Poole, M. (1990a), Science-and-religion: a challenge for secondary education, *British Journal of Religious Education,* 13 (1), 18-27.

Poole, M. (1990b), Beliefs and values in science education: a Christian perspective: Part 2, *School Science Review,* 71, 67-73.

Poole, M. (1992), Teaching about issues of science and religion, in B. Watson (ed.), *Priorities in Religious Education: a model for the 1990s and beyond,* pp 144-164, London, Falmer.

Poole, M. (1995), *Beliefs and Values in Science Education,* Buckingham, Open University Press.

Poole, M. (1996), *A Reply to Richard Dawkins,* Oxford, Farmington Institute.

Popper, K.R. (1974), *Conjectures and Refutations: the growth of scientific knowledge,* London, Routledge and Kegan Paul.

Popper, K.R. (1975), The rationality of scientific revolutions, in R. Harré (ed.), *Problems of Scientific Revolution,* pp. 72-101, Oxford, Clarendon.

Ramsey, I.T. (1957), *Religious Language,* London, SCM.

Ramsey, I.T. (1964), *Models and Mystery,* Oxford, Oxford University Press.

Rees, D.G. (1967), *A Psychological Investigation into Denominational Concepts of God,* unpublished MA dissertation, University of Liverpool.

Reich, K.H. (1989), Between religion and science: complementarity in the religious thinking of young people, *British Journal of Religious Education,* 11 (2), 62-69.

Reich, K.H. (1991), The role of complementarity reasoning in religious development, in F.K. Oser and W.G. Scarlett (eds), *Religious Development in Childhood and Adolescence,* pp 77-89, San Francisco, California, Jossey-Bass.

Reich, K.H. (1994), Can one rationally understand Christian doctrines? An empirical study, *British Journal of Religious Education,* 16 (2), 114-126.

Rolston, H. (1987), *Science and Religion: a critical survey,* New York, Random House.

Soskice J.M. (1985), *Metaphor and Religious Thought,* Oxford, Clarendon.

Stanesby, D. (1994), *Science and Christianity: friends or enemies?,* Oxford, Farmington Institute.

Swinburne, R. (1979), *The Existence of God,* Oxford, Clarendon.

Swinburne, R. (1983), Mackie, induction and God, *Religious Studies,* 19, 385-391.

Theobald, D.W. (1968), *An Introduction to the Philosophy of Science,* London, Methuen.

Tilby, A. (1992), *Science and the Soul: new cosmology, the self and God,* London, SPCK.

Tobacyk, J., Miller, M.J. and Jones, G. (1984), Paranormal beliefs of high school students, *Psychological Reports,* 55, 255-261.

Torrance, T.F. (1984), *Transformation and Convergence in the Frame of Knowledge: explorations in the interrelations of scientific and theological enterprise,* Belfast, Christian Journals.

Torrance, T.F. (1985), *Reality and Scientific Theology*, Edinburgh, Scottish Academic Press.

Trigg, R. (1993), *Rationality and Science*, Oxford, Blackwell.

Trigg, R. (1998), *Rationality and Religion: does faith need reason?* Oxford, Blackwell.

Vollmer, G. (1987), The status of the theory of evolution in the philosophy of science, in S. Andersen and A. Peacocke (eds), *Evolution and Creation*, pp 70-77, Aarhus, Aarhus University Press.

Ward, K. (1990), *Divine Action*, Collins, London.

Ward, K. (1996a), *God, Chance and Necessity*, Oxford, Oneworld.

Ward, K. (1996b), *Religion and Creation*, Oxford, Clarendon.

Ward, K. (1998), *Religion and Human Nature*, Oxford, Clarendon.

Watts, F. (1996), Are science and religion in conflict? *The Psychologist*, January, 15-18.

Watts, F. and Williams, M. (1988), *The Psychology of Religious Knowing*, Cambridge, Cambridge University Press.

Weil, S. (1959), *Waiting on God*, London, Collins.

White, A.D. (1922), *A History of the Warfare of Science with Theology in Christendom*, Volumes one and two, New York, Appleton.

White, L. (1967), The historical roots of our ecologic crisis, *Science*, 155 (3767), 1203-1207.

Wolpert, L. (1992), *The Unnatural Nature of Science*, London, Faber and Faber.

2

RELIGION AND VALUES: A QUANTITATIVE PERSPECTIVE

Leslie J. Francis

Introduction

The majority of research projects conducted in England and Wales during the past twenty years into the worldviews of adolescents have routinely chosen to ignore the potential role of religion in shaping values, attitudes and behaviours, as exampled by Department of Education and Science (1983), Furnham and Stacey (1991), Balding (1993; 1997; 1998; 1999), Hendry, Shucksmith, Love and Glendinning (1993), Woodroffe, Glickman, Barker and Power (1993), Roberts and Sachdev (1996) and Kremer, Trew and Ogle (1997). The implicit assumption is clearly that religion is both privatised and marginalised in the modern world to the point that information about religiosity is irrelevant in understanding and interpreting the social and public worldview of young people.

The first major empirical survey to challenge this assumption within England and Wales was a study based on over 13,000 adolescents reported by Francis and Kay (1995). According to this study, religion persists as an important predictor of adolescent values over a wide range of areas. A second more recent analysis, reported by Gill (1999), came to similar conclusions from data collected among adults in the British Social Attitudes Surveys. On this account, religion is neither fully privatised nor fully marginalised in the modern world of the adolescent.

Clearly in modern society there remains a place for religious belief, religious practice and religious affiliation. The key question concerns the extent to which these well-established dimensions of religion function as predictors of social values, attitudes and behaviours and the value of using any one of these indicators in isolation from the others.

Historically, one of the most commonly used markers of religiosity in social surveys was self-assigned religious affiliation. More recently, confidence in self-assigned religious affiliation as a socially useful indicator of religiosity has been undermined from three directions. First, one influential account of religion in contemporary society has emphasised the persistence of 'believing without belonging', (Davie, 1994). A misreading of this account seems to elevate the importance of religious believing over religious affiliation. This misreading is based on ambiguity in the word 'belonging', which is used somewhat oddly in the classic phrase 'believing without belonging' to refer to practice rather than to affiliation. Second, researchers who are more concerned with religious practice than with religious affiliation draw attention to the fact that affiliation is itself a relatively poor predictor of practice. While the majority of self-assigned Baptists may well be regular churchgoers, the majority of self-assigned Anglicans in England appear never to consider going to church. Herein is the problem of 'religious nominalism'. The mistake is to consider that religious affiliation is insignificant in its own right except as a surrogate for other religious measures. Third, a number of scholars, working particularly in the social psychology of religion, have refined instruments to distinguish carefully between finely nuanced dimensions of religiosity, as exampled by the distinction between intrinsic, extrinsic and quest orientations (Batson, Schoenrade and Ventis, 1993). The mistake is to consider that only a complex theoretical account of religion can provide an adequate basis for empirical enquiry.

Although self-assigned religious affiliation is currently neglected as a socially useful indicator of religiosity, this remains potentially the most publicly acceptable and the most generally available indicator in light of the routine inclusion of a religious affiliation question in many national censuses. Indeed, such a question is currently planned for inclusion for the first time in England, Wales and Scotland in the census scheduled for 2001.

An important and powerful attempt to rehabilitate self-assigned religious affiliation as a theoretically coherent and socially significant indicator has been advanced by Fane (1999). Fane draws on Bouma's (1992) sociological theory of religious identification, according to which he defines religious affiliation as a 'useful social category giving some indication of the cultural background and general orientating values of a person'. Then Bouma posits a process through which 'cultural background' and 'general orientating values' are acquired. Importantly, this process of acquisition is exactly the same for religious identity as it is for political or sporting or philosophical identities, and consists of: first, 'meaning systems', which Bouma (1992, p. 106) describes as 'a set or collection of answers to questions about the meaning and purpose of life', and second, 'plausibility structures' (borrowed from Berger 1967, 1971), which Bouma (1992, p. 107) describes as 'social arrangements which serve to inculcate, celebrate, perpetuate and apply a meaning system'. He maintains that all of us possess meaning systems from which we derive our existential purpose. He cites a living Church as being one example of a plausibility structure through which a meaning system is, literally, made plausible and then disseminated. Although a self-assigned religious identity might also imply commitment to a plausibility structure (practice) and adherence to its related meaning system (belief), Bouma (1992, p. 108) suggests that it might be equally, perhaps more, significant in terms of the exposure to the particular cultural background that it represents. Crucially, this alternative conceptualisation avoids the difficult terrain of religious affiliation as proxy for practice and belief by recognising that even non-churchgoers and non-believers 'may still show the *effect* of the meaning system and plausibility structure with which they identify' (Bouma, 1992, p. 108, emphasis added).

The value of Bouma's sociological theory of religious identification is that it allows us to perceive, and thus analyse, a self-assigned religious affiliation as a key component of social identity, in a way similar to age, gender, class location, political persuasion, nationality, ethnic group and others (see Zavalloni, 1975, p. 200). It informs our attitudes and, in turn, our modes of behaviour by contributing to our self-definition both of who we are, but equally importantly, of who we are not. This type of analysis is especially advantageous when interpreting census data, because it is inclusive of all those who claim a religious affiliation, not only of the minority who also attend church.

Alongside Bouma's theory of religious identification, Fane (1999) also draws on Bibby's (1985) theory of 'encasement' developed from his empirical surveys in Canada. Bibby argues that Canadian Christians are 'encased' within the Christian tradition. In other words, this tradition has a strong, influential hold over both its active and latent members from which affiliates find it extremely difficult to extricate themselves. Contrary to the claims of secularisation theorists that low levels of church attendance are indicative of the erosion of religion's social significance (see Wallis and Bruce, 1992), Bibby (1985, 1987) would argue that this trend is actually a manifestation of the re-packaging of religion in the context of late-twentieth-century consumer-orientated society. Consumers, as we all are, are free to select 'fragments' of faith, and we are encouraged to do this by the way in which the Churches have simulated the marketing strategies of the wider society.

The central point to glean from Bibby's analysis is that the potential for religion, in this case Christianity, to be a socially significant attitudinal and behavioural determinant has not necessarily disappeared. If anything, the Christian 'casing' may have been strengthened, because the accommodationist stance adopted by the Christian Churches has, according to Bibby, reduced the need for affiliates to look elsewhere.

Against this background, the aim of the present study is to test the power of self-assigned religious affiliation to explain individual differences in social attitudes in a database of nearly 30,000 adolescents living in the modernity of England and Wales. The present analysis goes beyond the earlier work reported by Francis and Kay (1995) and by Gill (1999) in two important respects. Both of the earlier studies were concerned to model the influence of religion entirely within a Christian framework. The present study fully recognises the multifaith and multicultural context of modernity in England and Wales and includes the other major faith traditions with significant presence in these communities. Both of the earlier studies gave emphasis to exploring the relationship between religious practice and values. The present study is concerned to explore the dimension of religious affiliation.

Method

A detailed attitude inventory, developed by Francis (1982a, 1982b, 1984) and Francis and Kay (1995), was completed by 29,124 secondary school pupils attending year nine and year ten classes throughout England and Wales. The schools were selected to be representative of the geographical and social distribution of schools and to contain an appropriate representation of state-maintained, denominational and independent schools. The questionnaires were administered by the class teachers. The pupils were assured of anonymity and confidentiality. They were promised that no one within their school would read their answers, but that the completed questionnaires would be despatched to the University of Wales for computer coding and analysis. All the pupils were within the age-range of thirteen to fifteen years. There was an equal number of girls and boys.

In addition to a range of background questions, the questionnaire presented 128 Likert-type items arranged on a five-point scale: *agree strongly, agree, not certain, disagree* and *disagree strongly.* The aim of the current presentation is to illustrate the three key areas of personal values, family values and social values by reference to exemplar items. For clarity of presentation, the *agree strongly* responses were collapsed into the *agree* responses, and the *disagree strongly* responses were collapsed into the *disagree* responses.

Religious affiliation was determined in the questionnaire by a multiple-choice question identifying the major world faith traditions and the main Christian denominations. The final category 'other, please specify' allowed respondents to expand the range of pre-coded options.

Results
Religious affiliation
The majority of the 29,124 respondents to the survey (98.7%) completed and gave intelligible answers to the question regarding religious affiliation. Of those who provided intelligible information on religious affiliation, 15,398 (53.5%) identified a recognised faith group and 13,360 (46.5%) checked the 'none' category. These data make it clear that over half of thirteen- to fifteen-year-olds in England and Wales continue to identify with a recognised religious tradition. The first question to be asked in the subsequent analysis concerns the extent to which identification with any religious group functions as a predictor of adolescent values.

The majority of the 15,398 respondents who identified with a faith group (94.1%) provided responses that could be subdivided into two categories: 'Christian' and 'other world faiths'. Of those who could be so subdivided, 13,676 (94.4%) came within the Christian category and 806 (5.6%) came within the other world faith category. These data make it clear that although England and Wales are properly regarded as multicultural and multifaith societies, the Christian tradition, historically bedded within the culture, remains overwhelmingly the predominant faith. The second question to be asked in the subsequent analysis concerns the extent to which adolescent values differ between those who identify with the Christian tradition and those who identify with a non-Christian tradition.

The 806 respondents who identified with the other world faiths included sufficiently strong representation of four faith traditions to facilitate further analysis. There were 349 Muslims, 227 Sikhs, 125 Hindus and 71 Jews. These data make it clear that young Muslims constitute the largest non-Christian faith tradition within the school system of England and Wales. The third question to be asked in the subsequent analysis concerns the extent to which adolescent values differ between these four major faith traditions.

The 13,676 respondents who identified with a Christian church named a wide number of different denominations. The majority of these respondents (91.7%) can be conveniently grouped into four main categories: Anglicans, Catholics, mainline Protestants and sects. The remaining 8.3% provided answers like 'Christian', 'ecumenical', 'St Peters', or identified smaller groups that were not able to sustain independent analysis, like Orthodox or Mormon. There were 8,159 Anglicans (including Church of England and Church in Wales), 2,393 Catholics, 1,561 mainline Protestants (including Baptist, Methodist and Presbyterian) and 427 sects (including Jehovah's Witnesses and independent house churches). These data make it clear that the historically established Church of England still commands a larger following than other Christian Churches among young people in England and Wales, at least in terms of religious affiliation. The fourth question to be asked in the subsequent analysis concerns the extent to which adolescent values differ between these different Christian groups. Although further analysis could distinguish between the different mainline Protestant Churches and the different sects, it is not the intention of the present paper to do so.

Personal values

From the wide range of items in the questionnaire, the present analysis has selected four examples of personal values: belief in God, the sense of purpose in life, attitude toward alcohol and relationship with mother.

Table 1 explores the relationship between religious affiliation and belief in God. Several previous surveys prepare us for the way in which young people in the UK are less likely to believe in God than older people (Greeley, 1992). When young people in England and Wales are classified into the three discrete groups of atheists, agnostics and theists, those who believe in God still emerge as the largest category. Two in every five (42%) young people claim to believe in God, compared with one in four (25%) who claim to be atheists and one in three (33%) who claim to be agnostics.

The data make it clear that there is no perfect match between religious affiliation and religious belief. One in every four (24%) young people who claim no religious affiliation nonetheless still believe in God. This personal belief is sustained outside faith groups. At the same time, two out of every five (43%) young people who claim affiliation to a religious group nonetheless deny belief in God. For them, religious affiliation is concerned with something other than personal religious belief.

The relationship between religious affiliation and religious belief is stronger among the non-Christian faith groups than among the Christian group. Thus 45% of those who claim affiliation to the Christian Churches do not believe in God, compared with only 19% of those who claim affiliation to other world faiths.

Among the non-Christian faith groups there is considerable variation in the proportion who do not believe in God. Only 8% of Muslims do not believe in God, compared with 35% of Jews. There is also considerable variation among the Christian groups in the proportion who do not believe in God. Only 13% of those affiliated to sects do not believe in God, compared with 51% of Anglicans.

Religious affiliation is, therefore, a significant predictor of levels of belief in God, especially when distinctions are made between different faith groups *and* different Christian traditions.

Table 2 explores the relationship between religious affiliation and a sense of purpose in life. Purpose in life is central to the meaning-making process and religion is often considered central to shaping goals and purpose (Francis and Evans, 1996).

Overall, the data demonstrate that 56% of young people feel that their lives have a sense of purpose. The difference between those who belong to a faith group and those who do not belong to a faith group is highly significant. While 50% of those who do not belong to a faith group feel their lives have a sense of purpose, the proportion rises to 61% among those who belong to a faith group. The simple comparison between those who belong to Christian groups and those who belong to other faith groups reveals no significant differences. However, this simple comparison disguises considerable variation both within the Christian groups and within the other faith groups.

Among the non-Christian faith groups, young Sikhs record a significantly lower sense of purpose in life than young Hindus, Jews and Muslims. Among the Christian groups, young people affiliated with sectarian groups record a significantly higher sense of purpose in life than young Anglicans, Catholics and Protestants.

Religious affiliation is, therefore, a significant predictor of adolescent life satisfaction, especially when viewed by faith group *and* by Christian denomination.

Table 3 explores the relationship between religious affiliation and attitude toward alcohol. Health educators have long been concerned with the effect of drugs, including alcohol, on adolescent health (O'Connor, 1978; Campbell, 1984). Recent research in the UK has drawn attention to the role of religion in shaping attitudes in this area (Francis, 1997a). In particular, the social acceptability of alcohol may vary considerably from one religious tradition to another.

Overall, the data demonstrate that 20% of young people consider that it is wrong to become drunk. The difference between those who belong to a faith group and those who do not belong to a faith group is statistically significant. While 16% of those who do not belong to a faith group consider that it is wrong to become drunk, the proportion rises to 22% of those who belong to a religious group. This simple comparison, however, disguises considerable variation between the young Christians and the young members of other faith traditions. While 20% of the young Christians consider that it is wrong to become drunk, the proportion more than doubles to 49% among the adherents to other world faiths.

Among the non-Christian faith groups there is further considerable variation from the alcohol-accepting Jewish young people to the alcohol-rejecting Muslim young people. Thus, 68% of the Muslims consider that it is wrong to become drunk, compared with 20% of the Jews. Considerable variation also exists among the Christian groups, from the alcohol-accepting Catholics to the alcohol-rejecting sects. Thus, 44% of the young people who belong to sects consider that it is wrong to become drunk, compared with 18% of the Catholics.

Religious affiliation is, therefore, a significant predictor of adolescent attitudes toward alcohol, especially when viewed by faith groups *and* Christian denominations.

Table 4 explores the relationship between religious affiliation and relationship with mother. Many thirteen- to fifteen-year-olds still turn to mother for support and for advice (Francis and Evans, 1997).

Overall, the data demonstrate that 50% of young people find it helpful to talk about their problems with their mother. The difference between those who belong to a faith group and those who do not belong to a faith group is statistically significant. While 47% of those who do not belong to a faith group find it helpful to talk about their problems with their mother, the proportion rises to 52% among those who belong to a faith group.

On this occasion, it is important to distinguish between those who identify with a Christian Church and those who identify with another faith tradition. Thus, 53% of the Christians find it helpful to talk about their problems with their mother, compared with 49% of the adherents to other faith groups. This simple comparison, however, disguises considerable variation within both the Christian group and the other faith group.

Among the non-Christian faith groups, 71% of young Jews find it helpful to talk about their problems with their mother, compared with 40% of the young Hindus and 45% of the young Sikhs. Among the

Christian groups, 58% of the young people associated with a sect find it helpful to talk about their problems with their mother, compared with 50% of the Catholics, 52% of the Protestants, and 50% of the Anglicans.

Religious affiliation is, therefore, a significant predictor of the support that young people receive at home, especially when viewed by faith group *and* Christian denomination.

Family values

From the wide range of items in the questionnaire, the present analysis selected four examples of family values: sexual intercourse outside marriage, homosexuality, divorce and abortion.

Table 5 explores the relationship between religious affiliation and attitude toward sexual intercourse outside marriage. The development of attitudes and values related to sexuality is fundamental to the process of adolescence (Rosenthal and Moore, 1993). Moreover, religion and sexuality are closely interrelated areas of human experience (Thatcher, 1993).

Overall, the data demonstrate that 14% of young people agree that it is wrong to have sexual intercourse outside marriage. The difference between those who belong to a faith group and those who do not belong to a faith group is statistically significant. While 11% of those who do not belong to a faith group feel that it is wrong to have sexual intercourse outside marriage, the proportion rises to 17% of those who belong to a faith group.

A more striking difference, however, concerns the comparison of those who identify with a Christian Church and those who identify with a non-Christian faith tradition. Thus, 38% of those identifying with a non-Christian faith tradition consider that it is wrong to have sexual intercourse outside marriage, compared with 15% of the Christians.

Further significant differences also emerge both within the Christian group and within the other faith group. Thus, 49% of the Muslim young people consider that it is wrong to have sexual intercourse outside marriage, compared with 27% of the Sikhs and 27% of the Jews. Over half (57%) of the young Christians associated with sects consider that it is wrong to have sex outside marriage, compared with 13% of the Anglicans and 15% of the Catholics.

Religious affiliation is, therefore, a significant predictor of adolescent views on sexual intercourse outside marriage, especially when viewed by faith group *and* Christian denomination.

Table 6 explores the relationship between religious affiliation and attitude toward homosexuality. Recent debate within the Christian community, for example, has identified considerable controversy over this issue (Yip, 1999). Some Christian groups take a more conservative line, emphasising continuity with tradition. Other Christian groups take a more liberal line, emphasising the acceptance of individual differences.

Overall, the data demonstrate that 38% of young people consider homosexuality to be wrong. The difference between those who belong to a faith group and those who do not belong to a faith group is statistically significant but very small, with 37% of those who belong to a faith group considering homosexuality to be wrong, compared with 38% of those who do not belong to a faith group.

Comparisons between those who belong to Christian groups and those who belong to other faith groups is also significant. While 36% of the Christians consider homosexuality to be wrong, the proportion rises to 42% among the other faith groups.

The variation between the different faith groups is highly significant. It is the Muslim community that stands out as holding the strongest position against homosexuality. Over half (55%) of the Muslims consider homosexuality to be wrong, compared with 31% of the Sikhs, 28% of the Hindus and 24% of the Jews.

The variation between the different Christian denominations is also highly significant. It is the members of the sects who stand out as holding the strongest position against homosexuality. Nearly three quarters (71%) of the members of sects consider homosexuality to be wrong, compared with 37% of the Catholics, 34% of the Protestants and 34% of the Anglicans.

Religious affiliation is, therefore, a significant predictor of adolescent views on homosexuality, especially when distinctions are made between different faith groups *and* different Christian denominations.

Table 7 explores the relationship between religious affiliation and attitude toward divorce. The issue of divorce is very relevant to the stability of family life and to the environment in which young people are reared. In turn, parental divorce has been shown to be reflected in the personal and social values adopted by their offspring (Francis and Evans, 1997).

Overall, the data demonstrate that around one young person in every five (19%) consider divorce to be wrong. Those who belong to a faith group remain significantly less in favour of divorce. Thus, 21% of the members of faith groups regard divorce to be wrong, compared with 17% of those who belong to no faith group.

While the difference between those who belong to a faith group and those who belong to no faith group is relatively small, a much larger difference emerges when comparison is made between the Christians and the members of other world faiths. Thus, 33% of those who belong to other faith groups consider divorce to be wrong, compared with 20% of Christians.

Considerable differences emerge between the different faith groups. Once again, it is the Muslim community that stands out as holding the strongest position against divorce. Over two fifths (42%) of the Muslims consider divorce to be wrong, compared with 28% of Sikhs, 21% of Jews and 20% of Hindus.

Considerable differences also emerge between the different Christian denominations. Once again, it is the members of sects who stand out as holding the strongest position against divorce. Nearly half (47%) of the members of sects consider divorce to be wrong, compared with 23% of the Protestants, 23% of the Catholics and 18% of the Anglicans.

Religious affiliation is, therefore, a significant predictor of adolescent views on divorce, especially when distinctions are made between different faith groups *and* different Christian denominations.

Table 8 explores the relationship between religious affiliation and attitude toward abortion. The question of abortion brings together concerns to do with sexual mores and concerns to do with the sanctity of life. Both of these concerns are fundamental to religious traditions (Emerson, 1996).

Overall, the data demonstrate that just over one third (36%) of the young people agree that abortion is wrong. The difference between those who belong to a faith group and those who do not belong to a faith group is in the expected direction. While 33% of those who do not belong to a faith group agree that abortion is wrong, the proportion rises to 38% among those who belong to a faith group.

Further information is clearly conveyed by distinguishing between those who belong to the Christian faith and those who belong to a non-Christian faith tradition. While 38% of the Christians agree that abortion is wrong, the proportion rises to 46% among those who belong to a non-Christian faith group.

Further differentiations between the different faith groups and the different Christian denominations also prove highly significant. Among the non-Christian faith groups, the Muslim community takes a stricter view against abortion than the other faith communities. Thus, 58% of the Muslims regard abortion as wrong, compared with 40% of the Sikhs, 31% of the Hindus and 27% of the Jews. Among the Christian denominations, members of sects take a stricter view against abortion than other denominations, with Catholics coming into second place. Thus, 65% of those who belong to sects regard abortion as wrong, compared with 50% of the Catholics, 38% of the Protestants and 31% of the Anglicans.

Religious affiliation is, therefore, a significant predictor of adolescent views on abortion, especially when distinctions are made between different faith groups *and* different Christian denominations.

Social values
From the wide range of items in the questionnaire, the present analysis selected four examples of social values: attitudes toward the police, concern for the environment, views on pornography and views on violence on television.

Table 9 explores the relationship between religious affiliation and attitude toward the police. Young people's attitudes toward the police in particular provide a useful indicator of the way in which they regard themselves in relation to law and order. In one sense, religion may be considered to promote civil order and obedience. In another sense, religion may contribute to the definition of minority status and alienation from the law (Cashmore, 1979).

Overall, the data demonstrate that 55% of young people consider that the police do a good job. The difference between those who belong to a faith group and those who do not belong to a faith group is statistically significant. While 51% of those who do not belong to a faith group feel that the police do a good job, the proportion rises to 58% among those who belong to a faith group.

In respect of this issue, however, the difference between the Christian group and the non-Christian group is highly significant. Among the Christian faith group, 59% consider that the police do a good job. Among the non-Christian faith group, 44% consider that the police do a good job.

At the same time, there are considerable variations within the different Christian groups and within the different non-Christian faith groups. Among the non-Christian faith group, the proportions of young people who consider that the police do a good job vary from 55% among the Jews to 35% among the Sikhs. Among the Christians, the proportions vary from 65% among the sects to 53% among the Catholics.

Religious affiliation is, therefore, a significant predictor of adolescent attitudes toward the law, especially when viewed by faith groups *and* Christian denominations.

Table 10 explores the relationship between religious affiliation and environmental concern. According to some commentators, religious traditions can detract from proper care for the environment. According to other commentators, religions traditions can promote care for the environment. A growing empirical literature has begun to map this area (Francis, 1997b).

Overall, the data demonstrate that 66% of young people are concerned about the risk of pollution to the environment. The difference between those who belong to a faith group and those who do not belong to a faith group is highly significant. While 63% of those who do not belong to a faith group are concerned about the risk of pollution to the environment, the proportion rises to 69% among those who belong to a faith group.

To regard all those who belong to a faith group as coming within one category is, however, misleading. A further significant difference emerges between those who identify with a Christian group and those who identify with a non-Christian faith group. While 70% of the Christians are concerned about pollution to the environment, the proportion falls to 64% among the non-Christian faith groups.

Quite large variation also exists between members of the non-Christian faith groups, although in view of the sample size this does not reach statistical significance. Thus, 75% of the Jews are concerned about the risk of pollution to the environment, compared with 62% of the Muslims and 61% of the Sikhs.

The variation among the Christian Churches reaches statistical significance. Thus, 67% of the Catholics are concerned about the risk of pollution to the environment, compared with 72% of the Anglicans and 73% of the Protestants.

Religious affiliation is, therefore, a significant predictor of adolescent attitudes toward the environment, especially when distinctions are made between different faith groups *and* different Christian denominations.

Table 11 explores the relationship between religious affiliation and attitude toward pornography. Religion's established role as guardian of sexual mores is likely to be expressed in a less tolerant attitude toward pornography (Jelen, 1986).

Overall, the data demonstrate that a third (33%) of the young people consider that pornography is too readily available. The difference between those who belong to a faith group and those who do not belong to a faith group is statistically significant in the predicted direction. While 30% of those who do not belong to a faith group consider that pornography is too readily available, the proportion rises to 36% among those who belong to a faith group.

There is also a statistically significant difference between those who belong to a Christian group and those who belong to a non-Christian faith group. Among the Christian group 36% consider that pornography is too readily available, compared with 40% among the non-Christian faith group.

The differences between Hindus, Jews, Muslims and Sikhs do not reach statistical significance on this issue. Among the Christian groups the real comparison is between the sects on the one hand and the Anglicans, Catholics and Protestants on the other hand. Nearly three fifths (57%) of those who belong to a sect consider that pornography is too readily available, compared with 38% of the Catholics, 37% of the Protestants and 34% of the Anglicans.

Religious affiliation is, therefore, a significant predictor of adolescent attitudes toward pornography, especially when distinctions are made between different Christian denominations.

Table 12 explores the relationship between religious affiliation and attitude toward violence on television. Several recent studies have demonstrated that religion is an important predictor of adolescent television-viewing behaviour and attitudes, alongside other demographic variables like age, sex and social class (Francis and Gibson, 1993).

Overall, the data demonstrate that one young person in five (20%) considers that there is too much violence on television. The difference between those who belong to a faith group and those who do not belong to a faith group is statistically significant. While 17% of those who do not belong to a faith group consider that there is too much violence on television, the proportion rises to 22% among those who belong to a faith group.

The difference between the Christians and those who belong to a non-Christian faith group is also statistically significant on this issue. Thus, 29% of those who belong to a non-Christian faith group consider that there is too much violence on television, compared with 22% of those who belong to a Christian group.

On this issue, strong differences also emerge between the different faith groups and between the different Christian denominations. Among the non-Christian faith groups, it is the Muslims who stand out as taking the most critical view of television. Nearly two fifths (38%) of the young Muslims consider that there is too much violence on television, compared with 24% of the Hindus, 21% of the Jews and 20% of the Sikhs. Among the Christian denominations, it is the sects who stand out as taking the most critical view of television. Over two fifths (43%) of the young people who belong to sects consider that there is too much violence on television, compared with 26% of the Protestants, 21% of the Anglicans and 20% of the Catholics.

Religious affiliation is, therefore, a significant predictor of adolescent attitudes toward violence on television, especially when distinctions are made between different faith groups *and* between different Christian denominations.

Conclusion

The data presented in the foregoing analyses have demonstrated the power of self-assigned religious affiliation to predict adolescent values over a wide range of issues, including personal values, family values and social values. According to these data, self-assigned religious affiliation is most powerful as a social indicator in England and Wales when proper distinctions are made both between major world faiths and between different Christian denominations. The fact that these data have been collected among teenagers strengthens two key conclusions.

The first conclusion supports the contention that religion remains a significant social influence in modernity. Even among young people, those most exposed to and shaped by the influences of modernity, religion shapes personal and social attitudes and behaviours. In the light of such overwhelming evidence, any attempt to understand modernity that ignores the influence of religion can be at best only partial and at worst grossly misleading. The view that in modernity religion is privatised and marginalised is clearly contradicted by the evidence.

The second conclusion supports the contention that self-assigned religious affiliation is itself a sufficient and adequate indicator of key aspects of the social significance of religion in modernity. That this is the case among young people, those inevitably shaped by the families and cultures into which they have been born, adds significant weight to the case advanced by Fane (1999). According to this case, self-assigned religious affiliation is not to be seen as a poor proxy to more perceptive measures of religious belief or religious practice, but as a key component of social identity, in a way similar to age, gender, class and ethnic group. In this sense, even in modernity, individuals remain encased within the religious tradition that they own through self-assigned religious affiliation. Such encasement carries with it deep-rooted values of considerable social and public significance.

Acknowledgement

I am grateful to Ros Fane for developing and sharing with me her argument for the social significance of self-assigned religious affiliation, which stimulated the analysis presented in this paper.

Table 1   I believe in God

overview

agree	42%
uncertain	33%
disagree	25%

belong to faith group?

no	24%	
yes	57%	(χ^2 = 3638.8, P<.001)

type of faith group

Christian	55%	
other	81%	(χ^2 = 276.5, P<.001)

non-Christian faith groups

Hindu	79%	
Jewish	65%	
Muslim	92%	
Sikh	74%	(χ^2 = 62.3, P<.001)

Christian groups

Anglican	49%	
Catholic	70%	
Protestant	63%	
sects	87%	(χ^2 = 694.7, P<.001)

Note: The overview statistics presents the percentage of young people who agree, who are uncertain and who also disagree. The remaining statistics compare the percentages within different categories who agree.

Table 2   I feel my life has a sense of purpose

---

overview

agree	56%
uncertain	35%
disagree	10%

belong to faith group?

no	50%	
yes	61%	$(\chi^2 = 376.1, P<.001)$

type of faith group

Christian	61%	
other	63%	$(\chi^2 = 1.3, NS)$

non-Christian faith groups

Hindu	62%	
Jewish	64%	
Muslim	68%	
Sikh	51%	$(\chi^2 = 23.1, P<.001)$

Christian groups

Anglican	59%	
Catholic	65%	
Protestant	63%	
sects	76%	$(\chi^2 = 89.2, P<.001)$

Table 3   It is wrong to become drunk

---

overview

agree	20%
uncertain	17%
disagree	64%

belong to faith group?

no	16%	
yes	22%	(χ^2 = 178.7, P<.001)

type of faith group

Christian	20%	
other	49%	(χ^2 = 486.3, P<.001)

non-Christian faith groups

Hindu	31%	
Jewish	20%	
Muslim	68%	
Sikh	35%	(χ^2 = 142.8, P<.001)

Christian groups

Anglican	19%	
Catholic	18%	
Protestant	26%	
sects	44%	(χ^2 = 267.1, P<.001)

Table 4   I find it helpful to talk about my problems with my mother

overview

agree	50%
uncertain	19%
disagree	31%

belong to faith group?

no	47%	
yes	52%	(χ^2 = 92.9, P<.001)

type of faith group

Christian	53%	
other	49%	(χ^2 = 4.8, P<.05)

non-Christian faith groups

Hindu	40%	
Jewish	71%	
Muslim	52%	
Sikh	45%	(χ^2 = 24.1, P<.001)

Christian groups

Anglican	54%	
Catholic	50%	
Protestant	52%	
sects	58%	(χ^2 = 17.2, P<.001)

Table 5   It is wrong to have sexual intercourse outside marriage

overview

agree	14%
uncertain	15%
disagree	71%

belong to faith group?

no	11%	
yes	17%	($\chi^2 = 258.5$, P<.001)

type of faith group

Christian	15%	
other	38%	($\chi^2 = 356.6$, P<.001)

non-Christian faith groups

Hindu	29%	
Jewish	23%	
Muslim	49%	
Sikh	27%	($\chi^2 = 53.3$, P<.001)

Christian groups

Anglican	13%	
Catholic	15%	
Protestant	19%	
sects	57%	($\chi^2 = 863.2$, P<.001)

Table 6   Homosexuality is wrong

overview

agree	38%
uncertain	24%
disagree	38%

belong to faith group?

no	38%	
yes	37%	$(\chi^2 = 8.0, P<.01)$

type of faith group

Christian	36%	
other	42%	$(\chi^2 = 13.3, P<.001)$

non-Christian faith groups

Hindu	28%	
Jewish	24%	
Muslim	55%	
Sikh	31%	$(\chi^2 = 71.1, P<.001)$

Christian groups

Anglican	34%	
Catholic	37%	
Protestant	34%	
sects	71%	$(\chi^2 = 325.2, P<.001)$

Table 7   Divorce is wrong

overview

agree	19%
uncertain	26%
disagree	55%

belong to faith group?

no	17%	
yes	21%	$(\chi^2 = 108.6, P<.001)$

type of faith group

Christian	20%	
other	33%	$(\chi^2 = 95.4, P<.001)$

non-Christian faith groups

Hindu	20%	
Jewish	21%	
Muslim	42%	
Sikh	28%	$(\chi^2 = 39.5, P<.001)$

Christian groups

Anglican	18%	
Catholic	23%	
Protestant	23%	
sects	47%	$(\chi^2 = 330.7, P<.001)$

Table 8	Abortion is wrong

overview

agree	36%
uncertain	30%
disagree	34%

belong to faith group?

no	33%	
yes	38%	(χ^2 = 80.3, P<.001)

type of faith group

Christian	38%	
other	46%	(χ^2 = 32.2, P<.001)

non-Christian faith groups

Hindu	31%	
Jewish	27%	
Muslim	58%	
Sikh	40%	(χ^2 = 59.6, P<.001)

Christian groups

Anglican	31%	
Catholic	50%	
Protestant	38%	
sects	65%	(χ^2 = 598.1, P<.001)

Table 9   The police do a good job

---

overview

agree	55%
uncertain	22%
disagree	24%

belong to faith group?

no	51%	
yes	58%	($\chi^2 = 147.7$, P<.001)

type of faith group

Christian	59%	
other	44%	($\chi^2 = 86.0$, P<.001)

non-Christian faith groups

Hindu	40%	
Jewish	55%	
Muslim	49%	
Sikh	35%	($\chi^2 = 18.1$, P<.001)

Christian groups

Anglican	61%	
Catholic	53%	
Protestant	63%	
sects	65%	($\chi^2 = 83.2$, P<.001)

Table 10 I am concerned about the risk of pollution to the environment

overview

agree	66%
uncertain	24%
disagree	10%

belong to faith group?

no	63%	
yes	69%	(χ^2 = 170.4, P<.001)

type of faith group

Christian	70%	
other	64%	(χ^2 = 16.2, P<.001)

non-Christian faith groups

Hindu	69%	
Jewish	75%	
Muslim	62%	
Sikh	61%	(χ^2 = 7.6, NS)

Christian groups

Anglican	72%	
Catholic	67%	
Protestant	73%	
sects	70%	(χ^2 = 38.8, P<.001)

Table 11   Pornography is too readily available

overview

agree	33%
uncertain	35%
disagree	31%

belong to faith group?

no	30%	
yes	36%	(χ^2 = 164.7, P<.001)

type of faith group

Christian	36%	
other	40%	(χ^2 = 6.2, P<.05)

non-Christian faith groups

Hindu	45%	
Jewish	36%	
Muslim	40%	
Sikh	40%	(χ^2 = 2.3, NS)

Christian groups

Anglican	34%	
Catholic	38%	
Protestant	37%	
sects	57%	(χ^2 = 144.4, P<.001)

Table 12   There is too much violence on television

overview

agree	20%
uncertain	22%
disagree	58%

belong to faith group?

no	17%	
yes	22%	(χ^2 = 154.4, P<.001)

type of faith group

Christian	22%	
other	29%	(χ^2 = 30.5, P<.001)

non-Christian faith groups

Hindu	24%	
Jewish	21%	
Muslim	38%	
Sikh	20%	(χ^2 = 33.9, P<.001)

Christian groups

Anglican	21%	
Catholic	20%	
Protestant	26%	
sects	43%	(χ^2 = 188.5, P<.001)

References

Balding, J. (1993), *Young People in 1992*, Exeter, Schools Health Education Unit, University of Exeter.

Balding, J. (1997), *Young People in 1996*, Exeter, Schools Health Education Unit, University of Exeter.

Balding, J. (1998), *Young People in 1997*, Exeter, Schools Health Education Unit, University of Exeter.

Balding, J. (1999), *Young People in 1998*, Exeter, Schools Health Education Unit, University of Exeter.

Batson, C.D., Schoenrade, P. and Ventis, W.L. (1993), *Religion and the Individual: a social-psychological perspective*, Oxford, Oxford University Press.

Berger, P.L. (1967), *The Sacred Canopy: elements of a sociology of religion*, New York, Doubleday.

Berger, P.L. (1971), *A Rumour of Angels: modern society and the rediscovery of the supernatural*, Harmondsworth, Penguin Books.

Bibby, R.W. (1985), Religious encasement in Canada: an argument for Protestant and Catholic entrenchment, *Social Compass*, 16, 287-303.

Bibby, R.W. (1987), *Fragmented Gods: the poverty and potential of religion in Canada*, Toronto, Irwin Publishing.

Bouma, G.D. (1992), *Religion: meaning, transcendence and community in Australia*, Melbourne, Longman Cheshire.

Campbell, G. (ed.) (1984), *Health Education and Youth*, London, Falmer Press.

Cashmore, E. (1979), *Rastaman: the Rastafarian Movement in England*, London, George Allen and Unwin.

Davie, G. (1994), *Religion in Britain since 1945: believing without belonging*, Oxford, Blackwell.

Department of Education and Science (1983), *Young People in the 80s: a survey*, London, Her Majesty's Stationery Office.

Emerson, M.O. (1996), Through tinted glasses: religion, worldviews and abortion attitudes, *Journal for the Scientific Study of Religion*, 35, 41-55.

Fane, R.S. (1999), Is self-assigned religious affiliation socially significant? in L.J. Francis (ed.), *Sociology, Theology and the Curriculum*, pp 113-124, London, Cassell.

Francis, L.J. (1982a), *Youth in Transit: a profile of 16-25 year olds*, Aldershot, Gower.

Francis, L.J. (1982b), *Experience of Adulthood: a profile of 26-39 year olds*, Aldershot, Gower.

Francis, L.J. (1984), *Teenagers and the Church: a profile of churchgoing youth in the 1980s*, London, Collins Liturgical Publications.

Francis, L.J. (1997a), The impact of personality and religion on attitude toward substance use among 13-15 year olds, *Drug and Alcohol Dependence*, 44, 95-103.

Francis, L.J. (1997b), Christianity, personality and concern about environmental pollution, *Journal of Beliefs and Values*, 18, 7-16.

Francis, L.J. and Evans, T.E. (1996), The relationship between personal prayer and purpose in life among churchgoing and non-churchgoing 12-15 year olds in the UK, *Religious Education*, 91, 9-21.

Francis, L.J. and Evans, T.E. (1997), The relationship between marital disruption, and adolescent values: a study among 13-15 year olds, *Journal of Divorce and Remarriage*, 26, 195-213.

Francis, L.J. and Gibson, H.M. (1993), The influence of age, sex, social class and religion on television viewing time and programme preferences among 11-15 year olds, *Journal of Educational Television*, 19, 25-35.

Francis, L.J. and Kay, W.K. (1995), *Teenage Religion and Values*, Leominster, Gracewing.

Furnham, A. and Stacey, B. (1991), *Young People's Understanding of Society*, London, Routledge.

Gill, R. (1999), *Churchgoing and Christian Ethics*, Cambridge, Cambridge University Press.

Greeley, A. (1992), Religion in Britain, Ireland and the USA, in R. Jowell, L. Brook, G. Prior and B. Taylor (eds), *British Social Attitudes: the 9th report,* pp 51-70, Aldershot, Dartmouth Publishers.

Hendry, L.B., Shucksmith, J., Love, J.G. and Glendinning, A. (1993), *Young People's Leisure and Lifestyles,* London, Routledge.

Jelen, T.G. (1986), Fundamentalism, feminism, and attitudes toward pornography, *Review of Religious Research,* 28, 97-103.

Kremer, J., Trew, K. and Ogle, S. (eds) (1997), *Young People's Involvement in Sport,* London, Routledge.

O'Connor, J.C. (1978), *The Young Drinkers: a cross-national study of social and cultural influences,* London, Tavistock Publications.

Roberts, H. and Sachdev, D. (eds) (1996), *Young People's Social Attitudes: the views of 12-19 year olds,* Barkingside, Barnardos.

Rosenthal, D. and Moore, S. (1993), *Sexuality in Adolescence,* London, Routledge.

Thatcher, A. (1993), *Liberating Sex,* London, SPCK.

Wallis, R. and Bruce, S. (1992), Secularization: the orthodox model, in S. Bruce (ed.), *Religion and Modernization: sociologists and historians debate the secularisation thesis,* pp 8-30, Oxford, Clarendon Press.

Woodroffe, C., Glickman, M., Barker, M. and Power, C. (1993), *Children, Teenagers and Health: the key data,* Buckingham, Open University Press.

Yip, A.K.T. (1999), Gay and lesbian Christians: the lived experiences, in L.J. Francis (ed.), *Sociology, Theology and the Curriculum,* pp 187-196, London, Cassell.

Zavalloni, M. (1975), Social identity and the recording of reality: its relevance for cross-cultural psychology, *International Journal of Psychology,* 10, 197-217.

3

BAUDRILLARD, SIMULATION AND THE DEBATE ABOUT COLLECTIVE WORSHIP IN SCHOOLS

J. Mark Halstead

Introduction

The opposition to the continuing legal requirement of a daily act of collective worship in schools in England and Wales is generally expressed within a liberal framework of values and takes for granted the assumptions of liberal education. The argument contains three main components. First, it is impossible to find a form of worship that is acceptable to all the faith groups in our pluralist, multifaith society, and therefore collective worship in the common school is an inappropriate activity because it would inevitably privilege one faith group over others (cf. DES, 1985: 497). Second, even if it were possible to find a form of worship that was acceptable to all faith groups at the same time, collective worship in schools would still be inappropriate within secular liberal education because it presupposes belief and thus involves promoting one particular conception of the good at the expense of others. This means that school worship has more in common with indoctrination than with education (cf. British Humanist Association, 1975). Third, worship should in any case be a voluntary act, a free response to personal belief in God, which cannot be compelled by means of legislation (cf. Hull, 1975: p 34).

It is very difficult to argue with this position, grounded as it is in the fundamental liberal values of liberty, equality and rationality and in the belief that free critical debate is the most rational way for the pursuit of truth (cf. Halstead, 1996). If we accept that education is about the development of personal rational autonomy, critical openness, equality of opportunity, rational morality, the celebration of diversity, democratic decision-making and the free market of ideas, then it is very hard to justify any activity in schools that involves siding with one particular definitive conception of the good and forcing children to engage in an activity that belongs to the domain of free personal choice. As Phenix (1965: 90) points out, 'The purpose of academic teaching is to increase understanding, not advocate a particular religious position'.

It is true that believers have sometimes tried to offer counter-arguments, including the following four points. First, those who object to collective worship should have the right to withdraw from it, but not the right to deny the experience to others. Second, the presence of Sikhs, Muslims and other religious minorities in schools should not be used as a justification for policies such as the abandonment of school worship, which are diametrically opposed to their own wishes (cf. Halstead and Khan-Cheema, 1987). Third, collective worship in schools opens up a new dimension of experience for many children which they would not gain elsewhere. Fourth, participation in common traditions with deep historical roots, such as religious worship, has an important contribution to make to the education of children and to their development of self-knowledge and knowledge about the origin of the shared values of society, irrespective of their personal religious faith (cf. Haldane, 1986).

But these counter-arguments are not strong enough to outweigh the basic liberal argument that public institutions should not promote any particular version of the good. Liberalism supports equally the freedom to worship and the freedom not to worship. Liberal schools may teach all children about worship as part of their general education, but children do not need to practise worship in order to learn about it. It is often claimed by its supporters that collective worship is an important educational activity (cf. Religious Educational Council, 1996: 44-6), but Thatcher (1997: 5-11) presents some convincing arguments that worshipping is one of very few human activities that are not educational. Teaching children about worship is quite different from forcing them to worship. It is there that the argument ends for many people who see it as just a matter of time until the law on collective worship in schools is brought into line with the liberal perspective. But is this really the end of the matter? There are growing numbers of people who have doubts as to whether liberal education and the values that underpin it provide the only justifiable way of thinking about education or the only adequate account of all that is important for children to learn. Postmodernism has emerged as the major challenge to liberal values in the new millennium. The aim of the present chapter is to examine the insights postmodernism offers into human nature and the nature of education, and then to apply these insights to the debate about collective worship.

Postmodernism is a hugely complicated set of interlocking ideas, and to make the topic more manageable, the discussion has been narrowed down to one postmodernist thinker, Jean Baudrillard, a former professor of sociology in Paris, whose writings are currently at the cutting edge of the postmodernism debate in both the United States of America and the United Kingdom. The present chapter will argue that from a postmodernist perspective, collective worship can most appropriately be viewed as 'simulated worship'. This understanding of collective worship has important implications for the debate about the justifiability of collective worship in schools, as well as for thinking about ways of making collective worship more meaningful for pupils as we move into the next millennium.

The chapter is divided into three sections. The first section sketches some of Baudrillard's central ideas and shows how these represent a significant challenge to liberal values. The second section focuses on one of Baudrillard's key ideas 'simulation' and considers its relevance to schooling generally and to collective worship in particular. The final section focuses on the current situation of collective worship and future possibilities are reviewed in the light of the emerging postmodern worldview.

The apocalyptic vision of Jean Baudrillard

Jean Baudrillard is one of the most discussed, most significant and most controversial social theorists in France today. He has increasingly turned away from sustained systematic analysis, preferring vast, unqualified generalisations which leave no room for argument. His contempt for facts and definitions makes it easy to criticise him from a rational, liberal perspective, and his manner of presentation is often clumsy (cf. Bertens, 1995, pp 156-7). In spite of these limitations, however, his writing is of unique importance to anyone interested in current thought. Unsatisfactory and unclassifiable though his work may be, it nevertheless throws up disturbing questions, which will be dismissed only with a bad conscience. To introduce his work, let me focus briefly on three recurrent ideas in his publications: fashion (see Baudrillard, 1993: chapter 3), consumerism (see Baudrillard, 1998) and simulation (see Baudrillard, 1983c).

Fashion

In the narrower sense, fashion refers to our attitudes to clothes, the body, objects, but in the broader sense we can see fashion in politics, morals, economics, science, culture, sexuality, even research priorities (Baudrillard, 1993: 87). There is something irrational about fashion, its sense of spectacle and squandering, its arbitrariness, its attempt to elevate sign over meaning, its narcissism, its subversion of order, its rejection of ideology, its lack of a moral focus (Baudrillard, 1993: 94). It is this irrationality that makes fashion a symbol of the resistance of many young people to the liberal values that Western education seeks to impart. It is perceived as an alternative route to self-esteem. Our lives easily become a patchwork constructed from scraps of fashionable images drawn mainly from the television. When we get hungry, for example, we can pop an Italian-style meal into the microwave and it cooks in minutes; it tastes awful, but the slim, sexy people who eat it on television seem to love it, and we are seduced into wanting a life like theirs. There is no escape from fashion: attempts to resist fashion become the new fashion, as the current trend in body-piercing shows.

Consumerism

Baudrillard (1983b: 46; 1998) argues that nowadays people are socialised into consumption from an early age. They learn in school, at home, from their peers and from the media about commodities and how to master their use and how to earn the money and leisure needed to purchase them and use them. Everything that is valued is now commodified. Even sex has become a commercial commodity that is an important part of modern industrial production (fashion and cosmetic industries, contraception, pornography, newspapers, satellite TV) and still more important in marketing nearly everything (cf.

Weeks, 1991). But commodities are no longer produced simply to satisfy needs; they confer status and prestige, and thus serve as indexes of social standing in the consumer society (cf. Sarup, 1996: 107). Objects or brands are no longer chosen over others because they are more useful, durable or attractive, but because of the way they are marketed, and because of their 'sign value', their socially constructed prestige value (cf. Hull, 1996). Symbolic value thus becomes more important than actual value. Signs and codes have become the primary constituents of social life, of the 'real'. To buy a coke is no longer to buy a fizzy drink to quench one's thirst, it is to enter a sexy, fun-loving, carefree, youthful world – so long as one buys the right brand (cf. Poster, 1995: 106).

Simulation

In the modern, liberal world we can readily tell the difference between representation and reality, between simulation and truth, between an idea and the thing it refers to. Objects have their own precise characteristics and differ from their images and representations (cf. Bauman, 1992: 150).

Baudrillard says that all these things now are hopelessly mixed up, and that simulation is dominant in many areas of life. I am grateful to Paul Muff for the following description of a Baudrillard-style postmodern holiday experience.

Kylie and Jason fly out to Marmaris in Turkey in August, where the temperature is 120 degrees in the shade. They go to a night-club with air-conditioning, where a band called Abbaesque is playing 'Dancing Queen'. Jason decides to play the video ski-race machine, and within seconds is gliding down the *piste* in an imaginary snow-scape universe. Kylie is wearing the headphones of a personal stereo which plays Kraftwerk's 'Autobahn', while at the same time exploring the effects of an Ecstasy tablet which Jason purchased from a drag queen outside the club. While 'skiing', Jason is thinking of a scene from the film 'Blue Velvet', and trying to remember the name of the Roy Orbison song in the movie which he is hoping to sing at the Karaoke later in the evening.

For Baudrillard, simulation removes the difference between the authentic and the fake, the real and the imaginary. There is no longer any objective test that can be applied in order to distinguish false from true, representation from reality. For Baudrillard, simulation is 'no longer a question of the false representation of reality (ideology), but of concealing the fact that the real is no longer real, at least no more real than the next thing, no firmer than the thing which feigns it' (Bauman, 1992a: 151). In the past we knew that a map represented a territory (Baudrillard, 1983c: 1-2), and that an opinion poll represented public opinion (Baudrillard, 1985: 578-582). But now we live in a state of 'hyper-reality', where we are faced with images that represent nothing but themselves, information that does not inform, experiences that only appear real (Baudrillard, 1983a). Hyper-reality does not set itself against the unreal, the illusionary, the fake, the imaginary; it absorbs them all equally into its own enlarged vision of the world. What is real politics, asks Bauman: 'the smiling faces on TV emitting headline-catching one-liners, or the profound visions and world-shattering deeds they simulate' (1992a: 151)? What is the erotic, we might add: the 'plastic sexuality' that is left once sexuality has been separated from reproduction (Giddens, 1992), or the 'sim-stim' (simulated sexual stimulation) of Gibson's (1993) classic cyberpunk story, *Burning Chrome*? It is also relevant to note how characters in this story save their money to have 'a face job' which converts them into virtual clones of cult figures. We can no longer say where reality and truth lie. In hyper-reality, 'truth has not been destroyed,' says Bauman (1992a: 151), 'it has been made irrelevant.'

This side-lining of truth combined with the rapid spread of the hyper-real through the media ushers in the collapse of both Marxist and liberal politics as dominant ideologies. As Poster (1995: 112) points out, individuals are no longer citizens of a rationally ordered state, eager to maximise their civil rights, nor yet proletarians anticipating the onset of communism, but merely passive consumers faced with a myriad of advertising images and self-referential signs. More ominously, perhaps, they are faced with a daily diet of simulated violence: by the time they leave school, most children will have witnessed tens of thousands of simulated murders, robberies, assaults and sexual attacks on the television screen and the playstation. Perhaps many children are passive consumers of these simulations too.

It is clear that Baudrillard fails to define terms, that he ignores contradictory evidence, that his arguments are not based on a sustained and systematic analysis, that his claims are open to criticism for deriving unqualified generalisations from particular examples (cf. Poster, 1988: 7-8; 1995: 113). Baudrillard (1992: 9) makes no claim to follow rational liberal standards of scholarship, but would argue that his grand visionary style is the only way of exposing the nature of hyper-reality. 'Since the world drives to a delirious state of things,' he says, 'we must drive to a delirious point of view.' Liberalism, he would claim, in its pursuit of rational distinctions, is part of a 'conspiracy to deny the absence of a line dividing the real from the unreal' (Bauman, 1992a: 153). In hyper-reality, rational distinctions begin to disappear, even distinctions between opposites: the left and right in politics, truth and falsehood in the media, beauty and ugliness in art and fashion, all tend to merge in a generalised simulation. To use a favourite example of Baudrillard's, by exposing Watergate as a scandal, the *Washington Post* journalists only served to conceal the fact that the whole political system is a scandal, because they implied that away from Watergate there are sound political principles in operation, such as truth and justice (Baudrillard, 1983c: 26-29). Similarly, the Monica Lewinsky affair raised interesting questions about the difference between truth and untruth, proper and improper, simulated and real.

Simulation in school

In respect of simulation in the school curriculum and collective worship, Baudrillard (1983c: 83ff; 1993) has identified three stages or orders of simulation.

The first stage is the straightforward counterfeiting or copying of an original as performed, for example, in paintings or in the theatre. Simulation of this type has always been a significant part of religion: Holy Communion is a simulation of the Last Supper, and Sukkoth is a simulation of the time the children of Israel spent living in the wilderness.

The second stage is the pure series. In the process of mass production, exact replicas are produced on assembly lines or through automated processes.

The third stage was described in the last section, where copies are not based on an original but on numbers, formulae and coded signals, where the difference between representation and reality is erased, where simulations come increasingly to constitute the world. What is real is what we are given on the television screen. Previously, the media were believed to mirror reality, but now, as we have seen, they are coming to constitute simulacra (i.e. reproductions of objects or events without originals: cf. Baudrillard, 1983c: 11), which together make up a 'hyper-reality'. We internalise messages from the media, with the result that we become 'merely terminals within the media system' (Sarup, 1996: 112). In television soap opera the referent becomes the reality, and it is so real that even Tony Blair in his first year as prime minister appealed for justice for Deirdre in the television soap *Coronation Street.* Culture consists of constructed realities, Disneylands, which are more real than the reality they are supposed to refer back to, so that in the end there is no reference back. What the fantasy of Disneyland conceals, according to Baudrillard, is the fact that all America is Disneyland (Baudrillard, 1983c: 23-26; 1988: 98-100).

It is not difficult to apply these stages to schooling, for school itself is in some respects a simulation of the outside world.

First, many children's games are based on simulation. The game of cowboys and Indians simulates what was once a popular topic of movies, which were themselves a simulation of real life on the frontiers in nineteenth-century America. The board game of Monopoly is a simulation of the real property market. The same kind of simulation is involved in more serious approaches to children's education. Books by Tansey (1971) and Taylor and Walford (1972) describe in detail a number of simulation exercises for use in the teaching of geography, history, English, mathematics and economics. The technique seems to be a particularly popular approach to art at the moment, with displays in many primary schools featuring children's simulations of paintings by the Impressionists, Lowry or Leonardo da Vinci.

Second, the way that National Vocational Qualifications (NVQs) are defined means that they have some similarities to the mass-production model. Perhaps the same is true of National Curriculum Assessment tests (SATs) and indeed all forms of assessment.

Third, collective worship in schools is not 'real worship', but 'simulated worship', and has much in common with Baudrillard's third stage of simulation. 'Real worship' means worship as understood and practised by religious communities (cf. Thatcher, 1997: 5), worship that occurs when 'people of the same faith willingly come together to participate in an act of religious devotion' (Muslim Educational Trust, 1995: 3), worship that involves, in the words of Circular 1/94, 'reverence or veneration paid to a divine being or power' (Department for Education, 1994: paragraph 57). 'Simulated worship', on the other hand, involves the performance of some of the same ritual acts as 'real worship' (such as prayer and hymn singing), but without one or more of the necessary conditions for the latter, such as voluntariness and shared belief. It may of course be that what some people engage in at church is 'simulated worship'. As we have seen, Thatcher (1997: 5-11) has argued convincingly that worship ('real worship') is not educational, but 'simulated worship' may be.

Collective worship in schools has been classified as belonging to the third stage or order of simulation because it no longer involves a conscious imitation of the public worship that goes on in churches, but has taken on a life of its own. For many children it is a simulation without any reality outside itself, certainly without any foundation in the reality of their own lives. In simulated artwork children have a picture that they copy, or that acts as a stimulus to their own creative output. In moral education they may be taught to simulate virtues that have no currency in their own social circles (cf. MacIntyre, 1999), but at least the teacher offers a living role-model which they can follow. However, these examples are in contrast to the 'simulated worship' that occurs in school, which is for most children their only experience of worship. The result is that there is no reference back in their minds from the simulated activity to the 'real worship' that it represents, and the difference between the two may mean that children are actually miseducated about the nature of worship in religion (cf. Brown, 1995: 4). However, to describe collective worship in schools as 'simulated worship' is not in itself a value judgement, but a statement of concept. It does not undermine the possible worth of collective worship for pupils, but rather reconceptualises it.

It seems that many writers in the last thirty years have been struggling towards this reconceptualisation. Hull (1975: 38, 107) argues that if children cannot comprehend the beliefs associated with worship, they cannot 'affirm or deny' or even 'pretend to affirm or deny' those beliefs; but if the beliefs are not affirmed, children cannot be said to be engaging in 'real worship' at all. Hull therefore speaks of 'pre-worship' and 'bringing children to the threshold of worship' (p. 39), a phrase that has proved very popular with religious educators in recent years (cf. Taylor, 1989: 56). Others have contrasted 'religious' with 'secular' worship (see, for example, Webster, 1995: chapter 3) or have tried to redefine worship in schools as the celebration of shared values or 'worth-ship', which is defined by McCreery (1993: 24) as 'that which is of worth to the community', though Trainor is quick to point out that this is 'not the same thing' as worship (quoted in RE Council of England and Wales, 1996: 72). 'Secular' worship involves such things as the celebration of values and achievements, opportunities for quiet reflection and the development of corporate identity (McCreery, 1993: 26-9; Attfield, 1996; Taylor, 1989: 56, 69; Gill, 1998). Circular 1/94, though widely condemned as unworkable (RE Council of England and Wales, 1996: 32-37), also recognises a distinction between 'worship in schools' and 'worship amongst a group with beliefs in common', but unfortunately confuses the issue by suggesting that collective worship in schools means worship in 'its natural and ordinary meaning' (Department for Education, 1994: paragraph 57). Each of these accounts of collective worship in schools goes some way towards acknowledging its basis in simulation.

One of the first consequences of a recognition of the fact that school worship is 'simulated worship' is that the liberal arguments with which this paper started, which assume that collective worship in schools is intended to be 'real worship', begin to lose their force. Simulation is a respectable technique in schools which can enrich children's experiences, develop their emotions, and teach them about many things, including religion, and it is a particularly useful technique in a pluralist society because it enables children to see things through the eyes of others without implying that any particular worldview is the correct one. Unlike 'real worship', 'simulated worship' does not presuppose belief, and therefore there is nothing indoctrinatory about it. Whereas worship is a free response to belief in God, 'simulated worship' involves entering into and sharing someone else's experience and is, therefore, among other things, an exercise in empathy, tolerance, understanding and respect.

A recognition that collective worship in schools is simulated rather than 'real worship' also helps to shed new light on some of the main problems to do with collective worship in schools at the start of the new century and to point to possible ways forward.

Rethinking collective worship

Any discussion of possible ways forward must start by identifying current problems, and it is hoped that the foregoing discussion will help to illuminate these. This chapter has referred to two hyper-realities in which children grow up, namely school-oriented hyper-reality and media/fashion-oriented hyper-reality, and unsurprisingly many children find the latter more seductive. The hyper-reality of the school is often viewed as boring, but those school activities that are perceived to have utility for the future (such as learning how to use products and how to earn the money to buy them) are tolerated or even appreciated. However, as we have seen, the 'simulated worship' that goes on in school is too self-referential, having no relation in most children's minds to any reality outside itself. Children, therefore, are not only bored, but come to resent continued exposure to the activity. Gill's (1998) research suggests that such resentment has often set in by the age of ten or eleven. The resentment appears in many cases to carry across to anything to do with religion. The self-referentiality even extends to those dimensions of collective worship that have nothing to do with religious belief, such as the celebration of community and the development of corporate identity. For the community that is celebrated is usually the school itself, and identification with the school community becomes an end in itself, rather than helping pupils to recognise the goal of responsible citizenship in broader society. The simulated community of the school comes to constitute the real world for children, rather than leading them towards the real world.

The 'simulated worship' that goes on in schools often bears no relation whatsoever to the excitement of the hyper-real world outside school: it is not media-generated, it is not fashionable, it is not linked to consumerist values. It is, almost literally, in the minds of many children (and adults), nothing. This sense of the alienation, the emptiness, the meaninglessness of collective worship for many children is captured very well in the words of a fourteen-year-old quoted by Gill (1998): 'After they start, you just drift away. You don't listen at all to what they are saying. You are just staring at the floor and wait until they finish and just go'. Other children link this alienation to the perceived lack of relevance in collective worship; Johnson (1997: 61) quotes a thirteen-year-old as saying, 'Things change. The world is changing. It's about time they [assemblies] changed as well; no-one listens, because it doesn't mean anything to us'. The fact that these are not isolated opinions is confirmed by Francis and Kay (1995) in a large-scale survey of the religious attitudes and values of thirteen- to fifteen-year-olds; they found that the vast majority did not want a daily religious assembly in school.

If we take the advice of the thirteen-year-old quoted by Johnson (1997), what direction should changes in collective worship take? The analysis drawn from Baudrillard's vision of the world points to the need to acknowledge the hyper-reality generated by fashion and the electronic media in particular, and work within the possibilities it legitimates, rather than to look back wistfully to an earlier age when decisions were justified in terms of rational coherence or religious authority. A Baudrillardian perspective in fact opens up several possibilities.

One possibility is to approach collective worship as an introduction to (or symbol of, or metaphor for) a spiritual way of life, defined as an alternative to the materialism and consumerism of hyper-reality on the one hand, and to the artificiality of media-driven hyper-reality on the other (Halstead and Taylor, 2000: 30-31). To use Baudrillard's exaggerated language, in the obscene delirium of communication, everything is transparent and over-exposed; there is no intimate interior. Collective worship could, theoretically, point children to this missing spiritual dimension, this intimate interior to their lives (cf. Parffrey, 1997: 38-39; Webster, 1995: chapter 5). Collective worship could become a metaphor for individual spirituality, a reinjection of reality into their lives. Of course, the need for a spiritual dimension is not a new idea. It is linked to what Wilson (1990: 82-88) sees as an important aspect of moral education, to do with 'the basic ecology . . . of human desires, emotions and deeds' and 'the state of our soul' (cf. McLaughlin and Halstead, 2000). Bauman (1992: 11), too, argues that if we want to regain truly human forms of moral agency in the postmodern age, we should look not to 'the learnable knowledge of rules' but to alternative conceptions of moral responsibility based on human spontaneity, ambiguity and wonder.

The problem is that there is nothing to make collective worship into a viable symbol or metaphor, a viable alternative, nothing to make it acceptable. It is currently popularly perceived, particularly at secondary school level, as unfashionable, traditional, backward-looking, out-of-date (cf. Kay, 1996). If one wants to be thought 'cool' by one's contemporaries one has to be seen to be choosing the correct cultural icons of the time and acting these out in the correct manner: there is nothing 'cool' about collective worship. For collective worship to be a successful metaphor for an alternative, spiritual way of life, perhaps the spiritual itself would have to be commodified and made fashionable. There have been few moves so far in this direction in the UK, but the USA has seen some success in the commodification of spirituality. Not long ago, a quarter of the titles on the *New York Times* bestseller list were on spiritual subjects. *The Road Less Traveled,* a book on spirituality by psychiatrist M. Scott Peck, was there for 571 weeks. The reinvention of popular mythologies such as the belief in angels (seen in the wearing of angel badges, the sale of model angels and pictures of guardian angels, and so on) is another example of the simulation and commercialisation of spirituality in America. According to Eugene Taylor (1994), the new spirituality is a popular phenomenon of epic proportions, in which people are swept along by powerful emotional commitments which provide them with a new optimism and hope for the future. Baudrillard would say it is fashion, but it need not be a cynical move for those responsible for the provision of collective worship in schools to pay attention to these trends and use them as a way of introducing children to the spiritual dimension of life.

Another possibility is to make collective worship more seductive (to use another of Baudrillard's favourite terms: cf. Baudrillard, 1990), to help pupils perceive it as appealing, interesting and forward-looking.

There are many ways of doing this, one of them being to adopt a more inclusive and girl-friendly approach in the worship in line with contemporary feminist theology (cf. Daykin, 1996). This might achieve a number of important objectives. It might generate interest and discussion even among pupils who normally show little interest in religious practice. It might encourage a certain pride among pupils that their school is at the cutting edge of theological debate. It might remove a stumbling block to worship for many girls by dismantling some of the tacit patriarchalism of current practice. The recognition that these changes were being incorporated into 'simulated worship' rather than 'real worship' might soften the opposition to such changes from more conservative quarters.

The only other way forward, I suspect, is to ban collective worship in schools, which might just possibly make it fashionable.

References

Attfield, D. (1996), Worship and religious education, *SPES*, 4, 21-27.

Baudrillard, J. (1983a), The ecstasy of communication, in H. Foster (ed.), *The Anti-Aesthetic: essays on postmodern culture*, pp 126-133, Port Townsend, Washington, Bay Press.

Baudrillard, J. (1983b), *In the Shadow of the Silent Majorities: or, the end of the social and other essays*, New York, Semiotext(e).

Baudrillard, J. (1983c), *Simulations*, New York, Semiotext(e).

Baudrillard, J. (1985), The masses: the implosion of the social in the media, *New Literary History*, 16, 577-589.

Baudrillard, J. (1988), *America*, London, Verso.

Baudrillard, J. (1990), *Seduction*, London, Macmillan.

Baudrillard, J. (1992), *The Transparency of Evil*, London, Verso.

Baudrillard, J. (1993), *Symbolic Exchange and Death*, London, Sage.

Baudrillard, J. (1998), *The Consumer Society*, London, Sage.

Bauman, Z. (1992a), *Intimations of Postmodernity*, London, Routledge.

Bauman, Z. (1992b), *Postmodern Ethics*, Oxford, Blackwell.

Bertens, H. (1995), *The Idea of the Postmodern: a history*, London, Routledge.

British Humanist Association (1975), *Objective, Fair and Balanced*, London, British Humanist Association.

Daykin, B, (1996), Feminist theology and collective worship in the 'broadly Christian' context, *SPES*, 5, 26-29.

Department for Education (1994), Circular 1/94: Religious Education and Collective Worship, London, Department for Education.

Department of Education and Science (1985), *Education for All* (The Swann Report), London, Her Majesty's Stationery Office.

Francis, L.J. and Kay, W.K. (1995), *Teenage Religion and Values,* Leominster, Gracewing.

Gibson, W. (1993), *Burning Chrome,* London, Harper Collins.

Giddens, A. (1992), *The Transformation of Intimacy,* Cambridge, Polity Press.

Gill, J. (1998), Spiritual and moral values in collective worship: conversations with pupils, *SPES,* 8, 5-11.

Haldane, J. (1986), Religious education in a pluralist society: a philosophical examination, *British Journal of Educational Studies,* 34, 161-181.

Halstead, J.M. (1996), Liberal values and liberal education, in J.M. Halstead and M.J. Taylor (eds), *Values in Education and Education in Values,* pp 17-32, London, Falmer Press.

Halstead, J.M. and Khan-Cheema, M.A. (1987), Muslims and worship in the maintained school, *Westminster Studies in Education,* 10, 21-36.

Halstead, J.M. and Taylor, M.J. (2000), *The Development of Values, Attitudes and Personal Qualities: a review of recent research,* Slough, National Foundation for Educational Research.

Hull, J.M. (1975), *School Worship: an obituary,* London, SCM Press.

Hull, J.M. (1996), The ambiguity of spiritual values, in J.M.Halstead and M.J. Taylor (eds), *Values in Education and Education in Values,* pp 33-44, London, Falmer Press.

Johnson, A. (1997), Pilot study: staff and student attitudes to and experiences of the act of worship at Key Stage 3, in T. Copley (ed.), *Collective Worship,* pp 49-63, Exeter, University of Exeter School of Education.

Kay, W.K. (1996), Religious education and assemblies: pupils' changing views, in L.J. Francis, W.K. Kay and W.S. Campbell (eds), *Research in Religious Education,* pp 267-277, Leominster, Gracewing.

MacIntyre, A. (1999), How to seem virtuous without actually being so, in J.M. Halstead and T.H. McLaughlin (eds), *Education in Morality*, pp 247-268, London, Routledge.

McCreery, E. (1993), *Worship in the Primary School*, London, David Fulton.

McLaughlin, T.H. and Halstead, J.M. (2000), John Wilson on moral education, *Journal of Moral Education*, 29, 247-268.

Muslim Educational Trust (1995), *Education in Multi-faith Britain: meeting the needs of Muslims*, London, Muslim Educational Trust.

Parffrey, V. (1997), Collective worship: 'And can it be. . .?', in T. Copley (ed.), *Collective Worship*, pp 35-40, Exeter, University of Exeter School of Education.

Phenix, P.H. (1965), Religion in American public schools, in *Religion and Public Order*, Chicago, Illinios, University of Chicago Press.

Poster, M. (ed.) (1988), *Jean Baudrillard: selected writings*, Cambridge, Polity Press.

Poster, M. (1995), *The Second Media Age*, Cambridge, Polity Press.

RE Council of England and Wales (1996), *Collective Worship in Schools*, Abingdon, Culham Educational Foundation.

Sarup, M. (1996), *Identity, Culture and the Postmodern World*, Edinburgh, Edinburgh University Press.

Tansey, P.J. (1971), *Educational Aspects of Simulation*, London, McGraw-Hill.

Taylor, E. (1994), Desperately seeking spirituality, *Psychology Today*, 27 (6), 54-68.

Taylor, J.L. and Walford, R. (1972), *Simulation in the Classroom*, Harmondsworth, Penguin.

Taylor, M.J. (1989), *Religious Education, Values and Worship: LEA advisers' perspectives on implementation of the Education Reform Act 1988*, Slough, National Foundation for Educational Research.

Thatcher, A. (1997), Educational arguments for collective worship, in T. Copley (ed.), *Collective Worship*, pp 5-23, Exeter, University of Exeter School of Education.

Webster, D. (1995), *Collective Worship in Schools*, Cleethorpes, Kenelm Press.

Weeks, J. (1991), *Against Nature: essays on history, sexuality and identity*, London, Rivers Oram Press.

Wilson, J. (1990), *A New Introduction to Moral Education*, London, Cassell.

4

GOD AND YOUTH IN THE GLOBAL VILLAGE: AN UPDATE

Brian V. Hill

Introduction

> Let us suspend . . . our grown-up function as role models and
> educators of our nation's youth. Rather than focusing on how
> we, as adults, should inform our children's activities with
> educational tidbits for their better development, let's . . . look to
> them for answers to some of our own problems adapting to
> postmodernity. . . . They are, already, the thing that we must
> become.

The words are those of Douglas Rushkoff (1997: 13), in *Children of
Chaos*, a book subtitled *surviving the end of the world as we know it.* He
identifies himself as a member of 'Generation X', thereby embracing
the label invented by Douglas Coupland (1991). Rushkoff maintains
that the world has changed so radically in the last few decades, that
those of us born in previous generations can no longer suppose that we
have the answers to what it will take to survive and prosper in the
future. If Rushkoff is right, then we might as well admit that donning
the mantle of religious educators has been an unjustified conceit on
our part, the more so if our date of birth precedes 1945!

Even the recent focus on Generation X is now being displaced by
attempts to understand the next 'generation' on, defined not by a
conventional twenty-five year cycle or so, but by the changes that a
mere decade has brought about, a decade that has seen the arrival of
the Internet. One writer has coined the term the 'NetGen' (Sweet,
1999: 375) for this new youth constituency.

Who do we think we are, presuming to know what meaning systems will be of most service to modern youth, inheritors, as they are, of the fragile and fractured world we have bequeathed to them (a reality that accommodates global warming, acid rain, and cyberspace pornography)? Even more absurd, how dare we dabble in *religious* education, an enterprise predicated on the value of ancient wisdoms, crafted for the most part in pre-industrial societies?

It is, therefore, with some trepidation that I undertake the task of looking for connections between religious education and modern youth. In speaking of 'modern' youth, I am focusing mainly on those young people whose social reality is being constructed from the messages they are incessantly exposed to by the commercial media and the Internet, those whom Rushkoff (1997: 3) calls the 'screenagers'. This necessarily narrows down my main focus to those present-day youth who live in highly industrialised countries, not because I do not care about the rest, but because, in terms of the globalised consciousness that is currently evolving, *they* are the ones at the leading edge of social change.

If only the same could be said for religious education. An English report in 1970 bore the title *The Fourth R* (Ramsey, 1970), implying that religious studies should have no less a priority in a young person's basic education than the traditional 'three Rs'. Even though the inclusion of religious education in the compulsory state curriculum was already legally obligatory at that time, the committee apparently felt the need to defend it in these terms.

Now, less than thirty years later, other basics have been set alongside the three Rs, including computer literacy, safe sex, and drug education. Where do religious studies stand in such company, and who cares? Have we been outflanked by the arrival of a generation of youth so acclimatised to living with uncertainty that they merely pity those of an older generation who are still beset by metaphysical anxieties, much as they also pity us for needing their help to programme the video-recorder? Are we in the unenviable position of marketing a sabre-tooth curriculum when sabre-toothed tigers have become extinct? (see Benjamin, 1939).

The first part of my argument will be that the credibility gap between youth and religious educators has grown much wider in the last few years than most of us are prepared to acknowledge. In particular, the Church has been relegated to the margins, being perceived by youth as a quaint relic of the past. This is a perception that clerics nostalgic for the Age of Authority have done little to counter.

Second, I will consider some of the revisionist attempts that have been made to re-establish the relevance of religion, including one that proposes to replace the fourth 'R' with 'S', that is, with an emphasis on something called 'spirituality.' Third, I will argue that not only do most of these attempts fail to intersect with the consciousness of modern youth, but that they ignore certain resurgent trends in the leading world religions. Finally, under the heading of 'Resonances', I will suggest some ways to re-establish connections with the 'NetGen'.

Relegations

First, then, we need to note the way modern youth have relegated institutional religion to the margins. Corresponding to this, Church leaders have relegated 'youth work' to the too-hard basket. They do not say that this is what they are doing. They profess to be 'toughing it out' by clinging to old liturgies and authority structures until youth 'come round'.

It's just a stage

Their trust in such practices is reinforced by a still popular version of adolescent psychology. After all, it has been 'well known', at least since G. Stanley Hall at the beginning of this century (Kett, 1977: 204f), that all young people go through a rebellious phase before settling into their adult roles. Who is not aware that, in the course of establishing their separate identities, adolescents tend to kick against their parents' values? Have not people been complaining about the skittishness of youth since the time of Socrates?

Hall (1904) regarded a period of *sturm und drang* during adolescence as inevitable, and based much of his educational theory on it. Many still do, so much so that one of my daughters once commented to me that she was feeling deprived because she appeared to have missed out on her teenage rebellion!

Hall saw this phase not only as inevitable, but also as the most appropriate prelude to religious conversion. In a similar spirit, many Christian youth organisations and school syllabuses earlier this century tended to interpret religious education as faith-enculturation, topped off by a 'second birth', albeit interpreted *à la* Rousseau in maturational rather than theological terms. At a popular level, such views of adolescent psychology *still* prompt many Church elders to tolerate the restiveness of teenagers, though with barely concealed impatience, believing that ministries with youth are in a holding mode until they 'grow out of' this 'stage'.

This is a head-in-the-sand attitude; and not only so because much social research has cast doubt on the universality of the *sturm under drang* phenomenon (Connell, 1962; Kitwood, 1980). In addition, there have been major shifts in cultural consciousness, combined with technological innovations at least as epoch-making as the invention of the steam engine. These have led to the emergence of a youth cohort the like of which has never been seen before.

Surely I exaggerate? Are we, for example, to relinquish the developmental stories told by such researchers as Piaget, Goldman, Kohlberg and Erickson just because the cultural terrain has been redefined by McLuhan, Foucault, Bill Gates and the drug lords? I would not want to suggest that the developmentalists have nothing to offer in enabling us to understand youth. They assuredly have. But in some ways they have been outflanked.

A new social reality

In several western countries, cultural analysts have been noting generational discontinuities of massive dimensions (Eckert and Willems, 1984; Coupland, 1991; Mackay, 1997). The majority have located the beginnings of these discontinuities in the social disturbances of the 1960s and 1970s. These were characterised by a high level of youth participation, fuelled by factors as diverse as the Vietnam War, the graphics and communications revolutions, the contraceptive pill and fibre-glass surfboards. Forms of activism ranged from anti-conscription rallies to alternative lifestyle movements.

Speaking to the Australian situation, social researcher Hugh Mackay (1997) developed a typology of three generations, each moving further away from the preceding one in its perception of social reality. The first he called the 'lucky generation'. These, paradoxically, were the people who experienced adolescence in the Depression and the Second World War, hardly suggestive of good luck. But his point was that they subsequently entered on adult life in a time of high material prosperity and full employment.

The children of the lucky generation were the widely acknowledged 'baby boomers', whom MacKay, speaking for the Australian culture, called the 'stress generation'. Raised in the good times, living for the 'now', with a mythical life expectancy of thirty, they were now finding themselves still alive at forty five, doubting whether they would be able to survive on their superannuation, and hurting because their children profoundly rejected their philosophies.

These, the children of the baby boomers, Mackay termed the 'options generation'. They were the Australian equivalent of what North Americans call Generation X, and Rushkoff (1997) the 'children of chaos'. Mackay demonstrated that their perception of the world was as different from that of their parents, as theirs was from the previous generation; in both cases, a quantum shift. Rushkoff goes further and argues that Generation Xers are far better at coping with the social realities of today's world than their parents and grandparents, because they have grown up in it. Uncertainty is the air they breathe and, according to him, they love it! And now we have the NetGen, juggling multiple realities with nonchalant flair.

Compare the different roles television has played in the lives of these generations. For those whose formative adolescent years were over by the end of the Second World War, television was a hypnotic marvel which turned many into addicts, typified by the cartoon showing a group of adults glued to a set that was only depicting visual static. Their children, however, that is, the baby boomers, were the first children in history to be baby-sat by 'the box', and some of their addiction to consumer pleasures must be attributed to it. Rushkoff argues that Generation X has evolved beyond the passive-viewer syndrome, assisted by the invention of the remote control, which enables a viewer to operate the television set from a distance. 'The [modern] viewer's weapon against programming', he says, 'is discontinuity' (Rushkoff, 1997: 40). Similarly, children of the NetGen have extended the skill of switching TV channels at will to 'surfing the Internet', with its infinitely greater range of virtual realities.

Having grown up with these facilities, the NetGen is adept at 'multi-tasking', that is, the ability to keep track at one and the same time of music on the radio, multiple web-sites, conversation in the room and, perhaps, the homework assignment in front of them. Because this juxtaposing of images reminds them of the way the media constructs these alternative realities, they have developed a sense of irony which partly shields them from the designs the programmers have on them. They sense the artifice, and process messages at speeds that leave older generations gasping. All this helps them to manage the information overload much better than their elders.

Coupland's initial description of Generation X was somewhat ambiguous, swinging between admiration and pity, whereas Rushkoff was unashamedly enthusiastic about their adaptability and self-confidence. They had found a way to live with uncertainty, to ride the wave of change for all it was worth, saved by a quality of irony from expecting the wave they were currently on to last for ever. Even more so for the NetGen, open transport on the Internet frees them from the grip of media moguls intent on controlling information, and unlike those raised on authoritative grand narratives, whether religious or modernist, they can perceive patterns in the chaos. Who dares say what their needs are, or how they ought to live?

An enduring need

I come from a country where the young by and large enjoy a casual and self-chosen lifestyle that few other countries can match, but where there is also a youth suicide rate higher than most. Perhaps for that reason I was arrested by one of the passages in the novel *Generation X*, where Claire says, to no one in particular: 'It's not healthy to live life as a succession of isolated little cool moments. Either our lives become stories, or there's just no way to get through them' (Coupland, 1991: 10).

There is little evidence that modern youth, having rejected traditional narratives as out of phase with the chaotic kaleidoscope of stimuli that they are experiencing, are framing for themselves better stories, or reasons for living. The cult film *Pulp Fiction* mirrored with telling effect the amoral and episodic reality they encounter, a reality heavily dependent on aggression and adrenalin surges. And how easily the young, having viewed this particular film with evident enjoyment, are able to dismiss it with ironic comment and go on to their next activity, while older generations continue trying to come to grips with it.

As police and social workers strive to pick up the pieces when young people collapse (whether through boredom, exploitation, abuse or unwise experimentation) they discover that needs *do* exist, even in this ebullient generation. The need for a story that makes sense, relationships that affirm, and a future hope that validates deferred gratification, is still there. The challenge for religious educators is to connect with it.

The Church militant or recumbent?

It is a challenge that many Churches are not willing to address. As noted earlier, if modern youth tend to relegate the Church to the past, no less do Churches tend to relegate 'the youth problem' to the too-hard basket. Churches, if they still have any attenders in the category of youth, expect conformity. In a take-it-or-leave-it frame of mind, they persist with their traditional liturgies and chorales undisturbed by the manifest restlessness of the young. Content to maintain a security blanket for the old and middle-aged, they take no thought for the morrow, when their church buildings will likely be transformed into restaurants and art galleries.

Similarly, I have encountered theological programmes in many places that are equally reactionary, albeit for different reasons often associated with academic aspirations. These programmes maintain that the traditional theological disciplines *must* flourish, even, if needs must, at the expense of that begrudged set of studies condescendingly referred to as 'practical theology' or 'pastoral studies'. Sometimes issues in developmental psychology and individual counselling are addressed, but little is done to understand the mind-set of modern youth, as they strive to comprehend a world of greater economic risks and social freedoms, whilst at the same time observing the Churches' struggle to re-establish their traditional authority structures, as though all that was needed was to turn the clock back.

Revisions

Have there been no efforts to bridge this gap? There have been some, based on attempts to revise present practice in one of three distinctive directions.

Global ethics

One has been the attempt to identify a global ethic that might re-establish community without demanding individual conformity to a particular worldview. For some, this has become a commitment to environmental rehabilitation: a commitment that has sometimes achieved the status of a religion, supported by appeal to 'the goddess' principle in creation, or to *Gaia* spirit of the allegedly sentient earth (Lovelock, 1988).

More soberly, perhaps, many pin their hopes on covenants and declarations of rights, both of animals and humans. I am personally happy to work in such arenas, sharing the aspirations for social justice that they represent, and welcoming dialogue on common values with those who think differently from myself (cf. Küng and Kuschel, 1993). However, if we want to encourage in our students a concern for the lives of others, this requires a compassion and hope for the future that are not always prominent in the mind-set of the NetGen. Such ideals spoke for a time to the flower-people of the 1960s, but they mean less to those who have been persuaded by postmodernism that everything is relative and transient. Why bother?

Religious universalism

Perhaps postmodernism points in another direction, implying that institutional religion, in its search for propositional truth, has missed the turning. Thus, the second kind of revisionism involves basing religious education on religious universalism. Perhaps we should be appealing to universal archetypes, reflected, as though through angled mirrors, in the symbols of many faiths; useful, not for what they say literally, but for the intuitions of transcendence that they evoke.

This was the approach adopted in the curriculum materials developed by Michael Grimmitt and others, called *A Gift to the Child* (Grimmitt, Grove, Hull and Spencer, 1991), which John Hull hailed as drawing not on the great religious traditions as such, so much as on 'the study of religion' in its more abstractive reaches (Hull 1996: 180). In this claim Hull was glossing over the fact that the direction from which he was coming in the study of religion was as distinctive a value-stance as that of the traditions he was discounting.

One of the problems with religious universalism is that, in discounting the propositional content of religions, it swings reliance on religion towards the aesthetic, converting the signals of transcendence (Berger, 1971) into personal feeling states. It is then a short step to the NetGen's perception that vivid experiences are all one can hope for and seek, in an otherwise uncertain and discontinuous reality.

Spirituality

The third kind of revisionism involves focusing on 'spirituality' rather than 'religion'. Heelas (1996) suggests that New Age talk of self-realisation is precisely the right 'spirituality for "baby boomers"' (see Hill, 1997). So a focus on 'spirituality' has the superficial advantage of tapping into the New Age as well as into older religious traditions.

Certainly, an agreement that the spiritual is a dimension that transcends the material or animal plane of human existence is a potentially useful place to start, though opinions vary as to whether the focus should be on our intuitive, rational, creative or relational capacities. But even more fundamental, as the reference to New Age thought shows, is the disagreement about whether it relates to something beyond or simply within ourselves.

I have attempted to argue elsewhere (Hill, 1989) that a relatively pragmatic decision to enhance our distinctively human capacities is a first step to giving spirituality its proper place in the curriculum, which is in every subject. Alongside this, however, there must also be earmarked curriculum time for studying theories as to the origin and nature of the spiritual. My argument was meant, in part, to validate religious education as a core study.

Prone to irony the younger generations may be, but they also show considerable willingness to entertain notions of occult entities, artificial intelligences in cyberspace (originally part of Gibson's fantasy in *Neuromancer*, 1986) and alien beings elsewhere in the galaxy. So spirituality may seem to be a promising candidate for bridge-building in religious education. But we must be wary of relying on this device; for Generation Xers, let alone the NetGens, such speculations often constitute merely a source of entertainment. Holding contradictory ideas at one and the same time is fun. In this, young people are to some extent protected from naiveté by their ability to keep such things at a humorously skeptical distance. On the face of it, they are not driven to seek closure as older generations were.

Furthermore, the tendency in New Age thinking is to divorce spirituality from obligation, whether to God or one's neighbour. Inner therapy replaces the confessional. The focus is on experience rather than responsibility. The 'rave' party has the same status as the adoration of God, especially since it is more ecstatic and makes no moral demands.

We must find some way of reaching in further, getting beyond the experiential to the existential; to the inner self on whom it sooner or later dawns that the irony that protects it from disillusionment also prohibits it from loving and being loved for itself. The search for personal meaning has not been superseded by the pleasure principle; it has only been deferred, and may even have been derailed.

In sum, the revisionisms I have touched on, namely global ethic, religious universalism and spirituality talk, look pale beside the synthetic novelties and ecstacies on which today's youth can call, using technology or drugs, and are not robust enough to restore those who sink into boredom and despair. Nor, we must recognise, do they allow for the drawing power of resurgent religious traditions and emergent cults.

Resurgences

This brings me to the curious fact that with the coming of industrial democracies, religion has *not* withered on the vine, as some commentators predicted. Many of the major religions of the world are resurgent. They are reviving their pre-modern narratives and offering them to a world adrift.

In some cases, religious strategists have cultural reconquests in mind, riding on the back of military conquest or economic superiority. Others, finding themselves in the minority in pluralised societies, have been motivated to find security in the reaffirmation of traditional religious dogmas. And many modern youth, alienated in the midst of plenty, are responding to the appeal of cults, which market certainty through submission to their unquestioned authority.

Social analysts, particularly those of liberal persuasion, have been slow to acknowledge the influence of resurgent religions, preferring to marginalise them as ideological throw-backs. But this will not do. In this respect, theses about Generation X and the NetGen are overly simplistic. While such terms may usefully identify one mainstream, they skate over the substantial numbers of modern youth who are themselves critical of the mainstream. Some have been hurt by it; some have been immunised against its worst features by good homes or enriching sub-cultural experiences. Not infrequently, religion has been part of this immunisation.

I need at this point to distinguish between two kinds of religious response: the fundamentalist and the renewalist. Liberal analysts are prone to run them together. The fundamentalist response is defensive, trying to turn the clock back even on modernity. It seeks to exercise political and cultural censorship in the interests of an unreformed tradition. Modern scholarship is wholly threatening to it. Where it cannot achieve political dominance, it withdraws into a separatist enclave, hostile not just to liberalism, but even to renewalists.

Renewalists, as I am applying the term, reaffirm the origins of their particular faith and the authority of its scriptures, but recognise a need to re-apply it to the conditions of contemporary society. Admitting that they live by faith, they insist that so does everyone, even liberals and other kinds of rationalist. The way ahead is to open up questions of basic assumptions in a spirit of dialogue and social problem-solving. They believe that they have a story to tell the world which will enable people to see life in more transcendent terms than can be accommodated by either rampant consumerism or ironic postmodernism.

In Christian terms, their numbers include what in the English-speaking world are referred to as 'Evangelicals', often with an adjective such as 'moderate' or even 'radical' (Wright, 1996) to distinguish them from co-religionists of more fundamentalist persuasion. The evangelical narrative affirms the biblical claim that the infinite God has communicated with the human species *in history,* myths have been transcended by divine acts, and basic questions of meaning, purpose and personal deliverance have been answered.

I number myself with this company, and the resonances I now propose to explore derive from my attempt to see the religious education of modern youth in the perspective of Evangelical belief. If it be supposed that I have suddenly become too party-political, my reply is to challenge all readers to put aside any claims to liberal neutrality that may prevent them from doing the same, and to own up to their presumptive starting points too!

Resonances

Religious educators must, if they are to remain contemporary and relevant without sacrificing the gifts of the religious heritage of humanity, address a number of challenges.

Enfranchisement

Religious educators must enfranchise young people in their own personal searches for personal meaning and affirmation. This probably sounds platitudinous, yet it needs saying. The typical religious education lesson, particularly when brought under the usual ethos of formal curriculum, is more directed to getting relevant content across to students than to finding out first what their primary concerns are. Since most other school subjects treat them the same way, it is not surprising if they expect no better from religious education.

What I am urging is not just the use of more effective techniques of motivation at the beginnings of our lessons, capitalising on our students' present focus of attention, after which we then settle down to teaching the prescribed syllabus content, but a genuine attempt to enter into their experience and travel with them in the religious issues that are arising in their lives.

Michael Grimmitt's proposal back in 1987 was to run two sets of curriculum topics in parallel: one about religious life-worlds, and one derived from the life-worlds of adolescents (Grimmitt, 1987). His suggestion gains added cogency when considering the needs of modern screenagers. Robert Jackson (1997) has also advanced valuable suggestions for exploring the religious life-worlds of our students.

A very practical consequence of starting a religious education course by identifying the *questions* of a religious kind that are on our students' minds is that when we then seek subsequently to acquaint them with some of the great religious traditions, it will be in the spirit of inviting them to see what help they can gain *in their own search* from the *answers* given by other people.

And they must be free to register their dissent if they find those answers insufficient in coping with present realities. It would be arrogant, in the light of the paradigm shifts that have occurred between recent generations, for religious educators to perpetuate the unchallengeable authority roles of a past era. Today, we are on this quest together.

Interrogation

Religious educators must help students to interrogate their own cultural conditioning, including the mind-set of their own generation, in order that they might entertain the possibility that enduring beliefs and values warrant their consideration. I have disputed the proposition that in a world of change everything is 'up for grabs'. The relativist postulate itself must be subject to critical scrutiny, in the interests of restoring something of that continuity of identity that enables not only the growing individual to function, but also cultures and communities.

The constants in human life are often obscured by surfing the Net and stabbing the remote control. Even schooling generally aggravates the problem through timetable policies that fracture interest by multiplying discontinuous lessons. But other choices are possible. Continuous experiences of relationship, for instance, fostered by travelling together with others, or in outdoor camps and expeditions, can act as an antidote.

Dialogue

Religious educators must develop forms of communication that encourage dialogue and values negotiation between persons of different faith. That is, we must establish a form of discourse in our classrooms that enables students to affirm their own beliefs whilst not denying space to students adhering to different beliefs. This is to be done not by pretending that the propositional content of such beliefs is a mere digression, but by talking about this content in ways that affirm the believer, even in the moment of dissenting from their belief.

Such a classroom climate is not going to evolve if the hegemony of one faith, such as Christianity or Islam, is asserted to such an extent that critical dissent is put off limits. Nor will it evolve if a focus on sincerity of feeling is substituted for an interest in the credibility of truth claims. Mutual respect and appreciation do not require that we deny 'those things most surely believed' in our own faith group. The authenticity of true dialogue is established by the extent to which it allows the sharing of our deepest commitments without either cloaked or naked power plays intended to impose conformity on another person.

In this connection, I am always happy to recommend the advice given to teachers by the authors of the Queensland Religious Education Curriculum (Religious Education Curriculum Project, 1983: 10-12). They urged that teachers avoid what they call 'presumptive language': presumptive, because it pre-empts the form of discourse in which the student is allowed to frame responses to the teacher's questions. They recommend the use of 'owning' and 'grounding' language, using phrases such as 'I think' or 'Christians say' to protect the student's personal space from invasion.

We may reasonably hope that when students see some teachers and fellow students testifying to deeply held convictions without rank-pulling or coercive intent, they will be motivated to hear them again on this matter. For ironic detachment cannot be the last word in a fulfilled life.

Social justice and environmental responsibility

Religious educators must valorise lifestyles that embrace social justice and environmental responsibility as well as personal satisfaction. This is an unashamedly value-laden guideline. It seeks, in the name of community, to overcome the self-centredness of Generation X and the NetGen. It will not be achieved by authoritarian moralisms, but by embracing their easy acceptance of diverse lifestyles, and their capacity for critical irony, and by applying them to social problems.

This will call for making a sharp distinction between 'live and let live' and 'live and let die'. Where these generations are concerned, stark images of good and evil may arouse more empathy for the oppressed than sanitised exemplars who seem out of touch with present reality. The environmental movement is giving a lead in this regard, especially by the way it challenges the phallic machines of industrial technology. I also perceive, in the student movements that are challenging oppression in many countries, that idealism is still latent in modern youth, awaiting the rise of causes and champions worthy of their critical attention.

Formal worship and Church government

Religious leaders must overhaul the anachronistic structures of formal worship and Church government that have chained the ageless gospel, in order to meet an egalitarian and electronic generation on its own ground.

This guideline speaks particularly to Christian educators. The baby boomers fled the Churches in the 1970s because they sensed the hollowness of culture-Christianity. Their children have no need to flee, because they were reared outside these structures. However, by the same token, they have even less reason to return, because the outward forms appear so irrelevant and out of tune with the world they inhabit. Religious educators and school chaplains must invest in new modes of interaction and communication, not waiting for the hierarchies to catch up, but educating for the future.

Nor should religious educators and school chaplains try either to trust in the powers of compulsion that the school gives them to enforce external conformity, or to make the gospel more palatable by playing down its distinctive truth-claims. Today's younger generations are highly capable of exposing such ploys as betrayals of the faith Christians claim to uphold.

References

Benjamin, H. (1939), *The Saber-Tooth Curriculum*, New York, McGraw-Hill.

Berger, P.L. (1971), *A Rumour of Angels: modern society and the rediscovery of the supernatural*, Harmondsworth, Penguin Books.

Connell, W.F. (1962), *Foundations of Education*, Sydney, Novak.

Coupland, D. (1991), *Generation X: tales for an accelerated culture*, New York, St Martin's Press.

Eckert, R. and Willems, H. (1984), Youth conflicts and public policy challenges in Western Europe, *Social change and family policies: Twentieth International CFR Seminar*. Melbourne, International Sociological Association, Australian Institute of Family Studies, 325-354.

Gibson, W. (1986), *Neuromancer*, London, Grafton.

Grimmitt, M. (1987), *Religious Education and Human Development*, Great Wakering, McCrimmons.

Grimmitt, M., Grove, J., Hull, J.M. and Spencer, L. (1991), *A Gift to the Child: religious education in the primary school*, London, Simon and Schuster.

Hall, G.S. (1994), *Adolesence: its psychology, and its relations to psychology, anthropology, sociology, sex, crime, religion and education*, New York, D. Appleton.

Heelas, P. (1996), *The New Age Movement: the celebration of the self and the sacralisation of modernity*, Oxford, Blackwell.

Hill, B.V. (1989), Spiritual development in the Education Reform Act: a source of acrimony, apathy or accord? *British Journal of Educational Studies*, 37, 169-182.

Hill, M. (1997), Book review of Paul Heelas, *The New Age Movement* (1996), *Australian Religious Studies Review*, 10, 76-77.

Hull, J.M. (1996), A gift to the child: a new pedagogy for teaching religion to young children, *Religious Education*, 91, 172-188.

Jackson, R. (1997), *Religious Education: an interpretive approach*, London, Hodder and Stoughton.

Kett, J.F. (1977), *Rites of Passage: adolescence in America 1790 to the present*, New York, Basic Books.

Kitwood, T. (1980), *Disclosures to a Stranger: adolescent values in an advanced industrial society*, London, Routledge and Kegan Paul.

Küng, H. and Kuschel, K.-J. (eds) (1993), *A Global Ethic: the declaration of the parliament of the world's religions*, London, SCM Press.

Lovelock, J. (1988), *The Ages of Gaia*, Oxford, Oxford University Press.

Mackay, H. (1997), *Generations: baby boomers, their parents and their children*, Sydney, Pan McMillan Australia.

Ramsey, I.T. (1970), *The Fourth R: report of the commission on religious education in schools* (The Durham Report), London, National Society and SPCK.

Religious Education Curriculum Project, (1983), *Religious Education: teachers' notes year 1*. Brisbane, Queensland Education Department.

Rushkoff, D. (1997), *Children of Chaos: surviving the end of the world as we know it*, London, Harper Collins.

Sweet, L. (1999), *SoulTsunami: sink or swim in new millennium culture*, Grand Rapids, Michigan, Zondervan.

Wright, N. (1996), *The Radical Evangelical: seeking a place to stand*, London, SPCK.

RICHNESS IN RELIGIOUS EDUCATION: ETHNIC, RELIGIOUS AND BIO-DIVERSITY

Mary Elizabeth Mullino Moore

The beauty of brilliance fills the sky;
Shadows of darkness creep down canyon walls,
Holding moisture and shade
        against the scorching noonday sun
And protecting shade-loving creatures in quietness
While their sun-loving friends dance in bright light.

The soft colors of a dawning sky
        Touch the earth lightly
While tall, craggy peaks reach high in the sky
        To kiss the heights of heaven;
Grasslands roll,
        And deserts blow.

In every landscape, Spirit is revealed –
Rolling, roaring,
        Shining, shading,
                Touching, reaching
Spirit!

Introduction

This poem by Moore (1998a) reveals the rich textures of the universe, although it describes only one small place in one moment of time. The earth is a rich and beautiful composition of diversity, but that reality is often identified as a problem to be solved rather than a gift to be appreciated, even within religious discourse, where one might expect a special delight in the stunning richness of divine creation.

The thesis of this chapter is that ethnic, religious and bio-diversity reveal the depths of life and contribute to the flourishing of life; thus, educational theory informed by diversity, and educational practice that engages people in diversity, are actually necessary for the flourishing of all beings in the third millennium. Such educational theory and practice will be informed by the richness of creation itself, by awareness of the pains and hurts within creation, and by the religious wisdom that stirs people to love the world fiercely. From all of these sources, education emerges with a fourth R of religion and values, and religious education emerges with a fourth R of richness. In addition to the sacred texts, ritual-devotional life and ethical practices of religious traditions, the very richness of creation is a source of revelation and guidance for educational practice. Thus, the central purposes of this chapter are: to identify some of the urgent cries that emerge in our complex world, to explore possibilities for respect that we need to nurture in that world and to identify future directions for education.

A crying world

We began with a poem, a reminder that we live in a world of delight; we also live in a world of pain. In this chapter I will lift up three kinds of pain that pervade our planet. Each of these pushes on communities and challenges our educational systems. Each of these is frequently neglected. Thus, I invite your attention to cries of pain from neglected persons, the neglected biosphere, and neglected peoples.

Cries of pain from neglected persons

Several months ago, an older woman went to her doctor with severe symptoms that proved to be shingles. After a few visits, the doctor was able to do little to relieve her symptoms or the disease. He explained to her that she would have to wait until the disease ran its course. Angrily, she said, 'You scientific and medical men have been able to send people to the moon and do all kinds of fancy things in space, but you have not done anything at all for us old people with shingles.'

When I first heard this story, I assumed that the woman of the story was speaking in extremes due to her pain. I certainly did not make any connections with religious education. Since that time, I have learned that shingles is one of those modern diseases about which there has never been one major medical study. If this is correct, it reveals that scientific research and practice are often designed to address dramatic questions and problems, or to respond to the majorities and averages of the population (majorities and averages in age, ability, ethnicity, socio-economic status or sexual orientation).

Similarly, educational systems are usually designed for the majorities and averages of student populations. Educators who engage with ethnically diverse and differently-abled students raise these concerns with particular pathos. They urge attention to the discriminatory and dehumanising practices that teachers and administrators perpetuate when they design education for dominant groups and for students with the most common or valued forms of intelligence and life experience (Beauboeuf-Lafontant and Augustine, 1996; Sleeter and Grant, 1987; Sleeter and McLaren, 1995; Goldberg, 1994; Hooks, 1989; Hess, 1997; Woyshner and Gelfond, 1997; Armstrong and Barton, 1999; Gardner, 1993, 1999). Unfortunately, educational writings on difference are themselves marginalised into specialisation areas, such as multicultural education or special education, with little attention given to how such expertise could reshape *all* of education, both in schools and religious communities.

These brief glimpses into medicine and education point to a common problem; social priority is given to needs and hurts of the largest or most influential segments of the human community. Considering these realities, how might religious education be responsive to cries of pain from the most neglected persons? Further, how might religious education engage people in evaluating priorities in the larger social world and inspiring people to ethical awareness and action?

Cries of pain from the neglected planet

We live on a planet where pain is evident wherever we turn; yet, some pains get considerably more attention than others. Consider some of the neglected cries of pain, such as the shrinking ozone layer, the rapidly decreasing layer of topsoil, and the desertification of large bodies of land. Consider the pollution of oceans and rivers and the deteriorating air quality over most cities of the world. Consider, also, the much-debated greenhouse effect, which seems to be warming the earth and shifting the ecological balance. The causes of global warming have been much debated, even in the international treaty negotiations of 1997 in Kyoto, Japan; the largest question is whether global warming is caused by high emissions or solar intensity. Debates also rage regarding whether preferable solutions are economic, technological or political (Grubb, Brackley, Ledic, Mathur, Rayner, Russell and Tanabe, 1991; Easterbrook, 1997; Carey and Arnst, 1997; Jachtenfuchs, 1996: 16-41).

Religious dimensions of this global pain have received far less attention than scientific and political dimensions. Religious silence, or near-silence, continues, although most religious communities have strong beliefs and practices related to the origins of the world and human responsibility toward it. Within Judaism, Christianity and Islam, for example, the creator of the universe is known to have deep compassion and strong guidance for the world. Such a God of compassion must surely care for the world as it suffers in this age. Furthermore, the religious perspectives that have been shaped over centuries of relating between God and the world might now shape the way that we ourselves understand environmental dilemmas and respond. According to Markus Jachtenfuchs (1996: 16-20), the very perspective that people have on global warming and other global and ecological issues is shaped by their culture and their social construction of reality. I suggest that religious issues are involved at the core of social constructions. If religion is a key to our human perspectives on the world, then religious education certainly needs to attend to issues of our planet, whether global warming, human poverty or racial warfare.

Cries of pain from neglected peoples
In addition to global ecological concerns, such as global warming and air and water pollution, cries of pain also come from neglected peoples. A story of the Haida people in Canada reveals something of the tragedy that they and many other indigenous people face across the world.

In 1985, a woman named Gwaganad appealed to the British Columbia Supreme Court (Canada) regarding the logging operations of a large company. Gwaganad appealed on behalf of the Haida people, her people, who had lived on the Queen Charlotte Islands for centuries. She told the court about her people, who welcomed foreigners two hundred years earlier and shared the land with them. She described how those foreigners urged them to adopt 'a better way to live, a different religion, education in schools', and how their traditional potlatches were outlawed (Gwaganad, 1993: 76). The potlatch was a festival meal in which everyone shared food and music and fun. Then Gwaganad described the ways of her people:

> I was taught to respect the land. I was taught to respect the food that comes from the land. I was taught that everything had a meaning. . . . We are a nation of people at risk today. . . . We almost lost ourselves as a people. . . . The only thing we can hold onto to maintain that pride and dignity as a people is the land. It's from the land we get our food, it's from the land we get our strength (Gwaganad, 1993: 77).

As Gwaganad continued her story, she expressed doubt that the logging company would ever provide the second growth of trees that they had promised (Gwaganad, 1993: 78).

Gwaganad then appealed to the court, by explaining how her people are attuned to the cycles of nature. She described her life as a food gatherer and, particularly, the spiritual experience she has in her body during the spawning season of the herring, when she and her friends go into the ocean to experience the spawning and to harvest the food. She concludes, 'And you don't quite feel complete until you are right out on the ocean with your hands in the water harvesting the kelp, the roe on kelp, and then your body feels right. That cycle is complete' (Gwaganad, 1993: 78).

I have shared Gwaganad's story in some detail because it reveals so much about the cries of neglected peoples. Her story reveals how people can be silenced by replacing their way of life, religion, educational system and traditional cultural practices. The Haida way is to live closely with the earth, use only what is needed for life, appreciate the ways of other creatures, and feel spiritual relationships in your body. The wisdom of Gwaganad and her Haida people is the kind of richness that is needed to support their lives and contribute to others as well. Theirs is a religious wisdom, which enables them to flourish as a people, and it contributes to the vision and hope of others.

A world where respect is possible

With these cries still ringing, we turn now to an extended case study that offers a note of hope for a world where respect is possible. I recently participated in the annual regional meeting of a large Protestant Christian denomination as the people prepared to make a decision about how the institution was going to respond to gay, lesbian and bisexual persons. The body was polarised regarding issues of homosexuality, and many gay and lesbian persons had been suffering for some years as they listened to debates. For some years, this religious community had been studying homosexuality and making alternate efforts to welcome, include, judge and transform these people. In the previous year, however, a small group had convinced the institution to enter a different kind of educational and discernment process.

In preparation for this year's regional meeting, much work was done in developing a process that would surface the various opinions that people held on the issue of homosexuality. Particular attention was given to mediating between 'extreme views on either end of a spectrum', as identified by the planning team. The hope was to find a middle ground or common ground. The plan was to begin in large groups, presenting the two views and two life stories (one person who accepted his or her homosexuality as natural and one who had been transformed). This would be followed by small group reflections, responses in the larger groups, and deliberation by the planning team, who would discern themes in the group discussions. The plan was carefully made; leaders then provided education so that people would understand the process and the rationale behind it.

Meanwhile small groups of people were very nervous about the process, and of the leaders who were leading it. These small caucus groups were meeting simultaneously to reflect on the issues, to discern a way ahead, and to influence the direction of discussions. In time, these small groups also contacted one another and sought ways to mediate their differences. All of this was happening during the year of preparation, as well as during the actual five-day conference.

When the conference time arrived, the leadership team led the process they had planned, and the religious leaders of the conference underscored its importance. The process was well received by the majority, who found the discussions meaningful and refreshingly open. The smaller caucus groups continued to be nervous, and they continued to meet on the side and reflect critically on the process and on their larger concerns. People in small conversational groups were also talking with one another as they met over meals or walked across campus. When the time for decision-making arrived, the community was led into a consensus decision with a small introduction to the process; people became confused. Many speeches were made, but the session ended with confusion as to how we were going to proceed. The planning team, along with conference leaders, met again and came back the next day with a proposal that reflected the views of many diverse people, expressed welcome to all persons regardless of sexual orientation, and proposed educational processes for the coming year. The body was not given another opportunity to discuss, but were invited to express their level of consent. They overwhelmingly expressed consensus and agreed to disagree beyond that. The body was moved, many to tears, and people with the varying positions, including those identified as 'the extremes', were happy (or reasonably content) with the consensus.

I have shared this case because it reflects much about diversity and education. The leaders of this discernment process were justifiably proud of their work in moving a large body of people to a joyous decision with minimal contention. They had successfully invited many people into a very open discussion, engaged people in listening to one another, and avoided much dichotomised rhetoric. At the same time, the body itself was justifiably proud of their work in discerning, listening, reflecting and deciding. At the same time, the smaller groups (which some would call caucus groups) were justifiably proud of their work in reflecting suspiciously on the process, even as they participated in it. One of those persons said to me later: 'One of the leaders of this process is taking all of the credit; he does not realise that it worked best when it fell apart and was not working at all. He also does not realise that the discernment that was done by some of our smaller groups was an important key to the good conclusion'.

I submit this case as an example of how diversity can function in human communities if allowed to surface and to be received as a welcome and vital part of community. In this case, everyone involved was somehow willing to participate in the dance of diversity, at least as a participant in the larger process of discernment. Some had designed that process to maximise the richness of the dance, and yet the spontaneous diversity of small groups and larger organised groups played their part as well. Without any one of these dynamics, something vital would have been lost. The vitality lay in the efforts to listen and reach consensus; it lay in the organised diversity; it lay in the failure of organised diversity; and it lay in spontaneous diversity that arose from suspicion, hope, critique and efforts to reform.

This case reveals a world where respect is possible. I do not mean this assertion naively, but I do mean it boldly. Some people were run over in this process, and some practised more control and arrogance than was healthy, but respect did emerge, at least for a moment, in a very complex religious institution. This is suggestive regarding efforts to live with diversity. It is also suggestive regarding epistemology and education. To know is to quest to know God and the world in a deep and responsive way (Moore, 1997: 234); thus, respect is a key to knowing. Respect is that which opens us to learn from one another, from the larger creation, and from the many communities with whom we share this earth. With that awareness, three aspects of respect will be identified here: respect for particularity, for the cosmos, and for the value of every being to the whole.

Respect for particularity

One focus of respect that is particularly countercultural in education is respect for particularity. Much of education pushes for general theories. Education is often designed to communicate basic ideas and concepts, to prepare students to pass tests, or to prepare people with the religious precepts they need for living in particular situations. Even the method of this chapter, drawing insights from particular events and cases, is countercultural. Whereas the purpose here is not to denigrate the search for broad trends through questionnaires, interviews and large qualitative studies, the purpose is to urge attention to every particular moment and being of God's creation. Particularity is often seen as the *context* in which general theories or values are applied, rather than a *source* of religious wisdom or a *contribution* to religious formation. It can be and needs to be all of these things.

I am arguing here that particularity is important for human wisdom, which I described above as the search to know God and the world in a deep and responsive way. Particularity is important in itself and, also, in relation to others. Consider the witness of creation itself. Consider the plant *Brighamia Insignis*, which grows on the cliffs of Hawaii. When the plant neared extinction, people wondered why. Scientists studied the problem and discovered that the birds responsible for pollinating the *Brighamia* had become extinct some time before; the plants, without a means of reproduction, were slowly becoming extinct themselves. Since that discovery, people have been cross-pollinating the *Brighamia Insignis* in order to preserve the species. This case reveals how vital every member of creation can be for the life of others. We will never recognise and nourish these connections if we do not attend to each distinctive part.

Drawing from this discussion, several challenges emerge for religious educators: to embrace particularity, to explore the ordinary realities of life, and to welcome the multiple stories and confusing questions of our religious traditions. We need to search the particularities of religious tradition, our own and others, and we need to explore the amazing world that is unfurled in ordinary particularities as well. This is risky in religious education because it can lead into chaotic interactions or reflection on apparent tangents, when the main subject is set aside long enough to explore a particular story or view that someone (teacher or student) feels compelled to share.

To practise such education, teachers are challenged to discern when to create space for particularities and when to allow them to emerge spontaneously. They are also challenged to seek ways for particularities to illumine the larger subject matter or the major questions and ideas with which a group has been struggling. This requires teachers and leaders to be skilled in discernment, in letting go of control at appropriate times and places, and in integrating ideas and practices within the dynamic interplay of a learning community. However overwhelming these challenges appear, many teachers have these skills in their everyday lives (as they engage in informal teaching); they need only to be encouraged to use the same gifts in their more formal educational settings.

Respect for the cosmos
In addition to respect for particularity, respect for the cosmos is urgent if education is to be practised with care for life. The cosmos here represents the whole of life. Although human beings cannot possibly grasp the fullness of the cosmos, and most of us are tempted to dwell on our own limited experiences, we *can* cultivate awareness of the largess of creation. We can even help people see how their personal decisions and experiences are connected with that larger whole. If we truly recognise that everything in the universe is interrelated, the cosmos is present in all of the ordinary particularities discussed above.

To speak of interrelatedness is to recognise that the environment is not a backdrop for the human drama. It is worthy in itself, as well as in relation to the particular communities and individuals that live within it. Human beings are also deeply connected in that web with animals, plants, water and soil. In the words of David Orr (1992: 148), 'our well-being is inseparable from that of nature' (cf. Orr, 1994). Indeed, we have much to learn of God from the ways of the cosmos. Consider a poem, by Moore (1983), 'Be Still and Know':

> The peaceful quiet beckons me
>   to be still,
> But I know not how.
> I think of things to do;
> They must be done,
> And yet, the quiet beckons still.
> I stop and sit and listen:
> I know —
>
> Walking with another on the path,
> Together we know —

The forest opens into space,
A vast meadow stretches down the gorge,
Tumbling into the river far below.
We cannot – will not – walk on;
We can only stop and listen
            and know —

Here is where we meet God;
We meet the grandness of God's creation
            in the grandeur of this gorge;
We do not understand,
            And yet we know —

Such an intimate sense of the cosmos can shape education in very practical ways. Ruth Conway and Brenda Watson (1998), for example, consider the cosmos when they analyse the tension between technological values in today's world and the passions that are required of people who seek a sustainable future. Rather than abandon technology or surrender their passions, they urge educators to choose and use technology in relation to their larger concerns for the world. They name three particular passions that are appropriate if educators care about the future: a passionate respect for nature and its delicately balanced eco-systems; a passion for social justice; and a passionate openness to others and to larger horizons (Conway and Watson, 1998: 170-175). In developing these ideas, Conway and Watson reveal their alertness to interconnectedness and their deep respect for the cosmos. Respect for the cosmos is not an optional extra for human well-being; it is necessary for connecting us with God and God's creation. Educationally, respect for the cosmos opens people to wonder and stirs humility; it also supports efforts to live in harmony with the complex sea of wonder in which we all live.

Respect for the value of every being to the whole
Reflecting on the cases of this chapter, I realise that one of the major needs in education is attention to the value of every being, or every part of the eco-system. The Haida people suffered when their value was ignored or actively suppressed. Their wisdom and agency were

denied; consequently, much of their dignity and livelihood was destroyed, not to mention their sheer enjoyment of the earth. In the case of the *Brighamia Insignis,* the dependence of this rare plant on a now extinct bird was not even known and, therefore, that reality could not be taken into account in the protection of either species. Only now, after the bird is extinct and after the relationship has been discovered, are scientists able to offer some protection to the plant until another bird or insect can assume the cross-pollination in an enduring way.

In the case of the regional Protestant conference, I am more intimately aware of the importance of respect for every being. One leader of the discernment and consensus process in that conference has been somewhat resistant to consultation processes in his home institution. In this large gathering, however, this person was leading the community to consensus on a matter that has been eruptive for many years. I found myself in this conference very suspicious of the leader's motives, fearful that some people would be hurt in the process, and yet hopeful that the discernment-consensus process would indeed lead us into a new era of political life. Having written on this very subject, and having committed myself to it for many years, I wanted the efforts to succeed. They did! And I had to be open to receiving a gift to the larger community, which was offered by one whom I did not fully trust. I was required to respect this leader as a member of the community, whose contribution was valuable. Respecting the value of every being requires people to face such delicate and challenging realities, and to recognise that plants, animals and stones are faced with challenging realities as well, each in its own distinctive way.

A world where education is urgent
In a crying world where respect is actually possible, even if it is not sufficiently common, education is urgent. The religious education needed in such a world will take seriously every cry from every part of the earth, and it will engender respect. Respectful education may actually be possible if it is grounded in cultural, religious and biological diversity.

William Doll (1993: 174-175) has proposed four Rs for postmodern education: richness, recursion, relations and rigour. At the same time, feminist theorists have analysed problems that emerge when difference is oversimplified or when social and political efforts are designed to transcend difference (Young, 1990; Mies and Shiva, 1993; Plumwood, 1993). Simultaneously, people are increasingly aware that bio-diversity is necessary for a sustainable eco-system. Drawing upon these analyses, this last section of the chapter will offer a construction of education that is grounded in diversity, drawing upon the fullness of God's creation in imaging the future of education. The practical purpose is to propose alternative educational approaches that enhance richness and empower people to engage critically and constructively with the issues of power and conflict that naturally emerge in an environment of diversity.

Dancing with difference
When people seek to respect particularity, the cosmos and the value of every being, they will find themselves dancing with difference. I am not talking here about simple diversity that falls into neat categories, such as England and Ireland, Israel and Palestine, women and men, rich and poor. The very choice of these pairs exemplifies the problem (Praetorius, 1998: 115-118); differences and similarities are too complex to be dichotomised. In fact, even talking in categories, or in the royal 'we', is problematic because many will not be included (Praetorius, 1988: 109-111) and some will be ambiguously included.

A certain humility emerges when we recognise that our view is not the only one. Sometimes this humility arises, as it did for me in the religious conference, when a person quite different from myself accomplished something that I had long valued; it may arise when one groups sees something in a situation that others completely miss. It will surely arise when hurricanes, tornadoes and earthquakes command our attention. It can also arise when people stop to watch a sunset, dig in a garden, or campaign against a plan to locate a toxic dump in the lower-income part of their city.

Such respect for difference is at the heart of community. According to Letty Russell (1993: 195), 'community is built out of difference'. Difference is a reality that cannot be denied. How then do we work with it? William Doll (1993) sees chaos at the heart of the natural world, so he advocates chaos as important to the educational process. Similarly, if difference is deep in the heart of the natural world, so dancing with difference is a way to engage that world in its fullness and respect the richness of divine creation, rather than to oversimplify it for the sake of human control.

If education is to help people dance with difference, we need faith communities and schools where people meet difference. We need communities and schools where people of different cultures, beliefs and values can meet and learn to dance, however awkwardly or angrily they begin. We also need teachers and administrators who value the dance, who have some experience in negotiating difference, and who are willing to be learners in the process. In such a dance, no one has all of the answers; if they did, the dance would cease and education would become stylised and rigid.

Diving into conflict

This discussion of difference leads into a second approach to education, which is diving into conflict. Conflict emerges wherever differences are really important to people, or where their values and needs run counter to one another. Even perspectives on difference can lead to conflict. For example, people of a majority ethnic group in a particular society often emphasise social similarities and unity, whereas people of minority groups frequently focus more attention on differences. The minority groups often fear, for good reason, that they will be pressured to assimilate to the dominant group's norms and values if the pressures of hegemony are too strong. Similarly, women and men often dispute theories of male-female difference, or of differences among men and among women. These issues are quite lively among women as they evaluate political strategies of equality and difference, and as they consider the several theories of difference within gender studies (Graham, 1996: 169-191).

One way to think about these conflicts is to recognise that they are inevitable and healthy within a diverse community. Conflict is not a new problem, especially within religion, but it is certainly a very present one. Diving into conflict does not mean doing battle, but confronting diversity, or facing together into differences. The religious conference of the case study was such an attempt, complete with rules for dialogue and attempts to encourage honest, personal and respectful conversation. Such an effort to engage the most challenging differences in a community is what I have named elsewhere as sacred confrontation (Moore, 1998b: 69-94). The very effort is diving into conflict.

Seeking convergence
If difference is so important, then separating disciplines of study or streams of students will not usually provide the most adequate education. If difference is so important, then neither enculturation nor assimilation can be the primary purpose of education either. Enculturation places primary emphasis on the existing culture, and assimilation places emphasis on the dominant culture. What may be more important is convergence: the meeting of cultures, ideas and ways of life in the shared life of a community; what may be most important is the revelation of the Holy in the midst of these meetings.

Some attention to difference is currently focused on conflict resolution, or resolving the problems that emerge from difference. While this approach is often urgent and valuable, the sole focus on resolving conflict can lead people to assume that difference is inevitably a problem, and tenuous compromises are our only options. Seeking convergence is a much deeper process, one in which people seek to understand one another deeply and to find directions for common life that their whole community (or most of it) can affirm, even as people continue to differ in many points of view and values. Convergence is a place of meeting in the ongoing movement of common life. Yesterday's convergence may need to yield to a new one tomorrow; yet, the search for convergence opens a community to discern God's calling to their shared vocation.

This discussion is not intended to oversimplify the values and challenges of introducing children and newcomers into an existing religious culture, or to deny the complexity and vitality of recent work in conflict resolution. It is, rather, to nuance the present practices of religious and educational communities. We can begin by recognising that neither children nor newcomers arrive in a community as blank slates. They are already a bundle of energy, feelings, ideas and experiences, to be respected and invited into convergence with the community, to be part of the common life, transformed by and transforming of the community. Further, we need to face the complexity and messiness of communal efforts to build agreement on critical issues. While the communal search for agreement can be very important, we will soon discover that agreement is allusive, and agreement is not really necessary for convergence. The wonder of God's world unfolds when differences and tensions are held respectfully, while the community converges on shared concerns and directions for living. Revelation thus continues (understood differently in different religious traditions), even as the flow of life continues, rising and falling through the canyons and across the plains of a living world.

Building community

A fourth critical approach to education is building community. This is vividly important in relation to the previous proposals regarding difference. Of course, communal needs vary. Communities will sometimes need to accent unity, and sometimes diversity. Even allowing for these differences, however, most bodies will frequently need to focus on building community. They will not necessarily be building intimate community. Sometimes they will be building partnerships related to specific purposes and projects; sometimes they will be supporting a community that keeps certain beliefs and values alive; and sometimes the relationships they build will be close and multifaceted.

At its base, building community is creating an educational ecology in which the formal and informal opportunities for learning enhance one another and in which people are encouraged to learn from traditional texts, from one another, from peoples far away and from the earth. They are further encouraged to learn from study and meditation, from action-reflection, from the stories of their elders, from the arts and cultural productions of their people, from the deliberations and practices of their community, and from every dimension of ordinary life. To accomplish such broad learning requires attention to community life, which is one of the most profound teachers.

This emphasis is particularly strong in C.A. Bowers and D. Flinders, who are concerned about non-relational approaches to education. Motivated by this problem, they propose an ecological perspective on general education, based in a relational view of people and the land (Bowers and Flinders, 1990: 233-50; Bowers, 1995). To grasp such a perspective and to build ecologically sensitive and closely related communities will be one of the most urgent challenges for educators in the next decade.

Acting boldly
One last educational approach will be identified here; that is, acting boldly. In a healthy eco-system, the various parts of the system are not abstractly related; they are in constant interaction. They are active agents, interrelated and dependent with one another. Such an eco-system provides a model for educational practice.

This focus on action echoes John Dewey's (1977) emphasis on education through experience or Paulo Freire's (1970) emphasis on praxis learning. The attention here is placed on a never-ending cycle of action, reflection, and action within the multifaceted contexts of social life. Such an affirmation is easily misunderstood by such code language as 'learning by doing' or 'experiential education', with the primary accent placed on individuals' actions; it can also be misunderstood as limited to the particular kinds of liberative action that concern Freire, or to unreflected, even trivial, experience. Such reductions are not true to Dewey or Freire, nor to my proposal.

John Dewey addressed such concerns over a period of many years, seeking to clarify the complexity of experience, and the ways in which certain kinds of action and experience can contribute to people being opened to future experience. He was particularly concerned with the social and purposive nature of experience (Dewey, 1977: 58-60, 67-72; cf. Dewey, 1962: 121-131). On the other hand, even Dewey fell short of seeing the thoroughly communal, interrelated nature of learning through action, or acknowledging fully the potential effects of such action beyond the immediate learning community. The interrelatedness of an eco-system offers a bolder image; whatever one does affects others in the system, and even affects the larger systems of which the learning community is part. Teaching and learning take place in the larger community, as well as in the smaller ones.

These concerns for bold action, understood interactively and complexly, have led me to include some kind of meaningful action in every course that I teach. Several of my classes have produced resource books, published desktop style. My Education and Story class produced an original play; the Liberative Pedagogy class led several workshops and learning events in local schools and churches. The purpose of these class actions was not simply to practise arts and skills that students can continue after they graduate. The students were seeking, as active learning communities, to contribute significantly to the larger community, and so they did!

This discussion of action leads back to the importance of richness in religious education, the beginning and ending theme of this chapter. Religious educators have unique opportunities to engage people in richness: by dancing with diversity, diving into conflict, seeking convergence, building community and acting boldly. Our action may not save the world, but I pray it will make a difference.

References

Armstrong, F. and Barton, L. (eds) (1999), *Disability, Human Rights and Education: cross-cultural perspectives,* Philadelphia, Pennsylvania, Open University Press.

Beauboeuf-Lafontant, T. and Augustine, D.S. (eds) (1996), *Facing Racism in Education* (second edition), Cambridge, Massachusetts, Harvard Educational Review, Reprint Series.

Bowers, C.A. (1995), *Educating for an Ecologically Sustainable Culture: rethinking moral education, creativity, intelligence, and other modern orthodoxies,* Albany, New York, State University of New York.

Bowers, C.A. and Flinders, D.J. (1990), *Responsive Teaching: an ecological approach to classroom patterns of language, culture, and thought,* New York, Teachers College.

Carey, J. with Arnst, C. (1997), Greenhouse gases: the cost of cutting back, *Business Week,* 8 December, 64-66.

Conway, R. and Watson, B. (1998), Green futures: the purpose and the passion that propels technology, and the implications for religious education, *British Journal of Religious Education,* 20, 166-177.

Dewey, J. (1977), *Experience and Education,* New York, Collier Books.

Dewey, J. and Dewey, E. (1962), *Schools of Tomorrow,* New York, E.P. Dutton and Co., Inc.

Doll, W.E. Jr (1993), *A Post-Modern Perspective on Curriculum,* New York, Teachers College.

Easterbrook, G. (1997), Brighter sun warms greenhouse debate, *US News and World Report,* 123 (13), 34.

Freire, P. (1970), *Pedagogy of the Oppressed* (translated by Myra Bergman Ramos), New York, Herder and Herder.

Gardner, H. (1993), *Frames of Mind: the theory of multiple intelligences,* New York, Basic Books.

Gardner, H. (1999), *Intelligence Reframed: multiple intelligences for the twenty-first century,* New York, Basic Books.

Goldberg, D.T. (1994), *Multiculturalism: a critical reader,* Cambridge, Massachusetts, Blackwell.

Graham, E.L. (1996), *Making the Difference: gender, personhood and theology,* Minneapolis, Minnesota, Fortress.

Grubb, M., Brackley, P., Ledic, M., Mathur, A., Rayner, S., Russell, J. and Tanabe, A. (1991), *Energy Policies and the Greenhouse Effect, Volume Two: country studies and technical options,* London, Royal Institute of International Affairs.

Gwaganad (1989), Speaking for the earth the Haida way, in J. Plant (ed.), *Healing the Wounds: the promise of ecofeminism,* pp 76-79, Philadelphia, Pennsylvania, New Society.

Hess, C.L. (1997), *Caretakers of our Common House: women's development in communities of faith,* Nashville, Tennessee, Abingdon.

Hooks, B. (1989), *Talking Back: thinking feminist, thinking black,* Boston, Massachusetts, South End.

Jachtenfuchs, M. (1996), *International Policy-Making as a Learning Process? the European Union and the greenhouse effect,* Aldershot, Ashgate.

Mies, M. and Shiva, V. (1993), *Ecofeminism,* Halifax, Nova Scotia, Fernwood.

Moore, M.E.M. (1983), Be still and know, unpublished poem.

Moore, M.E.M. (1997), Wisdom, sophia, and the fear of knowing, *Religious Education,* 92, 227-243.

Moore, M.E.M. (1998a), Spirit reveals, unpublished poem.

Moore, M.E.M. (1998b), *Ministering with the Earth,* St Louis, Missouri, Chalice.

Orr, D.W. (1994), *Earth in Mind: on education, environment, and the human prospect,* Washington, D.C., Island.

Orr, D.W. (1992), *Ecological Literacy: education and the transition to a postmodern world,* Albany, New York, State University of New York.

Plumwood, V. (1993), *Feminism and the Mastery of Nature,* London, Routledge.

Praetorius, I. (1998), *Essays in Feminist Ethics,* Leuven, Belgium, Peeters.

Russell, L. (1993), *Church in the Round,* Louisville, Kentucky, Westminster John Knox.

Sleeter, C.E. and Grant, C.A. (1987), An Analysis of multicultural education in the United States, *Harvard Educational Review,* 57, 421-444.

Sleeter, C.E. and McLaren, P.L. (eds) (1995), *Multicultural Education, Critical Pedagogy, and the Politics of Difference,* Albany, New York, State University of New York.

Woyshner, C.A. and Gelfond, H.S. (eds) (1997), *Minding Women: reshaping the educational realm,* Cambridge, Massachusetts, Harvard Educational Review, Reprint Series.

Young, I.M. (1990), *Justice and the Politics of Difference,* Princeton, New Jersey, Princeton University.

6

REPRESENTING FAITH TRADITIONS IN RELIGIOUS EDUCATION: AN ETHNOGRAPHIC PERSPECTIVE

Eleanor Nesbitt

Introduction

'*Ik onkar*', 'Sikhs have ten gods' and 'Sikhism stresses belief in One God'.[1] These three statements were made respectively by Guru Nanak, by Sikh pupils in British schools, and a Sikh 'working group', which was invited to advise the School Curriculum and Assessment Authority (SCAA) in drawing up 'Model Syllabuses' for religious education in schools in England.[2] Juxtaposition of these provides an impetus for examining the relationship between the Sikh tradition and community (which of course includes Sikh pupils in British schools), the representation of Sikh tradition in the religious education curriculum and for assessing the role of ethnographic insights in this enquiry. Although this chapter's principal focus is on the Sikh tradition, this is not meant to be in isolation from other faith traditions, as reference will also be made to data from studies of Hindu and Christian experience.[3] However, the ethnographic work to which I refer most often in this chapter was a study of eight- to thirteen-year-old British Sikhs in the West Midlands (Nesbitt, 2000).[4]

The term 'ethnography' is current with several related meanings: it is applied to anthropological fieldwork, to the report of such a study and to the theoretical underpinning of both of these. Usage in this chapter draws on all three areas of meaning and is particularly influenced by the interpretive approach of Clifford Geertz (1973) and my colleague Robert Jackson's (1977) application of this to religious education. Post-Saidian critiques of ethnography for its cultural imperialism by Arvind-pal Singh (1996) and others, and the deconstructive response of Crapanzano (1986) and others to Geertz, have also shaped my understanding.

This chapter summarises the characterisation of Sikhism, in particular in Model Syllabuses and curriculum books, and views this in relation to the concerns of recent ethnographic and historical studies. For example, divergence between ethnographers' and curriculum book writers' understandings of caste (*zat*) and *amrit* (sanctified water, water used in initiation) within the tradition problematises the representation of Sikhism in religious education and, more generally, the relationship between ethnography, religious studies, religious education and religious nurture. More fundamentally, the underlying 'world religions' model of discrete, reified religions is challenged, whether or not, with regard to the representation of the 'world faiths' that are studied in religious education, Sikhism is a special case. A plea is made for developing an enhanced awareness of the reflexive, interactive nature of human experience as evidenced in the related micro- and macro-processes of ethnographic research and of cultural reproduction in faith communities.

The nature of religious education

In maintained community (formerly 'county') schools, which constitute the vast majority of schools in England and Wales, religious education is statutory but must not be denominationally based. It is religious education, not religious instruction: in other words, it is distinct from the religious nurture, both informal and formal (in Sunday schools or in Gujarati or Punjabi language classes for instance), which members of faith communities provide for their young people. In this absence of a confessional base it resembles religious studies more closely than theology, although it is delusory to suppose that religious studies, or indeed any other academic discipline, is value free, as Arvind-pal Singh (1998a) has pointed out. The aim of religious education is not to perpetuate a particular faith tradition but to enable pupils to learn both about and from religions (SCAA, 1994: 7). This means providing opportunities both for the study of beliefs and practices and for personal reflection on the issues that these raise. These attainment targets for religious education are contextualised by the legal requirement that schools 'enhance [pupils'] spiritual, moral, cultural and social development' (SCAA, 1994: 4). Integral to this is the reinforcement and affirmation of each child's experience of religion (Ipgrave, 1999).

Sikh tradition: curricular presentation and ethnographic accounts
The Model Syllabuses
To take the example of Sikhism: Sikh tradition in the curriculum is mediated and determined by the syllabus, the resources used and the classroom delivery. In this chapter examples of just two aspects come in for scrutiny: the syllabus and resources; and, more specifically, the School Curriculum and Assessment Authority Model Syllabuses and curriculum books. The contents of syllabuses for public examinations, videos and electronic resources are not considered here.

The faith communities' working group reports and two Model Syllabuses (SCAA, 1994a, 1994b, 1994c) are intended as guidance for local agreed syllabus committees in designing locally agreed syllabuses. Moreover, they are required content for initial teacher training in religious education. Consequently, the Model Syllabuses are likely to be more influential than any of the locally agreed syllabuses. The recommendations of the Model Syllabuses are likely to be respected because they 'take into account an educational rationale for religious education' as well as 'present knowledge and understanding of religions as agreed by members of faith communities' (SCAA, 1994b: 3).

Consistently with the report of the Sikh 'working group' (SCAA, 1994a: 30-34) 'Sikhism' is presented as a distinct, internally coherent system. Clearcut 'beliefs and values' and statements about 'the Gurus', 'community' and 'practices' are presented in columns as bullet points in their report. In the syllabuses the use of such phrases as 'Sikh values', 'Sikh attitudes' (SCAA, 1994c: 46), 'distinctive Sikh principles' (SCAA, 1994b: 54), 'what Sikhism has to say' (SCAA, 1994b: 55) reinforce uncritically the reification and essentialising of faith traditions (see Jackson, 1997: 60). This distinctiveness is discussed below.

Curriculum books
It is left to resources, and to curriculum books especially, to provide flesh for the skeletal outlines of local agreed and Model Syllabuses. The

following survey of Sikh tradition according to curriculum books that are used in religious education in Britain is necessarily brief. Its focus is confined to definition and identity, caste and *amrit*, and these are set in the context of findings in a field study of young Sikhs. Curriculum books offer a particular view of what it means to be a Sikh, in some cases defining 'Sikh' as a disciple or follower of the Gurus, and then providing outlines of belief and practice (e.g. Arora, 1986; Coutts, 1990). With their focus on the maintenance of the five Ks (*panj kakke*, the five external markers of a Khalsa Sikh), many authors equate Sikh with Khalsa (those Sikhs who accept the discipline attributed to Guru Gobind Singh), and this accords with definitions drawn up by authoritative Sikh bodies during the twentieth century. Some contrast two sorts of Sikh, for instance anyone who has been through the *amrit* initiation ceremony, the *amritdhari* and *sahajdhari* (late developer)' (Butler, 1993: 41). Clutterbuck (1990: 59) acknowledged that 'Not all Sikhs will choose to take amrit', coupling this with a hint of exhortation or reproof 'they should still follow the code for living'.

Fieldwork, however, reveals that while many Sikhs are indeed *amritdhari*, and a much higher number are *keshdhari* (do not cut their *kesh*, i.e. hair, one of the five Ks), there is also a high incidence (varying from one caste or congregational community to another) of Sikhs (especially males) with short hair. Whereas some curriculum books, in both text and visual images, present the five Ks (and for males the turban) as part and parcel of being Sikh, ethnographic research among young Sikhs in Coventry suggested that a two-tier understanding was widespread. For these young people, the outward marks distinguished not so much Sikhs from non-Sikhs as (in their words) 'proper' Sikhs from Sikhs and others (Nesbitt, 1998b). Moreover, along with the *panj kakke*, Sikhs stressed vegetarianism as a requirement for a 'proper Sikh', again differing from the curriculum books which, in line with the Rahit Maryada (Sikh Code of Discipline), do not mention this.

In other words, ethnographic research suggests that the authors of curriculum books tend to present principles or norms as if they are practised universally, or at least more widely than they are, and so to marginalise those who identify with a tradition but do not regard these norms as defining or central. We find sweeping statements about the maintenance of the five Ks or the turban. Not only the text of curriculum books but also the illustrations present Sikhs as *keshdhari* and more often than not as turbaned males. It should of course be stressed that some authors do acknowledge clearly that not all Sikhs are *amritdhari* or even *keshdhari* (e.g. Cole and Sambhi, 1980: 5; Dhanjal, 1987: 61) and that some publications in which short-haired Sikhs appeared in photographs (e.g. Coventry Education Authority, nd) have met with protest from concerned members of the community.

To move to 'caste', curriculum books tend to emphasise the Gurus' teaching of 'equality', and this is certainly true to the conviction and practice of informed and devout Sikhs.[5] However, the cumulative impression from many curriculum books obscures two facts that merit consideration in the processes of learning about and learning from Sikhism. First, since the Gurus married within caste (*zat*) and arranged their children's marriages with caste-fellows, they must have accepted caste as a socially useful convention, although they recognised its irrelevance to humans' ultimate goal of being liberated from rebirth, *mukti* (see McLeod, 1997: 231-232). Second, as ethnographic data suggest, not only do Sikhs continue to prefer marriages (i.e. horizontal linkages) to be within *zat*, but also young British Sikhs internalise caste-based stereotypes (in a vertical hierarchy) at least as much as their Hindu peers (Nesbitt, 1997a).

The tension between official-insider and ethnographic-outsider understandings is evident from comparing two recently published statements. According to Weller (1997: 234), in a statement negotiated with Sikhs, 'Sikhism teaches that there are no distinctions between people and rejects the concept of caste (or *zat*), which therefore has no religious significance for Sikhs . . .'). Baumann (1996: 122) states by contrast, 'Where the Sikh community divides into caste-articulated congregational communities, the multi-caste Hindu community shades into an encompassing set of practices which defies hermetic community boundaries'. Both statements are 'true' and indeed compatible, but only if the commensal and matrimonial aspects of caste are distinguished and the Gurus' declaration of the irrelevance of birth/status to attaining *mukti* (release from being repeatedly reborn) is distinguished from the twentieth-century concept of equality. The complex contemporary social reality (as detailed by Kalsi, 1992) is usually not adequately represented or addressed in syllabuses or curriculum books. Whether it should be, for older pupils at least, and if so how, will be differently answered in accordance with individuals' views on religious education's relationship to religious nurture, theology, religious studies and ethnography. Certainly this, and the matters to which we now turn, could provide input for both cognitive and affective aspects of religious education.

Amrit

For the writers of curriculum books, *amrit* is the sweetened water with which Sikhs are initiated at the ceremony variously called *amrit sanskar, amrit pahul* and *khande-di-pahul*. They also mention as *amrit* the sweetened water with which a baby's tongue is touched when receiving his or her first name.[6] Only Dhanjal offers another usage of *amrit* as the nectar of immortality in Hindu mythology relating to Amritsar (1993: 13).

Many of the young Sikhs in my ethnographic study, however, used the term *amrit* not only for the sweetened water used in initiation but also for water that had been imbued with healing and protective power by being blessed by a Baba (a charismatic leader, see Nesbitt, 1997b) or by having been placed close to the Guru Granth Sahib during an *akhand path* (the continuous reading for forty-eight hours of the complete scripture), a practice firmly prohibited by the Rahit Maryada). Fieldwork in Coventry revealed the importance of amrit in these young Sikhs' experience as a transformed and transforming medium whose use, through sipping or splashing, brings a variety of benefits and affects individual behaviour. None of this appears, to my knowledge, in any syllabus or curriculum book.

The fact that, by contrast, none of the children or adults knew of *amrit* being given to infants, a lifecycle rite described in so many textbooks, suggests the dangers inherent in generalising from what may be very infrequent practice. More field study is needed. It is possible that the injunction in Rahit Maryada has led to a very infrequent ceremony being described as the norm. Furthermore, the familiarity of the writers of religious education curriculum books with parallel rites in other faith communities, notably with the infant baptism of children born into many Christian families, may have influenced their perception of Sikh tradition. The demands of the religious education syllabuses followed for the General Certificate of Secondary Education (GCSE) may have a similar origin.

Issues of content

Discrepancies such as these between curriculum-book content and ethnographic data raise the issue of content, and this in turn raises questions of representation and authority. Who decides the definition and content of the 'world religions'? To use Marion Bowman's (1992) model, what is the basis for including or excluding either 'official' or 'folk' religion, and can such analytic distinctions be sustained in practice? The relationship between religious nurture, the processes whereby children acquire the beliefs and practices of their elders, or some adaptation of these (Bushnell, 1967; Hull, 1984), and religious education's presentation of a faith tradition, need to be clarified. Should religious education be using uncritically material that corresponds closely to that used in gurdwara classes? Lastly, how is religious education regarded by members of faith communities?

Certainly, to take this last question first, concerned members of faith traditions are aware of the potential of religious education to further or misrepresent their faiths, as evidenced by Zaki (1982) and Das (1994). Although little has been written by Sikhs, some have campaigned against publications that contain pictures of 'Sikhs' with short hair (e.g. Coventry Education Authority, nd). Particularly vigilant in monitoring curriculum books is the British Sikh Educational Council, whose members are in some cases consulted by authors. The Council also exerted influence at national level through the Sikhism Working Group, whose report shaped the School Curriculum and Assessment Authority Model Syllabuses. Moreover, some Sikhs are concerned enough to be actively involved in the shaping of religious education locally, whether as members of local Standing Advisory Councils on Religious Education (SACREs) and Agreed Syllabus Committees (Taylor, 1991) or in the faith communities' working groups set up by the Schools Curriculum and Assessment Authority. Only future research will reveal the processes whereby the 'representatives' of a faith community arrive on the local SACRE.[7]

In practice, the influential voice of the Sikh representative on SACREs and Agreed Syllabus Committees seems likely to rule out controversial material (material that does not present the Khalsa model and conform to the rulings and Tat Khalsa ethos of the Shiromani Gurdwara Parbandhak Committee). One example is the significant exclusion of the role of *sants* (charismatic and controversial Sikh religious, and sometimes political, leaders), although Butler (1993: 58) devotes a sentence to them. What is at stake is authority: as things stand, can only those aspects of Sikh practice that are endorsed by the Shiromani Gurdwara Parbandhak Committee in Amritsar be included in the Sikh component of religious education? Can or should advisory groups represent a wider spectrum of Sikh outlook, thereby 'reducing the risk of portraying any religious tradition as monolithic, or of claiming generalisability for accounts of the essentials of religions written by small groups of insiders' (Jackson, 1997: 135). Does 'multicultural' allow no space for diversity within 'cultures'?

Issues of language

Attention to ethnographic study of the Sikh tradition in Britain alongside its presentation in religious education also highlights issues of language and issues of boundary-drawing, which I suggest are, *mutatis mutandis*, of relevance to other traditions too. To take the linguistic issues first, these are: translation as transformation; whether religious education should be conservative and purist or reinforce change; and the need for awareness that terms can mask conceptual shifts.

To start with translation as transformation: religious education texts include translations of the *mul mantar* (literally 'root formula', the verse commencing *ik onkar* with which the Guru Granth Sahib begins). With exceptions (e.g. Clutterbuck, 1990; SCAA, 1994a: 33), these renderings use 'he' to refer to 'God' at least until the last line 'realised through His grace'. Not only are there no gender-specific personal pronouns and possessive adjectives in the original (although the nouns are masculine), but there is no single term for 'God' in the Guru's utterance. What results is an arguably more masculine version than the original warrants (Singh, 1993; Nesbitt, 1994) and one with all the European, Judaeo-Christian connotations of 'God'. Of course, the replacement of masculine terms with the gender-free 'Sovereign', one translator's solution (Singh, 1996), is also open to question. Here, clearly at issue are the distorting powers of translation, the cultural and theological burden of religious language and the gendering of language. The wider philosophical issue of whether 'monotheism' is an appropriate term for Guru Nanak's experience is discussed by Arvind-pal Singh (1998b).

Another linguistic example raises the second issue: whether religious education should be reinforcing, restraining, ignoring or drawing attention to change. In some cases (in the media, for example, as well as textbooks) terms such as 'priest' and being 'baptised' are used for *granthi* and *amrit chhakna*. Indeed 'priest' is used by Sikh scholars too, for example in the Jallianwala Bagh entry of the Encyclopaedia of Sikhism (Singh, 1996). The fact that (like a priest) the *granthi* reads the scriptures publicly does not justify using a word that carries many inappropriate connotations: brahminical caste or theological training, ordination and pastoral responsibilities. Ethnographic research reveals, however, that Sikhs themselves use these translations, even when speaking English with other Sikhs, or as terms embedded in Punjabi discourse. Thus, data illustrate the changing use of language within the community and the changing range of meaning that English words now bear as a result of the twentieth-century emigration of South Asians to Britain. Should curriculum books endorse such shifts or more strictly promote Punjabi terms?

Both these examples (the English versions of *mul mantar* and the use of 'priest' and 'baptise') demand attention to the relationship between terms and concepts. Moreover, the same term can be used for concepts with only a partial overlap. Usage of 'God' by Sikhs and in curriculum books provides the example with which this paper started. When asked about the Gurus, a seven-year-old Sikh girl in Coventry responded:

> Of the ten there's two very special ones . . . Guru Nanak . . . and Guru Gobind Singh. Now we have a modern god which normally lives away from us but sometimes he comes to the temple and he's really special. (Sarah Davies: written communication.)

Ethnographic research throws light on my Sikh pupils' insistence that they had ten gods and that they had visited and received *amrit* from God (Nesbitt and Jackson, 1995). Young people (and their elders) were clearly using 'God' as a rendering of the Punjabi word 'Baba', which applies to the ten Gurus, the Guru Granth Sahib and (as in the above quotation) to venerated, more recent and living spiritual teachers *(sants)*. Much of the time when they said 'God', young Sikhs meant not *onkar, parmatma, hari, ram, khuda* or the other terms that writers have translated as God, but Guru and Baba. But how is use of 'God' for 'Guru' and 'Baba' extending or shrinking the concept 'God'? What is the role of religious education in acknowledging or unpicking popular usage? In accordance with the Schools Curriculum and Assessment Authority's attainment target two, could older pupils be 'learning from' such linguistic issues, for example learning to examine critically the relationship between term and concept, and to observe the shifts that can occur?

Distinctiveness and boundaries
The issue of boundaries emerges starkly from the Model Syllabuses: SCAA (1994b: 6) has an introductory section headed 'The Distinctiveness of Religions', and, as noted above, 'Sikhism' and other faiths are presented as distinctive. This accords with pronouncements from within the tradition, but it takes no account of recent historical analysis which has problematised the boundaries between the faith traditions on which the world religions' approach is predicated (Jackson, 1997; Oberoi, 1994; Smith, 1978). Ethnographic research among Sikhs and others in Britain lends weight to this deconstruction of religions and religious boundaries. Thus, our ethnographic research shows that some Hindus regard Sikhs (as well as Buddhists and Jains) as Hindus (a widely held view expressed by Prinja, 1996) and that many Punjabi families (certainly from Valmiki and Ravidasi zats) identify with both Hindu and Sikh tradition (Nesbitt, 1990). On the basis of his study of devotion to Baba Balaknath and Shri Pir Nigaha, Geaves (1998) and Geaves and Barnes (2001) have demonstrated that the spatial model of religions as bounded is unhelpful, since diversity and syncretism are at the heart of religions and the evolutionary nature of religion is aptly paralleled with the development of languages.

From this ethnographic base, religious studies suggest that nothing short of a reconceptualisation of the relation between Punjabi, Hindu and Sikh is needed in religious education. The perception of Sikhism as 'a derived religion' (Cole and Sambhi, 1993) is of only limited value, since it misleadingly suggests that only the historic origins of Sikh tradition need to be located in a wider 'Hindu' context. It is, however, arguably illuminating to consider contemporary variations in Sikhs' religious behaviour as continuously arising in a Punjabi Hindu matrix (Nesbitt, 2000a, 2000b). Ballard's (2000) analysis usefully (though unacceptably to many 'insiders') dismantles the received structure, with historical support from Oberoi (1994: 1-2). Once the categories of Hindu and Sikh are set aside, or at least challenged, the currents of Punjabis' religious activity can be observed afresh and possibly reconceptualised with, for example, the sort of 'dimensions' suggested by Smart (1971) and, in Indic dress, more recently by Ballard (2000).

Our particular focus in this chapter on Sikhs *vis-à-vis* Hindu tradition should not distract us from the wider scene with its many other ambiguous boundaries: the third millennium, like the closing years of the second, will be characterised by an increasingly pluralist individual spirituality (see, for example, Ward, 1991) and by an increasing number of children being brought up in mixed-faith, intercultural and interdenominational families and, certainly in the case of Christians, with multiple intrafaith influences (Nesbitt, 1993a). The assumption underpinning so much religious education of clear, agreed boundaries separating faith traditions and communities will be more and more anachronistic. This is by no means to deny the equally clear (and closely related) tendencies of certain groups to assert impregnable boundaries and to reinvent sharply delineated tradition in high profile ways. What I am arguing for is greater openness in religious education to exposing the dynamics of religious and cultural evolution. I recall a school in which a language awareness course preceded the study of any particular language. Could religious education in the first century of the third millennium risk the wrath of vested interests by similarly making more explicit (or at least raising the matter of) the linkages, overlaps and interactions? The perspectives of psychology and social anthropology are as valuable for religious education as they are for religious studies.

Ethnography and religious education

Ethnography has, I suggest, a multiple contribution to make at the beginning of the third millennium to the articulation of faith traditions in religious education for a multifaith society.

First, actual field studies show how religious education and the nurture of young people in their faith impinge on each other. We need to recognise that religious education contributes to the religious nurture of pupils from Sikh and other faith backgrounds (Nesbitt, 1998a, 1998c). In fact, some of what the child can articulate of her/his tradition may result from the intervention of school, perhaps as a result of a teacher's enquiries prior to a particular assembly. To take an instance of this from the Warwick data: when asked during an interview, 'Have you heard the word *karma*?', a sixteen-year-old Gujarati responded, 'Yes . . . I did it in my exam'. As I have illustrated elsewhere, some young people's identification with a religious label comes first on a teacher's authority (Nesbitt, 1991: 31; Jackson and Nesbitt, 1993: 162-3). Of course, the role of school in young people's developing awareness of their tradition is not confined to religious education. The painfully negative reaction of some peers has also to be recognised.[8]

Second, despite its colonial pedigree and the risks of cultural imperialism, ethnography does provide interpretive tools for understanding individuals in the context of heterogeneous, ever-changing groups and traditions. Accordingly, the Warwick Religious Education Project, consistently with Jackson (1997), emphasises the internal diversity and fluidity of faith traditions, constituted as they are of membership groups that are themselves aggregates of varied and changing individuals. It advocates an ethnographic and interpretive method whereby pupils 'build bridges' between their own individual experience and the experience of young people from a particular tradition, including those who are presented in the curriculum books. Thus, the ethnographic process can usefully inform religious education not only by providing data for curriculum materials, but by involving teachers with their pupils in making connections between aspects of their own and another's experience and understanding individuals in context.

Third, the challenges posed by ethnography to the foundational assumptions of religious education ginger up debate and could even herald an eventual paradigmatic shift in the subject. Meanwhile the interpretive approach continues to sit uncomfortably with world religions and Model Syllabuses. Only a censored ethnography is possible, with curriculum material being filtered through a 'world religions', SCAA-compatible mesh. Otherwise the untidy world that pupils meet will leave them with a very different sense of plural allegiance and waxing and waning heterodoxies and heteropraxes from the 'Sikhism', 'Hinduism' et cetera of the syllabuses.

In this connection Sarah Davies reports the dilemma of an ethnographer conducting fieldwork that was to provide the basis for a curriculum book on Sikhs:

> The experience of Sikh children represents their personal contact with the tradition rather than an overview. They may belong to a group, some of whose beliefs and practices lie outside those of other Sikhs. This may raise controversy, especially where Sikhs might wish their tradition to be portrayed in educational material as unified and conformist. (Personal communication.)

Are religious education texts to include only carefully vetted encounters with individuals who look, worship and express themselves in particular ways, even though – to take a Sikh example – it is the inspiration of *sants* (absent though they are from the syllabuses) that is a driving force for many of the most devout and 'committed' Sikhs? Or, to take another example, which raises the hotly contentious question 'who is a Christian?', how are influences on individuals' spirituality such as yoga or an increasing openmindedness to reincarnation to be acknowledged in religious education (Nesbitt, 1993b).

As long as curriculum books and syllabuses adhere to an approach that assumes discrete, relatively homogeneous world religions, teachers' awareness of the varieties of experience of their Sikh (and other) pupils needs to be informed by ethnographic insights. For example, as the Schools Curriculum and Assessment Authority syllabuses and the curriculum books stand, there is the clear likelihood that it will be the pupils' insider 'knowledge' of the tradition that appears as a straightforward 'misconception' or 'mistake' (as of course it would also to many spokespeople for the tradition) unless teachers are acquainted with the lived reality. Indeed, the framework for the assessment of quality and standards in Initial Teacher Training (OFSTED 1997: 10 d vi) stipulates that 'For all courses, those to be awarded Qualified Teacher Status must, when assessed, demonstrate that they . . . know pupils' most common misconceptions and mistakes in the subject'.

Furthermore, ethnographic insight points up the problematic nature of affirming each pupil in his/her faith (Ipgrave, 1999) since the affirmation of, say, one Sikh's Khalsa identity as Sikh risks marginalising the experience of the many pupils, identified by ethnographic research, whose families identify themselves as Sikh without observing or feeling the need to observe Khalsa discipline (see Nesbitt, 1998b).

Conclusion

The issues raised by examining the relationship between Sikh tradition (complex and developing) and the presentation of that tradition in religious education exemplifies issues for other faith traditions. This is not to deny that, in some respects at least, Sikhism is arguably a special case. Sikhs' minority status and insecurity, even in the country where their numbers are greatest, and the resultant sensitivities of many Sikhs to 'misrepresentation' by hostile or conspiratorial scholars (Helweg, 1996; O'Connell, 1996), plus the significance and emotive implications of 'the Sikh look' may arguably necessitate a higher degree of sensitivity in deciding the visual content of curriculum books (Nesbitt, 1997c).

Ethnographic research can benefit the curriculum, and its interpretive character can inform the processes of classroom pedagogy. At the same time, ethnography must challenge religious educationists' assumptions and extend the possibilities for the subject. To be more specific, as noted above, the Model Syllabuses provide teachers with model attainment targets of 'learning about religions' and 'learning from religions'. Currently, the portrayal of Sikhism in curriculum materials is homogeneous in a way that the reality is not. Attainment target one (learning about) 'includes the ability to: . . . explain similarities and differences between, and within, religions'. Here,

clearly, is an opening to enrich the syllabus from the internal diversity
. . . sant-influenced gurdwaras. For a glimpse of the profound impact
of sants on particular sectors of Sikh society, see Nesbitt (1985) and
Barrow (1999).

Is the faith of Mormons, Jehovah's Witnesses, Ahmadiyyas and
Radhasoamis to be invisible to a non-confessional religious education
because these groups fall foul of certain 'orthodoxies'? These questions
necessitate a consciousness of where one is positioning religious
education in relation to theology and nurture on the one hand, with
their doctrinal and confessional stance, and to religious studies on the
other hand, with its disciplinary affinity to social anthropology,
sociology and psychology.

Leaders, pupils, religious educators, ethnographers, writers and
researchers of religious studies texts are caught up in reflexive processes
that are themselves interacting. Examination of the tensions between
ethnography and the representation of one 'world religion', Sikhism,
as it is represented in religious education, on the one hand, and the
overlap between this representation and Sikh nurture, on the other,
suggests the need for a heightened awareness of the nature of insider-
outsider interactions in the dynamics of cultural reproduction.

Notes

1. For '*ik onkar*', in place of the widespread 'There is one God', N.G.-K Singh suggests 'There is one being' and 'one reality is' (1996: 1).

2. See respectively Adi Granth 1, Nesbitt and Jackson (1995) and SCAA (1994a). It needs to be noted that the Model Syllabuses are intended as guidance for local Agreed Syllabus Committees but do 'not constitute an authoritative legal interpretation of the provisions of the Education Acts' (SCAA, 1994b: 5).

3. These studies were funded by the Leverhulme Trust and the Economic and Social Research Council (Project no R000232489) respectively.

4. This was funded by the Economic and Social Research Council (Project no R000232489).

5. See Bains and Johnston 1995: 32 for instances from a Canadian Sikh's life.

6. Butler (1993: 38), Clutterbuck (1990: 48-9), Cole (1985: 83), Emmett (1994: 19), Penney (1988: 43), Sambhi (1989: 18), Thorley (1989: 22).

7. Sikhs, Hindus etc may serve on SACREs not only as members of 'Group A' (representatives of 'other religions'), but also on Group C (teachers' associations) or Group D (councillors and education officers). See Rose 1998 for issues raised by this 'representation'.

8. For example, Runnymede Bulletin (1997, June: 9) printed this poem by Kiran Chahal, a primary school pupil:

    They call you names for the fun of it
    To make your insides weak
    To injure all your happiness
    And tell you you're a Sikh.

References

Arora, R. (1986), *Religions of the World: Sikhism*, Hove, Wayland.

Bains, T.S. and Johnston, H. (1995), *The Four Quarters of the Night: the life-journey of an emigrant Sikh*, Montreal and Kingston, McGill-Queen's University Press.

Ballard, R. (2000), Panth Kismet Dharm te Qaum: continuity and change in four dimensions of Punjabi religion, in P. Singh and S. Thandi (eds), *Punjabi Identity in a Global Context*, pp 7-37, Oxford, Oxford University Press.

Barrow, J. (1999), Religious authority and influence in the diaspora: Sant Jaswant Singh and Sikhs in West London, in P. Singh and N.G. Barrier (eds), *Sikh Identity: continuity and change*, pp 335-348, Delhi, Manohar.

Baumann, G. (1996), *Contesting Culture: discourses of identity in multi-ethnic London*, Cambridge, Cambridge University Press.

Bowman, M. (1992), Phenomenology, fieldwork and folk religion, *Occasional Papers 6: British Association for the Study of Religions*.

Bushnell, H. (1967), *Christian Nurture*, New Haven, Connecticut, Yale University.

Butler, R. (1993), *Themes in Religion: Sikhism*, London, Longman.

Clutterbuck, A. (1990), *Growing Up in Sikhism*, London, Longman.

Cole, W.O. (1985), *A Sikh Family in Britain*, Oxford, Pergamon.

Cole, W.O. and Sambhi, P.S. (1980), *Meeting Sikhism*, London, Longman.

Cole, W.O. and Sambhi, P.S. (1993), *Sikhism and Christianity: a comparative study*, London, Macmillan.

Coutts, J. (1990), *Living the Faith: Sikh lives*, Harlow, Oliver and Boyd.

Coventry Education Authority (nd), *How a Sikh Prays*, Coventry, Coventry Education Authority.

Crapanzano, V. (1986), Hermes' Dilemma: the masking of subversion in ethnographic description, in J. Clifford and G. Marcus (eds), *Writing Culture: the poetics and politics of ethnography*, pp 51-76, Berkeley, California, University of California Press.

Das, Rasamandala (1994), The Western educationalists' perspective on the Vedic tradition, *ISKCON Communications Journal*, 4, July-Dec, 51-68.

Dhanjal, B. (1987), *Sikhism*, London, Batsford.

Dhanjal, B. (1993), *Amritsar*, London, Evans.

Emmett, P. (1994), *The Sikh Experience*, London, Hodder and Stoughton.

Geaves, R. (1998), The borders between religions: a challenge to the world religions approach to religious education', *British Journal of Religious Education*, 21, 20-31.

Geaves, R. and Barnes, C. (2001), The legitimization of a regional folk cult: the transmigration of Baba Balaknath from rural Punjab to urban Europe, *Journal of Contemporary Religion*, in press.

Geertz, C. (1973), *The Interpretation of Cultures*, New York, Basic Books.

Helweg, A. (1996), Academic scholarship and Sikhism: conflict or legitimization, in P. Singh and N.G. Barrier (eds), *The Transmission of Sikh Heritage in the Diaspora*, pp 253-268, Delhi, Manohar.

Hull, J.M. (1984), *Studies in Religion and Education*, Lewes, Falmer Press.

Hull, J.M. (1989), *The Act Unpacked: the meaning of the 1988 Education Reform Act for religious education*, Isleworth, University of Birmingham School of Education and the Christian Education Movement.

Ipgrave, J. (1999), Issues in the delivery of religious education to Muslim pupils: perspectives from the classroom, *British Journal of Religious Education*, 21, 147-158.

Jackson, R. (1997), *Religious Education: an interpretive approach*, London, Hodder and Stoughton.

Jackson, R. and Nesbitt, E. (1993), *Hindu Children in Britain*, Stoke on Trent, Trentham.

Jackson, R. and Nesbitt, E. (1995), Sikh children's use of 'God': ethnographic fieldwork and religious education, *British Journal of Religious Education*, 17, 108-20.

Kalsi, S.S. (1992), *The Evolution of the Sikh Community in Britain: religious and social change among the Sikhs of Leeds and Bradford*, Leeds, Community Religions Project, University of Leeds.

McLeod, W.H. (1997), *Sikhism*, Harmondsworth, Penguin.

Nesbitt, E. (1985), The Nanaksar movement, *Religion*, 15, 67-79.

Nesbitt, E. (1990), Pitfalls in religious taxonomy: Hindus and Sikhs, Valmikis and Ravidasis', *Religion Today*, 6 (1), 9-12.

Nesbitt, E. (1991), *'My Dad's Hindu, My Mum's Side are Sikhs': issues in religious identity*, Arts, Culture, Education, Research and Curriculum Paper, Charlbury, National Foundation for Arts Education.

Nesbitt, E. (1993a), Transmission of Christian tradition in an ethnically diverse society, in R. Barot (ed.), *Religion and Ethnicity: minorities and social change in the metropolis*, pp 156-169, Kampen, Kok Pharos.

Nesbitt, E. (1993b), Children and the world to come: the views of children aged eight to fourteen years on life after death, *Religion Today*, 8 (3), 10-13.

Nesbitt, E. (1995), Punjabis in Britain: cultural history and cultural choices, *South Asia Research*, 15, 221-40.

Nesbitt, E. (1997a), 'We are All Equal': young British Punjabis' and Gujaratis' perceptions of caste, *International Journal of Punjab Studies*, 4, 201-18.

Nesbitt, E. (1997b), 'Splashed with Goodness': the many meanings of Amrit for young British Sikhs, *Journal of Contemporary Religion,* 12, 17-33.

Nesbitt, E. (1997c), Religious education and Sikh identity: is this a special case? *World Religions in Education,* 32-36.

Nesbitt, E. (1998a), Bridging the gap between young people's experience of their religious traditions at home and school: the contribution of ethnographic research, *British Journal of Religious Education,* 20, 98-110.

Nesbitt, E. (1998b), Sikhs and proper Sikhs: young British Sikhs' perceptions of their identity, in P. Singh and N.G. Barrier (eds), *Sikh Identity: continuity and change,* pp 315-334, Delhi, Manohar.

Nesbitt, E. (1998c), How culture changes: British Sikh children and the Vaisakhi festival, *Journal of Sikh Studies,* 22, 95-118.

Nesbitt, E. (2000a), *The Religious Lives of Sikh Children in Coventry,* Leeds, Community Religions Project, University of Leeds.

Nesbitt, E. (2000b), Young British Sikhs and religious devotion, unpublished paper presented to Dharam Hinduja Institute for Indic Research conference, University of Cambridge, 8 July.

Nesbitt, E. and Jackson, R. (1995), Sikh children's use of God: ethnographic fieldwork and religious education, *British Journal of Religious Education,* 17, 108-120.

Oberoi, H.S. (1994), *The Construction of Religious Boundaries: culture, identity and diversity in the Sikh tradition,* Delhi, Oxford University Press.

O'Connell, J.T. (1996), The fate of Sikh studies in North America, in P. Singh and N.G. Barrier (eds), *The Transmission of Sikh Heritage in the Diaspora,* pp 269-288, Delhi, Manohar.

OFSTED/TTA (1997), *Framework for the Assessment of Quality and Standards in Initial Teacher Training 1997/98,* London, Office for Standards in Education/ Teacher Training Agency.

Penney, S. (1988), *Discovering Sikhism,* London, Heinemann.

Prinja, N.K. (1996), *Explaining Hindu Dharma,* Norwich, Religious and Moral Education Press.

Rose, D. (1998), A study of representative groups on SACRE, *Journal of Contemporary Religion,* 13, 383-393.

Sambhi, P.S. (1989), *Sikhism,* Cheltenham, Stanley Thornes.

SCAA (1994a), *Model Syllabuses for Religious Education: faith communities' working group reports,* London, School Curriculum and Assessment Authority.

SCAA (1994b), *Model Syllabuses for Religious Education: Model 1, living faiths today,* London, School Curriculum and Assessment Authority.

SCAA (1994c), *Model Syllabuses for Religious Education: Model 2, questions and teachings,* London, School Curriculum and Assessment Authority.

Singh, A.-P. (1996), Interrogating identity: cultural translation, writing and subaltern politics, in G. Singh and I. Talbot (eds), *Punjabi Identity: continuity and change,* pp 187-227, Delhi, Manohar.

Singh, A.-P. (1998a), Have we heard the last of religion? Towards a post-secular Sikh studies, unpublished paper, Workshop on New Perspectives in Sikh Studies, School of Oriental and African Studies, University of London, 28-29 May.

Singh, A.-P. (1998b), *Thinking between Cultures: metaphysics and cultural translation,* unpublished PhD dissertation, University of Warwick.

Singh, N.G.-K. (1993), *The Feminine Principle in the Sikh Vision of the Transcendent,* Cambridge, Cambridge University Press.

Singh, N.G.-K. (1996), *The Name of my Beloved: verses of the Sikh Gurus,* San Francisco, California, HarperSanFrancisco.

Smart, N. (1971), *The Religious Experience of Mankind,* London, Fontana.

Smith, W.C. (1978), *The Meaning and End of Religion,* London, SPCK.

Taylor, M. (1991), *SACREs: their formation, composition, operation and role on RE and worship,* Slough, National Foundation for Educational Research.

Thorley, S. (1989), *Sikhism in Words and Pictures,* Exeter, Religious and Moral Education Press.

Ward, K. (1991), *A Vision to Pursue: beyond the crisis in Christianity,* London, SCM.

Weller, P. (ed.), (2nd ed 1997), *Religions in the UK: a multi-faith directory,* Derby, University of Derby in association with the Inter Faith Network for the United Kingdom.

Zaki, Y. (1982), The teaching of Islam in schools: a Muslim viewpoint', *British Journal of Religious Education,* 5, 33-38.

7

RELIGIOUS EDUCATION BEYOND THE NATION STATE: THE CHALLENGE OF SUPRANATIONAL AND GLOBAL DEVELOPMENTS

Friedrich Schweitzer

Introduction

According to many politicians and economists, we have entered a new era: the age of supranational and global unification. There are high hopes, not only for a better future of international co-operation, of higher productivity and greater wealth, but also for the establishment of international peace and justice.

One of the key terms in contemporary discussions is 'globalisation'. The concept of globalisation is to take over from earlier interpretations of our contemporary situation. In this view, we should now speak of globalisation or of the 'global age' rather than of modernisation or postmodernity. Globalisation then is much more than a popular term. It is one of the main perspectives that are offered by social scientists for our journey into the third millennium.

While religious education has long been aware of the need for worldwide perspectives of peace, justice and mutual respect, the more recent discussion on globalisation has yet to receive much attention in this particular field of study. This may be due to the popular understanding of globalisation only in the sense of a worldwide open market. As long as globalisation is seen as no more than another step within the development of capitalist economy, it does not seem to imply much new for religious education. According to the analysts of globalisation, however, a purely economic understanding clearly falls short of its real impact. (For helpful introductions, see Waters, 1995; Beck, 1997; Beck, Giddens and Lash, 1996; Albrow, 1998; Beck,

1998a, 1998b; Tetzlaff, 2000). In their understanding, globalisation also entails a cultural process that may deeply change our lives, and it must be considered a social force that may influence our religious beliefs and deepest loyalties. It is in this sense of a 'global age' dawning upon us that globalisation may be considered a fundamental challenge for religious education.

It should be noted from the beginning, however, that the relationship between globalisation and religion does not only work in one way. While globalisation affects religion, religion may also affect globalisation. There are different ways of conceiving the unity of the world, and religion clearly has played a role in shaping such conceptions. Since globalisation is often reduced to an economic process, it will be important to point out the religious implications of a more comprehensive understanding of supranational unification.

In this chapter, we want to take up some perspectives from the emerging discussion on the relationship between globalisation, culture and religion. More specifically, we will try to show that globalisation implies a new situation for religious education, and why we might not yet be prepared to meet this situation. In a final section, a number of suggestions will be offered for how religious education may become able to take up the new challenges. In all of this, we will address supranational developments and globalisation in general, but we will also give some special attention in the second section to what sometimes is called the 'mini-globalisation' of European unification.

Globalisation and religion: perspectives from an emerging discussion

In today's discussions, globalisation is first of all understood as an economic process (Butterwege, 1999). It refers to the internationalisation of the market and, as a consequence, to worldwide competition between enterprises as well as between workers. As such, it is often used as an argument against the welfare-state, which supposedly has become an obstacle in this competition. In addition to this, globalisation is seen as a major challenge to the idea of the nation state. The globalisation of the international economy is no longer controlled by national governments (Albrow, 1998). Rather, the political unit of the nation state seems progressively to lose its influence on the factors and processes that shape the life of the people in a particular country. In this sense, globalisation poses serious problems for democracy since most democracies have been established at a national level.

While we have to keep all these issues in mind, our main focus will be on the less-well-known *religious* aspects of globalisation. And since the relationship between globalisation and religion is not obvious, we first need to become clear as to why we should be interested in this relationship. A good starting point for this may be found within the social-scientific discussion on globalisation. Roland Robertson (1992: 8), one of the leading analysts of globalisation, has coined the much-quoted phrase that globalisation means the process of turning the 'world into a single place'. It is important to note that, for Robertson, there are two sides to this process. Globalisation 'refers both to the compression of the world and the intensification of consciousness of the world as a whole' (Robertson, 1992: 8). In other words, globalisation may be considered an objective, mostly economic process, but it also includes a subjective side that refers to human consciousness.

At a first glance, this reference to a 'consciousness of the world as a whole' sounds like a new version of the familiar catchphrase 'Think globally: act locally', but there are important differences to be noted. Quite contrary to earlier discussions on global thinking, for example within ecological education, global consciousness in the sense of Robertson (1992) is not the result of education and enlightenment. Rather, we are dealing with an impact of economic and cultural influences. These influences are embodied, for example, in the modern media, whose global symbol has now become the *WWW* of the *World Wide Web*, they are embodied in worldwide mass transportation as well as in modern consumer culture and its international products, which are consumed all over the world. All this contributes to what has aptly been called, at first in the context of postmodernity (Harvey, 1989: 201), the 'compression of space and time'. The world as a 'single place' is based on the empty and abstract concepts of worldwide standardised time and space (Giddens, 1990: 18).

If the understanding of globalisation is thus widened in order to include not only the economic processes but also the cultural aspects connected to them, we may also see why globalisation has important religious implications. Some observers have pointed out that the idea of globalisation itself has religious roots. Robertson, for example, raises the question 'of the degree to which globalisation is or has historically been guided by religion'. In his view, religion contributes to the 'metacultural framing of the world as a whole', by which he means 'the ways in which basic categories of space (such as global map-making) and time (such as the universalisation and particularisation of calendars), as well as 'logic' and language, have been intimately bound-up with religion' (Robertson, 1991: 220). Others observe a religious dimension in the perception of the future aims of globalisation. According to Peter Beyer (1994: 7f.), the reference to the 'whole world' and the idea of a 'common social environment shared by all people on earth' bear 'a clear resemblance to the religious quest' because they include an 'eschatological' dimension. Such observations indicate that it makes sense to think of globalisation as a religious concept, and that consequently there is a need for critical re-examination of religious and pseudo-religious images of global unification and oneness. Globalisation may be subjected to a theological critique of its potential ideological implications.

On a more concrete level, several researchers have pointed out the effects of globalisation on religion. In this kind of analysis, the sociology of religion is extended to a global level by asking what globalisation does to religion. The first and main effect is often seen in a thorough *relativisation of religion*. When cultures and identities are brought closer together, says Peter Beyer (1994: 2), it becomes 'much more visible that the diverse ways of living are largely human constructions'. As a consequence, the life-worlds and worldviews that formerly could be taken for granted, 'appear to a significant extent arbitrary'. The multiplicity of different possibilities that sometimes is seen as an option of postmodern thinking now becomes an inescapable fact on a global level. Religion is perceived as a human construction, and the question of religious truth appears to be a purely subjective matter.

A similar argument may be found in the work of Anthony Giddens who analyses the role of tradition and of traditional knowledge in the process of globalisation. According to his results, it is one of the main effects of globalisation that all traditions lose their authoritative status and importance. Globalisation proceeds on the basis of what Giddens calls expert knowledge, and this type of knowledge comes to replace the authority of tradition, at least in many fields (Giddens, 1996).

A second effect of globalisation on religion results from what Giddens (1991: 144ff.) has called the *sequestration of experience*. Giddens maintains that globalisation is based on the abstract systems that have developed in modernity. More and more areas of contemporary society are determined by so-called self-referential systems like modern administration, which claim autonomy from the individual person and from personal feelings. Consequently, such systems leave no space for certain moral and existential experiences. Phenomena like 'madness; criminality; sickness and death; sexuality; and nature' are removed 'from the regularities of day-to-day life established by the abstract systems of modernity', an effect that is intensified by their global spread (Giddens, 1991: 156). Life without such experiences is not likely to raise questions of faith or ultimate meaning. Global experts are experts of technology or of the economy, not of religion.

A third effect of globalisation grows directly out of the second, the *privatisation of religion*. If everyday life functions without religious authority and without existential questions, such authority and questions become more and more removed from public life. They may still have their place but only in the private sphere. This effect of the privatisation of religion is further aggravated by the fact that 'traditional religious forms are no longer definitive for the society as a whole' (Beyer, 1994: 70). Religion is pluralised and individualised.

Yet as globalisation confronts religion with demands of relativisation and privatisation, with the constraint for religious communities 'to offer interpretations of that development and of their place in it' (Robertson, 1989: 18), there is also the response of *religious fundamentalism* (Marty and Appleby, 1991-1995). This fundamentalism, which may be considered a fourth effect of globalisation, is interpreted as counter-globalisation and as an attempt to uphold traditional authority. Often, the basic choice posed by globalisation for religion is said to be between a fundamentalist response and a globalising reorientation of religion (Beyer, 1994: 10).

In this view, fundamentalism is not a psychological aberration but is due to the fear of losing one's personal or religious identity.

While most observers agree that the main effects of globalisation on religion may be summarised with these terms, namely relativisation, privatisation, fundamentalism, at least some analysts like Roland Robertson (1989), Peter Beyer (1994), and José Casanova (1994) have attempted to describe an *alternative future for religion*. Even if the structural effects of globalisation clearly work in the direction described above, there are still important respects in which religion may play a significant *public role* within the process of globalisation. Contrary to the traditional secularisation thesis, these authors maintain that the confrontation with the systemic powers of globalisation may in fact create new possibilities for a public role of religion. Examples that may support this understanding are taken from a variety of countries and situations, including the Christian Right in the United States of America, liberation movements in Latin America, Islamic countries, and religious environmentalism in Europe. According to Casanova (1994), it is at the level of civil society that religion may play its public role, that is, with social movements and interest-groups outside the traditional political parties.

At this point we also need to take note of the *religious and theological visions* that have been developed in response to the process of globalisation. Examples of such visions may be found in the project of a 'global ethics', as Hans Küng (1990) calls it, with the idea of a 'new catholicity' set forth by Robert Schreiter (1997), or in a renewal of ecumenical perspectives in relation to globalisation, as for example Douglas Meeks (1992) suggests[1]. The common thread in these religious and theological responses to globalisation is the attempt to develop perspectives for the integrity of life in a global world. This includes models for a peaceful and dialogical relationship between the various forms of Christianity and other religions around the world which are to encounter each other with tolerance, respect and mutual understanding. Moreover, it includes the commitment to the 'humanity and dignity of the people' which is jeopardised by uncontrolled economic globalisation and unrestrained competition (Meeks, 1992: 7; also see Stackhouse,

Berger, McCann and Meeks, 1995). If such visions could become the guiding ideas for social movements and interest-groups within Churches and religious communities, they might function as an important basis for a non-fundamentalist response to globalisation.

Summarising the theological and sociological arguments for a new need for religion in the situation of globalisation, three points can be made. First, there are the so-called '*residual* problems of globalising systems' which go unanswered in the process of globalisation (Beyer, 1994: 97). These problems may include existential needs and experiences as well as questions of cultural and religious identity. Religion may contribute to an adequate response to such problems. Second, there are justice issues and, speaking more generally, ethical issues that do not disappear in a global world. Religion may play an important role in keeping such issues on the agenda of public life, and it may also contribute to their solution. Globalisation does not necessarily bring about justice in the world. Third, globalisation brings together people from very different backgrounds, culturally as well as ethnically and religiously. If globalisation is not to end with the now famous 'clash of cultures' (Huntington, 1996), models of peaceful encounter and of mutual respect and understanding are much needed, especially in respect of religion.

From this it is clear that the relationship between globalisation and religion is not only a question of what effects globalisation will have on religion. The question also is what kind of global world we need and about religion's potential to give shape to a global future of justice and dignity. Before taking up the question of what this means for religious education, I want to consider a somewhat more concrete example of supranational developments, namely European unification in its relationship to religious education.

European unification and religious education

One of the most important supranational developments in Europe is the establishment of the European Community. This community comprises most of the western, northern and southern countries of Europe but none of the eastern countries, at least not at this point. After a number of earlier phases, the European Community has now decided to take another step towards unification, the introduction of a single currency called the 'Euro', which will replace a number of the traditional currencies like the Deutsche Mark and the French Franc.

While the introduction of the new currency is considered a major step, which may not only bring economic growth but eventually political unity as well, it is not accompanied by corresponding political or cultural innovations. There is, of course, the European Parliament and there are administrative and political institutions at a European level. But transnational unification has largely progressed on an economic level. In this respect, European unification clearly follows the pattern of economic globalisation. Political decisions on questions of education and culture, for example, are to remain with the national governments in each of the participating countries. They are not included in the transnational process of unification. While this may be greeted as a positive opening for cultural diversity, it also creates a clear imbalance between transnational economy and national politics, an imbalance that works against democracy.

This way of achieving European unity, almost exclusively in economic terms, may explain why Europe has not become a major topic in religious education and why religious education has not received much attention in European politics. As far as European politics have become involved with education and research, this interest has been focused on the natural sciences, on technological innovations and on economic studies.

It is true that official statements sometimes make mention of religious education, for example, recommendation 1202 of the Council of Europe (1993) concerning religious tolerance. This recommendation demands that the teaching of religion and ethics be part of the school curriculum and work towards a better understanding of religions other than one's own. In January 1999, the Council of Europe (1999) adopted recommendation 1396 on Religion and Democracy. But so far, such statements have not led to political or financial consequences. For example, it is almost impossible to find support for research on religious education from sponsoring institutions of the European Community.

At the same time, it is obvious that, historically, religion, or to be more specific, Catholicism, Protestantism, Judaism and Islam, have strongly influenced European cultures and identities. And even today, in a situation of religious individualisation and pluralisation, this influence has not disappeared from the public scene. It is well known that religion may still create tensions and difficulties in Europe. For example, while in Germany (Daiber, 1995) the relationship between Protestants and Catholics has lost most of its former potential for hostilities, the Muslims living there, who are mostly of Turkish origin, have to a large extent not been accepted as fellow citizens by their German neighbours. However, there is also a positive side to the continuing influence of religion in Europe. Empirical studies on political and moral (for example, Schmidtchen, 1993) values have shown that many values that are considered politically and democratically desirable, correlate with religious attitudes. Religion still lends support to important community values. On the basis of data from the United States of America, a similar case has been made concerning the relationship between civil society and Christian religion (Wuthnow, 1996). Again, Christian religion is to be considered an important source of desirable values, and there can be no doubt that shared values and a strong civil society will be needed if the European Community is to become a democratic institution. European unification is in need of a cultural basis, and this includes religion. It seems, however, that so far, this point has not really been accepted in European politics or in economic circles.

This is not a statement of general scepticism towards European politics and European unification. Rather, the example of the European unification demonstrates the challenges religious education will probably have to face in a future that is shaped by supranational and global developments. Obviously, there is no clear awareness at a political level that economic co-operation presupposes more than a common market and that it needs a cultural basis.

However, it would be wrong to criticise only politics. We also have to admit that up to now, religious education theory in Europe is not in a position really to address policy questions at an international level (cf. Schweitzer, 1998). There are, of course, several European associations of religious education, like the Intereuropean Commission on Church and School (ICCS) or the European Forum for Teachers of Religious Education (EFTRE), to mention only two of the more well-known examples (see Schreiner and van Draat, 1998).

Most of them are professional associations, sometimes working in conjunction with Churches and other religious communities. But none of these associations may really claim to represent the official voice of religious education in Europe, a voice that is to speak for the majority of the professionals or for the parents in Europe.

At an academic level, the most influential institution at this point probably is the International Seminar on Religious Education and Values (ISREV). However, this standing seminar is not an exclusively European enterprise but includes members from many countries around the world. Nevertheless, with its large representation at least from Central and Northern Europe, it allows for important contacts and serves as a basis for joint discussion and research.

The importance of such international associations and co-operative enterprises in religious education is clearly growing. Yet the existing structures are not strong enough to influence the general public or to shape political decisions. Nor are they in a position to establish specific standards for religious education, including issues like insisting on the availability of religious education as a right of the individual child (Schweitzer, 2000), adjudicating between the different and sometimes contradictory approaches in religious education, or determining the inclusion or exclusion of religious education in the curriculum of the state school.

So what may we learn from a consideration of European unification as an example of present and future supranational developments? Two points are of special importance. First, so far there has clearly not been sufficient awareness of the cultural, ethical and religious dimensions and tasks which the process of supranational unification entails. Second, there are new tasks and challenges for religious education in theory and practice which might force us to rethink and to redirect our work in this field.

New challenges for religious education theory and practice in a globalising world

In the first two sections of this chapter we have tried to demonstrate that the supranational and global developments that accompany our entry into the third millennium, entail important and far-reaching consequences for religion and religious education. In this section we want to summarise and to some degree systematise the challenges that have become visible so far.

The first and most obvious challenge consists in strengthening ecumenical and interreligious education. If globalisation means that the world has become a 'single place', then all denominations and all religions have in fact become neighbours. In this situation, ecumenical and interreligious education may no longer be considered additional aspects of religious education, which can be left to special interest-groups or which may be limited to a small segment of the curriculum. Rather, ecumenical and interreligious education must become a central and continuous dimension of all religious education, at all ages and in all possible settings (cf. van der Ven and Ziebertz, 1994; Nipkow, 1998; Hull, 2000).

Ecumenical and interreligious education should not be reduced to a purely religious affair. The religious visions of ecumene, global ethics and 'new catholicity' include a fundamental challenge to all understandings of globalisation that idealise the dynamics of the market. By itself, the international market will not bring about justice. Rather, it will reinforce the split between rich and poor, between those who profit from globalisation and those who do not. Therefore, the vision of economic globalisation must be widened to include religious and ethical aspects.

My second point concerns the question of how religious education may achieve peaceful ecumenical and interreligious relationships (cf. Schweitzer, 1999). Traditionally, the approach to this task has often been framed as consciousness-raising, helping people who live in the limited context of their specific regions, nations, congregations or denominations, to become aware of the wider (if possible, global) context of living and believing. If there is any truth to globalisation theory, this situation has changed dramatically. The traditional parochial consciousness is no longer in existence. Rather, as mentioned above, international media culture and consumer goods, long-distance mass tourism and international communication have now brought about a consciousness of global scope quite independently of education. Unfortunately, this is not the type of consciousness that educators have been wishing for. It is not shaped by moral criteria like justice or mutual understanding. Yet it is not hard to see that this globalisation of consciousness has created a situation that calls for different educational strategies. We are no longer dealing with people who need education in order to become aware of a world beyond their own narrow confines. Rather, we are now dealing with people who have been overwhelmed by global influences and who are overpowered by the paralysing effects of worldwide information without a chance to influence the course of this world.

Third, religious education will have to be prepared for dealing with the worldwide effects of the relativisation of religion. The more globalisation proceeds by spreading abstract systems that are based on expert knowledge, the less people will rely on traditional wisdom, at least not for their everyday life. At the same time, the greater the variety of religious orientations or possible religious 'preferences' (to use this distinctively modern designation), the less any one of them may claim to be naturally given or to be revealed. In this situation, the relationship between 'religious nurture' and 'religious education' needs to be reconsidered. In a sense, there is no more room for simple nurture in religion. Even the most confessional religious education comes to depend on the dialogical and critical inclusion of other religious traditions and truth claims. Otherwise it will be perceived as arbitrary and as only subjective. If children and youth are constantly exposed to other options than those of the religious community of their parents, it is never enough just to tell them about the traditions of this particular community. Rather, other religious orientations must be taken up in order to become clear about what religious traditions have in common but also about the differences and divisions between them.

Fourth, religious education needs to address the issue of religious privatisation. If religion is to play a vital role as a humanising factor in the process of globalisation, we must claim a public role for religion. Privatised religion that pertains to individual life, remains important, but it will be in no position to meet the ethical and political challenges of globalisation. Therefore, religious education will have to raise directly and explicitly the question of how religion may play a public role, how religious values can in fact come to bear on political and economic decisions, and what institutions, for example, of civil society, may serve as carriers for a public influence of religion. Of course, these questions cannot be answered by education, especially not by religious education in a state school setting. They necessarily remain personal life-decisions which only the individual person can make for himself or herself. That someone becomes involved in religious environmentalism, for example, is not a legitimate aim of education. What religious education should do is to show the importance of a public role for religion and to point out what options one might have to become involved with this role.

In a certain sense, this brings us to our fifth point, the question of religious fundamentalism. If fundamentalism is a possible effect of globalisation, religious education will have to deal with this issue as well. When politicians make this demand of religious education they often seem to assume that the task of religious education should involve warning and alarming students against fundamentalism. But as we have seen in this chapter, fundamentalism is not like a disease against which people could be vaccinated. Rather, fundamentalism is a misguided response to globalisation and it is based on understandable motives, like the fear of losing one's personal or religious identity. It does not make sense just to refuse fundamentalism. Its motives have to be taken seriously. So if religious education introduces people to civil and democratic ways for religion to claim a public role, this will also contribute to taking up the challenge of fundamentalism.

The five points that I have taken up so far all refer to tasks that affect religious education theory as well as praxis. The remaining points refer to future research questions of religious education on the one hand and to political issues on the other. For research and theory-building I want to emphasise two points:

First, research on religious education may no longer be limited to a particular country. The national context should no longer be allowed to define the focus of research. We obviously need an internationalisation of religious education. If there is any truth to globalisation theory, the decisive influences may no longer be expected from institutions and systems at the national level alone. For example, the legal frameworks of national states in Europe will continue to play a role for religious education but their influence may well be more and more superseded by international influences of the European

Community. Or, to mention another example, youth culture may be less and less understood as a national phenomenon and more as an international culture. So religious education will have to widen its theoretical scope in order to include systematically the international dimension.

Second, if the effects of international influences on religious education are to be studied, we also need a new type of research, a type that may be described as international comparative research (Osmer and Schweitzer, 1997; Schweitzer, 1998; also cf. Moran, 1989). Effects of globalisation on religious education can hardly be studied in one national context alone. Convincing results will depend on comparing the situation in at least two countries. Only such research will produce the grounds for evaluating policies at a European or global level.

The results that one may expect from this kind of religious education theory and research could then form the basis for taking up new political and professional tasks. I have already mentioned the idea of working towards international standards for religious education which may be presented to governments as well as to religious bodies. Among others, such standards would concern the right of the individual child to have access to religious education, and they should also concern the quality of religious education itself. In addition to this, the question of the representation of religious education in a professional or political sense becomes an issue. As mentioned above, there is a confusing number of religious education associations in Europe alone but there is no single voice with which religious education might speak. If there is to be such a voice and if religious education is to be heard and to be taken seriously beyond individual countries, there is a need for bringing such associations into closer contact with each other and to coordinate their activities. This is not to suggest that the differences between the educational traditions in different countries should disappear for the sake of globalisation. There probably can never be a universal approach to religious education. Such an approach would necessarily be very abstract and of not much use for anybody. Yet excluding the universalist misunderstanding, there may be more room for international criteria than we expect. And given the impact of globalisation, it seems more than worthwhile to make the attempt of finding out about such criteria.

Conclusion

The supranational and global developments in economy and politics that have been mentioned in this chapter, clearly entail important and far reaching consequences for religious education. If religious education is to play a role in the changing world of the third millennium, it must develop a different praxis, claiming a public role for religion and finding new ways of ecumenical and interreligious understanding. In order to analyse and to guide such praxis, religious education theory itself, in line with the supranational and global developments, must become more international in terms of its theorising and research.

The title of this chapter speaks of 'religious education beyond the nation state'. Negatively speaking, this is to say that religious education needs to go beyond its traditional focus on national politics and on religious bodies at a national level because the nation state may no longer be considered the only context of decisive importance for politics or education. Positively speaking, it means that international co-operation and comparative research of international, interdenominational and interreligious scope will be needed if religion is to be operative as a humanising factor in the process of globalisation.

Globalisation affects religion and religious education but religious education may also affect globalisation. The human face of a global world will not come from the unifying dynamics of the economy alone. It will also have to come from the deep respect for the other which is the promise of true faith.

Note

1. In Germany, there is a considerable body of literature on ecumenical education; for recent summary statements cf. Koerrenz (1994), Goßmann, Pithan and Schreiner (1995).

References

Albrow, M. (1998), *Abschied vom Nationalstaat: Staat und Gesellschaft im globalen Zeitalter*, Frankfurt/M., Suhrkamp.

Beck, U. (1997), *Was ist Globalisierung?*, Frankfurt/M., Suhrkamp.

Beck, U. (ed.) (1998a), *Politik der Globalisierung*, Frankfurt/M., Suhrkamp.

Beck, U. (ed.) (1998b), *Perspektiven der Weltgesellschaft*, Frankfurt/M., Suhrkamp.

Beck, U., Giddens, A. and Lash, S. (1996), *Reflexive Modernisierung: Eine Kontroverse*, Frankfurt/M., Suhrkamp.

Beyer, P. (1994), *Religion and Globalisation*, London, Sage.

Butterwegge, C. (1999), *Globalisierung, Neoliberalismus und Sozialstaat*, Neue Sammlung, 39, 497-512.

Casanova, J. (1994), *Public Religions in the Modern World*, Chicago, Illinois, University of Chicago Press.

Council of Europe (1993), *Recommendation* 1202.

Council of Europe (1999), *Recommendation 1396 (Religion and democracy)*.

Daiber, K.-F. (1995), *Religion unter den Bedingungen der Moderne: die Situation in der Bundesrepublik Deutschland*, Marburg, Diagonal.

Giddens, A. (1990), *The Consequences of Modernity*, Cambridge, Polity Press.

Giddens, A. (1991), *Modernity and Self-Identity: self and society in the late modern age*, Stanford, California, Stanford University Press.

Giddens, A. (1996), Leben in einer posttraditionalen Gesellschaft, in U. Beck, A. Giddens and S. Lash (eds), *Reflexive Modernisierung: Eine Kontroverse*, pp 113-194, Frankfurt/M., Suhrkamp.

Goßmann, K., Pithan, A. and Schreiner, P. (eds) (1995), *Zukunftsfähiges Lernen? Herausforderungen für Ökumenisches Lernen in Schule und Unterricht*, Münster, Comenius-Institut.

Harvey, D. (1989), *The Condition of Postmodernity: an enquiry into the origins of cultural change*, Oxford, Basil Blackwell.

Hull, J.M. (2000), *Glaube und Bildung*, volume 1, Berg am Irchel, Kik-Verlag.

Huntington, S.P. (1996), *The Clash of Civilizations and the Remaking of World Order*, New York, Simon and Schuster.

Koerrenz, R. (1994), *Ökumenisches Lernen*, Gütersloh, Gütersloher Verlagshaus.

Küng, H. (1990), *Projekt Weltethos*, München, Piper.

Marty, M.E. and Appleby, R.S. (eds.) (1991-1995), *The Fundamentalism Project*, 5 volumes, Chicago, Illinois, University of Chicago Press.

Meeks, M.D. (1992), Globalisation and the oikumene in theological education, in R.E. Richey (ed.), *Ecumenical and Interreligious Perspectives: Globalisation in Theological Education*, pp 3-16, Nashville, Tennessee, United Methodist Board of Higher Education.

Moran, G. (1989), *Religious Education as a Second Language*, Birmingham, Alabama, Religious Education Press.

Nipkow, K.-E. (1998), *Bildung in einer pluralen Welt*, 2 volumes, Gütersloh, Gütersloher Verlagshaus.

Osmer, R.R. and Schweitzer, F. (1997), Religious education reform movements in the United States and in Germany as a paradigmatic response to modernization, *International Journal of Practical Theology*, 1, 227-254.

Robertson, R. (1989), Globalisation, politics, and religion, in J.A. Beckford and T. Luckmann (eds), *The Changing Face of Religion*, pp 10-23, London, Sage.

Robertson, R. (1991), The globalisation paradigm: thinking globally, in D.G. Bromley (ed.), *Religion and the Social Order: new developments in theory and research*, pp 207-224, Greenwich, Connecticut, JAI Press.

Robertson, R. (1992), *Globalisation: social theory and global culture*, London, Sage.

Schmidtchen, G. (1993), *Ethik und Protest: Moralbilder und Wertkonflikte junger Menschen*, Opladen, Leske and Budrich.

Schreiner, P. and Draat, H.F. v. (eds) (1998), *Who's Who in RE in Europe*, Münster, Comenius-Institut.

Schreiter, R.J. (1997), *The New Catholicity: theology between the global and the local*, Mary Knoll, New York, Orbis.

Schweitzer, F. (1998), Towards comparative research on religious education in Europe: reasons, obstacles, methodological considerations, *Informationes Theologiae Europae*, 7, 143-152.

Schweitzer, F. (1999), Global issues facing youth in the postmodern church, in K.C. Dean (ed.), *Growing Up Postmodern: imitating Christ in the age of 'Whatever'. The 1998 Princeton Lectures on Youth, Church, and Culture*, pp 67-78, Princeton, New Jersey, Princeton Theological Seminary.

Schweitzer, F. (2000), *Das Recht des Kindes auf Religion*, Gütersloh, Gütersloher Verlagshaus.

Stackhouse, M.L., Berger, P.L., McCann, D.P. and Meeks, M.D. (1995), *Christian Social Ethics in a Global Era*, Nashville, Tennessee, Abingdon.

Tetzlaff, R. (ed.) (2000), *Weltkulturen unter Globalisierungsdruck: Erfahrungen und Antworten aus den Kontinenten*, Bonn, Dietz.

Ven, J.A. v.d. and Ziebertz, H.-G. (eds) (1994), *Religiöser Pluralismus und Interreligiöses Lernen*, Kampen, Kok, Deutscher Studienverlag.

Waters, M. (1995), *Globalisation*, London, Routledge.

Wuthnow, R. (1996), *Christianity and Civil Society: the contemporary debate*, Valley Forge, Pennsylvania, Trinity Press.

8

IS THERE A WAY BEYOND FUNDAMENTALISM?
CHALLENGES FOR FAITH DEVELOPMENT
AND RELIGIOUS EDUCATION

Heinz Streib

Introduction

The global occurrence of fundamentalist developments and their highly political and sometimes scandalous quality call for a global perspective. The Chicago Fundamentalisms Project (Marty and Appleby, 1993a, 1993b, 1994a, 1994b, 1995) has the merit to address fundamentalism in such a global perspective across cultures and religious traditions. The global and highly political perspective, however, should not divert attention from the fact that there are also currents within fundamentalist movements that are not political. Moreover, it can be argued that, at the basis of any fundamentalist orientation, there are religious attitudes. The global and political perspective should furthermore not obscure the possibility of individual biographical developments which may open up opportunities to change and to find new biographical trajectories, to engage in deconversion and transformation. The study of biographies opens such a perspective. The two ex-fundamentalist case studies that will be portrayed in the first section of this chapter demonstrate not only the possibility of change, but also very different paths of deconversion and transformation.

Change, development and transformation are the hopes and expectations not only from a political, societal and educational standpoint, but also from the perspective of the scientific study of religion. Fundamentalism presents a challenge for education in general and for religious education in particular, if it is true that at the core of any fundamentalist orientation there is a religious dimension.

Fundamentalism presents a challenge for religious education that must be recognised. It is my thesis that religious education could provide decisive transformational potential, if it remembers its proper aims.

For that reason, we shall clarify and elaborate what fundamentalism is, how it develops, and what exactly we understand as specific developmental transformation, which may lead beyond fundamentalism. This chapter will also propose a structure and aims for religious education.

Case studies

Political concern about so-called sects and psychogroups led the Federal German Parliament to set up the Enquête Commission. The final report of the Commission (Deutscher Bundestag, 1998: 284), however, arrived at the moderate conclusion that new religious movements, fundamentalism and psychogroups 'do not pose a threat for government and society or for any of the relevant domains in society'. Such a moderate conclusion is in part due to a closer investigation of the biographical dynamics involved in joining and leaving such groups as it is presented in the results of qualitative-biographical research, which has been initiated by the Enquête Commission itself.

The aim of my research project on Christian-fundamentalist converts and deconverts was to compare and contrast biographies or careers of members and ex-members of Christian-fundamentalist milieus and organisations. The project took a qualitative approach and followed the method of biographical-reconstructive research, which means that the biographies are reconstructed in various dimensions from the data (narrative interviews with an average length of approximately two hours). Of the twenty-two interviews conducted, twelve were selected for analysis. Our analytical interest was focused on the relationship between 'religious career' and biography, on the question of personality change and continuity, and on questions of identity in the situation of dramatic processes of conversion and transformation. More details on the method are provided by Streib (1999a, 2000a) and on the results by Streib (1998a, 1999b, 2000a, 2000b).

The advantage of qualitative-biographical research is that it offers insights into the deep structures of the biographical dynamics in a diachronic perspective which is reflected in the narrative dynamic. Thus, it may contribute to a fresh understanding of fundamentalist conversion and deconversion. Before summarising some of the results, discussing its implications for an understanding of fundamentalism and drawing conclusions for religious education, I shall present two of the case studies.

Sarah

Sarah (twenty-one), born in 1976, grew up in a fundamentalist family together with three older and three younger siblings. Her mother took care of the household; her father worked as a clerk in a firm. Sarah remembers her father as an authoritarian and cruel person. As members of a fundamentalist small Church, Sarah's parents raised their children in the thought system and rules of this Church. After leaving high school, Sarah left home and began training as a nurse, but she had to abandon it because of psychological problems, and moved back home. Not long after her return, the entire family left this Church: her father because he considered it not truly Christian enough; Sarah deconverted from the fundamentalist milieu altogether, was driven from home by her parents, moved to a female friend's house and later moved in with her boyfriend. She began vocational training as an ergo-therapist and expected to take the exam soon after the time of the interview.

The dynamic of Sarah's narrative reveals her present problems to make something of her life, her anxiety over the challenges she faces and her hatred of her own biographical past. Her elementary need to feel at home in a warm, caring and unconditionally loving environment was not fulfilled by her family. On the contrary, she tells us about having been beaten and driven from home. Religion, for Sarah, is coloured by patriarchal authoritarianism and by fundamentalism. Sarah considers herself to have been oppressed and exploited. She continues to have difficulties in developing initiatives and in coping with conflicts.

In contrast to these negative experiences and developments, Sarah also reports positive experiences within the fundamentalist milieu: feelings of community in the Church, which compensated for the devastating atmosphere in the family. For years, Sarah lived in the milieu and thought-system of that fundamentalist group and was convinced that she was on the right track.

It was due to conversations in school and to the model of her older brother (who rebelled against this religious orientation and was also expelled from home), that Sarah gradually came to question the narrow-mindedness of the family's Church. An important factor in her final decision to leave the Church and home was Sarah's (delayed, but all the more vehement) adolescent process of detachment, especially from her father, who was both one of the leading figures in their Church and an authoritarian parent. Sarah's rebellion against the contradictions she saw between word and deed in her father was parallel to her rebellion against his faith.

While Sarah did not possess the resilience and strength to challenge her father's worldview and dissociate herself from it during late childhood and adolescence, she had mustered the courage only a few years before the interview to criticise the inconsistencies in the worldview of her Church and the lack of warmth in the relations between Church members. As a result of her ever more acute criticism and her increasing independence, Sarah was shunned and emotionally rejected by Church members and family alike. This suffering, which resulted in suicidal tendencies, induced her to risk limited confrontation with her environment and, more importantly, to escape from it.

In retrospect, Sarah refers to some rare but highly significant situations that helped her develop a mode of thinking that differed from that of her fundamentalist milieu and that helped her finally to find a way out. In particular, she refers to elucidating moments with her mother, providing opportunities to talk about questions that Sarah had heard in religious education classes.

Thomas

Thomas (forty-eight) lived, during his childhood and adolescence, in a big city in northern Germany. After graduating from high school, he studied biology at university to become a science teacher. Having passed his first examination and having completed his training as a teacher, he did not obtain full-time employment as a teacher for reasons we do not know. For the following twenty years he earned his living by doing different jobs here and there. At the time of the interview, Thomas lived with a woman, her two little children and an eight-month-old infant who was their own child.

As the reason for his attraction to sects and fundamentalist groups, Thomas told us that, as a student at the university, he found it both strange and appealing to have a sign hung on the door of his next door neighbour's flat 'do not disturb – meditation'. Thomas explains his attraction with his feeling at that time:

> I had the feeling, about myself, that this is not all, how I live. Well, it was the search for more intensity . . . for a certain kind of release from burdens which I felt . . . were perhaps not always clear . . . what it was. But a little lack of freedom, together with guilt, being dependent on . . . my family, uh, perhaps also a lack of self-confidence, I would say, was a kind of basic structure.

Years later, as Thomas was approaching his second exams in practical teacher-training and felt the stress and pressure of these exams, he was introduced to Bhagwan meditation by a friend. After a first-time visit, he remained in the Bhagwan movement for three or four years, living in various communes. As reasons for leaving, Thomas mentions that the ideology of the movement had become too narrow for him and that he felt too oppressed and was not satisfied with open sexuality. After this time, when his girlfriend had gone to India, Thomas moved back to his home town. There, through an old friend, he found his way into a bio-energetics group (which went by this name, but was a hardcore encounter group). Thomas tells us about a seven-day workshop, where everybody was confined to a room without eating or sleeping, and about having similar exercises every week. Surprisingly, however, his account is not completely negative:

> Standing without moving which after some time hurts so much that you begin to scream and to tremble . . . uh and then there come such basic feelings, there comes the screaming of a three-year-old . . . uh, or a rage or this and that, then this system of

this person was uh actually a therapeutic village . . . always living in therapy . . . uh, to liberate yourself.

Thomas also tells us that he has had good experiences in this group. After the group leader's death, Thomas left and went on to live a rather quiet life, belonging to the church choir of a mainstream Protestant parish, and earning his living as a taxi-driver and as a market salesman once a week. Then he met Scientology agents on the street and agreed to take a 'personality test'. And, unlike one of his friends who left Scientology after a first visit, Thomas became involved:

> Yes I took these tests and somehow I had been caught, though I really did not want to go there. I wouldn't have gone there at all first . . . but once I was there I said, well, what of it, then also I got somewhat curious and certainly this . . . this desire again for that . . . uh redemption, liberation from the past, from a very burdensome past . . . yes, that was it and they promised me something . . . they had also some sort of therapy: . . . they certainly now uh they are certainly harder, let's say more intransigent, more sectarian than anything I have ever seen before.

Thomas describes his attitude toward this new group, in contrast to his attitude toward the previous groups, in terms of cost and profit. And although Thomas talks extensively about a positive experience in Scientology 'therapy', the healing of a falling trauma that had plagued him very often in his dreams, his portrait of Scientology is generally negative and critical. He felt particularly uncomfortable with the lie-detector. Thomas, however, was not able to leave the organisation of his own volition. This was possible for him only in the context of joining a new group.

This began again by accident, when Thomas read an advertisement 'Tonight: Gospel Meeting' and followed this invitation. He went to this meeting in a charismatic Church, his feeling of strangeness dissipating fast and being replaced by deep fascination. Thomas was especially impressed by a nice young woman's account telling him about Jesus, who was alive and had helped her; and Thomas was not sure whether he was infatuated with this woman or attracted by her faith. In any case, he decided to come back for Sunday service. Thomas remembers that during his first visit to this gospel Church he had to go to the bathroom to cry, so emotionally overwhelmed was he when the group started to dance and praise the Lord. This experience affected Thomas so deeply that he stayed and became a member of this fundamentalist charismatic Church. This is where he met a woman who urged him to terminate his relationship with Scientology; Thomas responded immediately, by cancelling a cheque and never returning to Scientology.

It appears surprising that, after his extensive tour through groups that were rather critical of Christianity, Thomas obviously had no problem with fundamentalist thinking in this group. This points to a characteristic attitude that we can observe throughout Thomas' tour: the ideology or doctrinal truth did not play a decisive role in joining a group and does not seem to have made any difference to Thomas. Only when Thomas was required to submit, then he had to get away. Rather, motivation and fascination for Thomas consisted in the feelings of relief and in the therapeutic effect the group provided for him.

At the time of the interview, Thomas was living a rather secluded life together with his new partner and their children. Faithfulness to this woman is important to him, and he tells us that he reads to the children from the children's Bible. Looking back upon his tour through the various groups and organisations, Thomas uses biblical language, a quote from Paul to explain in what sense he regards himself as a Christian, maintaining that he does not want to be a prisoner of Christ.

> I did not want to be a prisoner of Christ so to speak . . . that uh, I have decided against that. I am not a disciple of Jesus . . . in that sense . . . uh . . . but I would not say Christianity is the worst there is, but I would say that I have experienced liberation, but I have said also . . . uh can say also Scientology . . . has helped me and . . . Bhagwan . . . has helped me, because in each . . . a good friend she says I have taken a little bit from everywhere, from Anthroposophy this, from Bhagwan that.

We have no reason to doubt Thomas' self-reflective summary: in each group he found, at least temporarily, some relief. For Thomas, conversion is not a once-in-a-lifetime experience, but rather a repeated experience of getting deeply involved. He was repeatedly able to find a temporary solution, and his rebellion against demands for submission repeatedly motivated him to leave these groups. Thomas' self-reflective account leads us to call him, in my terms, an 'accumulative heretic' (see below).

Is Thomas, however, both a compulsory convert and a compulsory heretic without any change? Upon following his narrative carefully, a transformation process becomes visible, which has developed through the long tour through all the different groups and movements, at the end of which a more self-assertive, more individual person emerged. His almost restless search has come to an end not only in warmth and embeddedness, but also in responsibility, with a nuclear-family situation.

Research results in broader perspective

The two case studies of Sarah and of Thomas are part of our research project on fundamentalist biographies, but they have implications beyond the primary political focus and scope of the Enquête Commission. The case studies yield insights into the biographical dynamics and developments of fundamentalists, into their processes of transformation and deconversion, which scientific reflection in general and developmental psychology in particular must sort out and investigate further. These are basic research results in regard to religious education, which does not want to ignore and exclude the non-mainstream forms of contemporary religious orientations (cf. Streib, 1999a; Streib and Schöll, 2000). I shall now summarise the most important results.

Themata

In our analysis of life themes, we did not find (as some in the Enquête Commission had expected us to find) a single typical 'sect biography'. We could identify neither a single typical biographical pattern of fundamentalist converts or deconverts, nor a typical bundle of motivational factors. Certainly, we did search the biographical narratives for motivational factors, for 'life themes' or 'themata' (Noam, 1990) which the subjects bring with them into fundamentalist milieus. While we were able to identify childhood traumata, childhood anxiety or unsatisfied hunger for love and acceptance, the motivational factors we found were only of the same kind found in non-fundamentalist biographies as well.

Typology
Comparison of the cases locates them within a typology. We were able to identify three types of fundamentalist 'careers'. The first type were those 'governed by tradition' who, innocent of alternatives, had been born into or grown into a fundamentalist orientation. The second type were the 'mono-converts' who convert once in a life-time into a religious orientation that they did not have before. The third type were the 'accumulative heretics' (Berger, 1979) whose biographies are a tour through different religious orientations. The latter I regard as a new type of religious socialisation.

Sarah is a typical case for the tradition-guided type of fundamentalist and Thomas is a typical case of an accumulative heretic. Accumulative heretics nevertheless convert to fundamentalist belief systems, albeit only temporarily. This typology suggests a clarification of the nature of fundamentalist conversion and deconversion.

Biographical dynamics and developments
The analysis of the interview material included a special focus on the biographical dynamics, developments and consequences and on indicators of transformation and de-compensation. Despite the subjects' struggle with often traumatic themata and despite some signs of de-compensation, the case material also revealed problem-reducing effects, or indications of developmental transformation.

Thomas is a typical case who has undergone a transformation during his journey through a variety of religious milieus, which finally enabled him to cope with his unrelieved desire for unconditional love. Sarah has experienced times of crises up to some severe episodes of de-compensation; only after deconversion has she entered into transformation.

Comparison of the cases (and also comparison between Thomas and Sarah, because I have chosen these two cases as examples of the extremes) reveals that transformation and de-compensation are not distributed equally among them. The tendency could be demonstrated that the 'type governed by tradition' suffers more negative consequences and in some cases de-compensation, while the 'accumulative heretics' develop more easily into transformation. I consider the documentation of these transformation processes the most important result of our research, which parallels other analyses.

Our observation that the 'accumulative heretic' type fundamentalists develop more easily into progressive transformation can be related to Kilbourne and Richardson's (1985) observation about such effect in 'social experimenters'. Another parallel can be drawn to Generation X biographies. In his stimulating analysis, Beaudoin (1998) portrays the specific way in which Generation X adopts religious orientations, remains suspicious toward institutions and traditions and puzzles together its own religiosity. Though Beaudoin's portrait of Generation X's 'irreverence as a spiritual gift' does not focus on fundamentalist orientations, the irreverent tendencies may serve as a safeguard against total submission in certain cases of fundamentalists as well; and they may be present in Generation X above the average.

Implications for intervention, counselling and education can be drawn from such an analysis. Certainly, therapy should be provided to help the troubled individual to work on and cope with traumatic life themes that he or she took into the fundamentalist or new religious milieu and that did not find resolution there. It is necessary to assist these transformation processes and there are some valuable contributions to consider (cf. Streib, 2000c), but the need for therapy is rather the exception. The prophylactic aspect of education in school and public education seems to be more important. Religious educators are called upon to make explicit their own contribution to the prophylactic response to the fundamentalist challenge. But what should people learn? What are the specific goals of religious education when it tackles the fundamentalist challenge? This is what I would like to make explicit in the final part of this chapter. First, however, I shall

highlight some features of the concept of fundamentalism from which
I draw my educational conclusions.

Fundamentalism: concepts and explanations

For clarification of the concept of fundamentalism in respect to the
chances of transformation in a biographical and religious educational
perspective, I refer to contributions from sociology and developmental
psychology.

Fundamentalism and modernity

Fundamentalism is 'anti-modernism'. Such understanding follows
from sociological analysis, as Küenzlen (1994, 1996) suggests. When
we trace fundamentalism's basic orientations back to its origin, to the
point where the first people and publications proudly identified
themselves as 'fundamentalists', it appears as a reaction against
developments in science, in theology, in society and in the Churches.
For an adequate description of fundamentalism, we can draw on the
four basic claims of the fundamentalist manifesto: infallibility and
literal understanding of the scripture; literal understanding of some
basic propositions such as virgin birth, bodily resurrection and the
return of Jesus; rejection of the results of modern science wherever
they contradict this literal understanding; the claim that only people
subscribing to this manifesto are truly religious. From this self-
description, it is obvious that fundamentalism, is a reaction to
modernity. However, this reaction to the processes of modernisation
itself is using rather advanced 'modern' scientific arguments, means of
communication and organisational strategies: it is modern anti-
modernism.

In a wider philosophical perspective, fundamentalist revivals appear
as indications of disturbances to which the project of modernity is
exposed. With reference to Lyotard's (1984, 1988, 1993) analysis, we
could say that the smooth teleological meta-story of modernity, which
is a meta-story of development, is challenged by postmodern
disturbances. Such disturbances also include individual and global
fundamentalisms, which again are based to no small degree on meta-
stories themselves.

The cognitive-structural theories of development in their traditional shape of a structural, hierarchical, sequential and irreversible logic of development can be seen as the developmental psychology variant of the modern meta-story. If unchanged, they neither account for fundamentalism, nor can they provide us with an explanatory framework for the individual fundamentalist revivals. A solution, therefore, derives from a modification of the developmental model which should allow us to take account of and explain the developmental dynamics of the fundamentalism problem. From such a different developmental perspective, implications follow for religious education.

Fundamentalism as revival of the 'Do-ut-des' style

A new perspective emerges from the following question: How does the thesis 'fundamentalism is modern anti-modernism' translate into terms of developmental psychology? At first glance, such a translation appears impossible, since the structural-developmental theories at hand appear to be in line with the progressive-teleological myth of modernity and therefore seem to be incapable of regression. Oser's theory of religious development (Oser and Gmünder, 1991) and Fowler's (1981) faith-development theory are no exception here. A new model, however, while certainly originating in the family of theories that consider the Piagetian developmental model for various other domains, tries to take a broader perspective and to qualify the cognitive and structural one-sidedness in the Piagetian family of theories. Taking up the thread of my doctoral dissertation (Streib, 1991), I have recently proposed a modification of structural-developmental theory of religion (cf. Streib, 1997), especially of Fowler's faith-development theory, from which a plausible explanation of fundamentalism can be advanced (Streib, 2001): the religious-styles perspective.

The most significant qualifications of structural-developmental theory that the religious-styles perspective suggests result from a decided focus on interpersonality, from a deeper account for the psychodynamic dimension, and from special attention to the religious milieu. For a revision of structural-developmental theory by focusing on the interpersonal, I refer to Noam (1985, 1990) and to Noam, Powers, Kilkenny and Beedy (1991). The new model proposes to describe religious development not in terms of stages, but rather in terms of styles. Development, then, appears as a cumulative sequence of styles, which supposedly peak at a certain point in life. These styles, however, are not assumed to disappear, but rather to decline and form a layer in one's psychic resources, which can be recalled and revitalised later when the need arises.

The religious-styles perspective can be described briefly as follows. First, the *subjective religious style* is predominant in early childhood when the symbiotic relation to the caretakers still prevails and the development of basic trust is crucial.

Second, the *reciprocal-instrumental religious style* or *'do-ut-des' religious style* develops when the child becomes aware of his or her own needs and interests as opposed to those of other people. *Do-ut-des* is the basic pattern for both the interpersonal and the God-human relationship. Good is what God and the authority persons wish and demand, bad and immoral is what results in punishment: a *do-ut-des* economy. Means of trade are obedience and observation of religious commandments. The characterisation of this style's understanding pattern as 'mythic-literal' (Fowler) means that an awareness of the metaphoric or symbolic meaning has not yet developed, that we must not modify any detail of the story or of the religious rules. Literally everything happened precisely as told in the story, literally everything has to be observed exactly as the religious rules prescribe.

Third, during puberty and adolescence, the *do-ut-des* style normally recedes to the background and is superseded by a new orientation, which we call *mutual religious style*, when the widening of the interpersonal horizon, for example in the adolescent peer group, and the mutuality of relations permit such development. The new style rests on mutuality in one's religious group and prefers an image of God as a personal partner. The unquestioned security in one's religious group (or its contrary, the dependence on their judgement) reveals that it is difficult to transcend the ideological and institutional group limits. The capacity to establish one's own critical and reflective point of view has not yet been developed.

Fourth, in the *individuative-systemic religious style* the social world is understood as a system in which I have to look for, take and defend my own place. It is the style of identity formation in which, through reflection, we have to find our place in society. And this is also true for religious matters: God, society, Church, the human being, all have their well-defined places and roles.

Fifth, we hope for the development of the *dialogical religious style,* which is able to realise that contradictions and differences need not result in exclusion and hostility towards others, but are opportunities to open up to, and learn from, other people with religious orientations different from our own.

It is obvious that the description of the reciprocal-instrumental or *do-ut-des* style characterises exactly what the fundamentalist worldview maintains. Fowler (1987: 85), too, has paralleled mythic-literal faith and fundamentalist communities: mythic-literal faith can in fundamentalist groups 'constitute the modal level for the community'. Moreover, Fowler distinguishes between two kinds of settings: 'It makes a considerable difference whether this stage is experienced in a community as a way station on a longer journey or as having the characteristic of a final destination'. We do not call children fundamentalists, however, but regard this style as one adequate for childhood. We regard as characteristic for fundamentalism only the persistence or revival of the *do-ut-des* style in adolescence and adulthood, when most people have already developed mutual or systemic orientations. The systemic style stands for modernity's competencies and requirements, it parallels the sociological notion of modernity. When in the midst of systemic or mutual style development, which is applied to most issues except for religion and 'existential issues' (Hunsberger, Pratt and Pancer, 1994; Hunsberger, Alisat, Pancer and Pratt, 1996), the *do-ut-des* style re-emerges and gains influence, we can speak of a fundamentalist revival. As the fundamentalist orientation grows stronger, so the *do-ut-des* style gains ground and dominates. In this way, the interpretation of fundamentalism as modern anti-modernism translates well into the terms of developmental psychology.

The challenge to religious education

Imagine Sarah and Thomas sitting in your religious education class! What would you expect them to learn? How would you react? Before the teacher is able to do anything, however, he or she must become aware of the fact that a student may have a fundamentalist orientation.

After identifying fundamentalist orientations, what are the basic aims of religious education? In short, religious education, despite all subject orientation, should be a place for talking personally, *for care of souls,* but also for reflecting and transforming one's religious orientation.

Care of souls in religious education

Religion involves the person very deeply, its 'content' concerns us ultimately (Tillich, 1929, 1931, 1957). The interview material has great value in demonstrating the deep personal involvement in themes and questions which only the ignorant would treat as mere content. Especially for the sake of fundamentalist students, we need to pay new and careful attention to the students' needs. Therefore, I propose to (re-)consider approaches of counselling and pastoral care for religious education. In an atmosphere of mutual perception and encounter, students will be able to disclose their own religious orientation, and fundamentalists will not need to hide their opinion, *care of souls* can take place, and deconversion has an opportunity to develop in this environment.

Transformation and the goal of religious autonomy

Fundamentalists, as our case material demonstrates, are able to engage in transformation. This might encourage religious educators to bear in mind that this potential exists. But can religious education continue to hold on to goals of reflection on religious matters only? Should individuative reflectiveness (Fowler) or religious autonomy (Oser) still be our main educational goals? The answer is yes, but only if there is a decisive qualification of structural-developmental goals.

The explication of the concept of fundamentalism that I have developed above has implications for religious education. If we understand fundamentalist orientations as a revival of the *do-ut-des* religious style, we look back from the actual state of development and enquire how previous orientations can be integrated. We deal with the difference, the clash, the split. And we ask how such 'dislocation of styles' can be overcome to the effect that the present mutual or systemic styles cover more ground. Here, the developmental expectation of religious autonomy is adequate, with the following important qualification. Religious autonomy must not be identified with the strict and narrow systemic style of a rational worldview, but rather stands opposed to the fundamentalists' humourless one-dimensionality. Religious autonomy involves a playful ease which is aware of the fact that knowledge is preliminary and that we think in models. Finally, integration or 'healing the dislocation' means to develop the ability to tell and re-tell, to read and re-write the story of one's life in one's latest available style.

In sharp contrast to the 'revival' that is characteristic for fundamentalism, responsive religious educators may develop some appreciation for 'regression', which, when it is in the service of the ego (cf. Blos, 1967; Henseler, 1994), can become a helpful perspective in counselling and in religious education, when the individual re-visits patterns of thought and feeling in his or her life in order to work on them and hopefully to integrate them into present thinking. Viewed from this perspective, what fundamentalist students need is not developmental impatience and provocative confrontation with the goal of religious autonomy, but rather *time*. Kegan (1982: 276) powerfully advocates such intervention, which he calls *joining the person*. It is one of the tasks for religious educators to join the fundamentalist meaning-makers, since they face a world that threatens their own opinions and beliefs. This means allowing fundamentalist students to hold their own views and to be integrated, even if these views are strange to the teacher and to the other students. Then it means cautiously inviting reflection.

Some goals of religious education

Explicating the above reflections in educational goals leads me to conclude with a wider perspective, because I suppose that fundamentalism can be taken as a challenge reminding religious education to become again what it should be in the first place. I shall state this in seven theses:

First, religious education should be a process dealing with *perplexity* and *astonishment*, rather than providing a flood of answers to questions that are unknown to the students.

Second, religious education should be a 'creative laboratory for thought experiments' (Ricoeur, 1992) and for fiction (cf. Streib,

1998b), rather than a curriculum of clear-cut lessons about the facts of one's own religion or another.

Third, religious education has the task of overcoming *literal faith* (Tillich, 1957: 244), and nurturing the *conflict of interpretations,* leading to an understanding of theological truth as *outline, model* and *thought experiment* for our time. Therefore, acquaintance with the diversity of theological thinking is an important goal for religious education in response to fundamentalist tendencies.

Fourth, religious education needs to promote *playful ease,* rather than humourless narrow-minded factual knowledge. Playful ease is a habit that we expect to be available in an unrestricted and unspoiled way in childhood. Religious educators, however, may need to develop or regain it for themselves and for their students as a prophylactic competence against fundamentalism. Are we not invited to 'become like the children'?

Fifth, religious education should nurture the ability to tell and re-tell, to read and re-write the story of one's life in one's latest available style.

Sixth, religious education should put in motion the *Protestant Principle* (Tillich, 1929) and transcend the concreteness of one's own Church, community and religious tradition (which even exceeds the sphere of religion) in order to reflect on nature, culture and history *under the aspect of ultimate concern.* In short, according to Tillich, religious education has the goal of opening the students' minds (as deeply as in their unconscious dimension) for the *ultimate mystery of being* (Tillich, 1931:234).

Seventh, religious education, thus understood, is an *aesthetic* adventure, rather than an instruction as it were in hermeneutic objectivity (Zilleßen, 1994, 1995).

Outlook

Our reflection on the concept of fundamentalism has focused on the remark that fundamentalist revivals indicate that the project of modernity is exposed to grave disturbances. Further, we noted that the developmental psychology variant of the modern meta-story, namely the cognitive-structural theories of development in their traditional shape of a structural, hierarchical, sequential and irreversible logic of development (if unchanged), do not provide us with the explanatory framework for the individual fundamentalist revivals. A solution derives from a modification of the developmental model: the religious-style perspective allows us to take account of fundamentalism and opens a perspective of development and transformation beyond the fundamentalist orientation.

Such modification is part of a paradigmatic shift and re-balancing which exceeds, of course, the domain of cognitive development of religion and of faith development, but has decisive consequences for them. It implies the re-balancing of disconnected reason with relational knowing, of universality with bodily being-in-the-life-world, of objectivity with object relation, of decentred subjectivity with openness for the Other. It is the task, to mention a few names, to revise the Piagetian and Kohlbergian structural teleology in the light of the hermeneutic of Ricoeur (e.g. 1992), the phenomenology of Merleau-Ponty (e.g. 1988), and Tillich's philosophy of religion and his theory of the religious symbol. From these accounts, as I have tried to demonstrate, a modified perspective on development and transformation emerges. This provides an answer to the question of whether there is a way beyond fundamentalism and has decisive implications for religious education. This may help to prepare religious education for the millennium that has just begun and in which we can not expect a decline of fundamentalist revivals.

References

Berger, P. (1979), *The Heretical Imperative: contemporary possibilities of religious affirmation*, New York, Doubleday.

Beaudoin, T. (1998), *Virtual Faith: the irreverent spiritual quest of Generation X*, San Francisco, California, Jossey-Bass.

Blos, P. (1967), The second individuation process of adolescence, *The Psychoanalytic Study of the Child*, 22, 162-186.

Deutscher Bundestag. (1998), *Final Report of the Enquête Commission on 'So-called Sects and Psychogroups'. New Religious and Ideological Communities and Psychogroups in the Federal Republic of Germany*, Bonn, Deutscher Bundestag.

Fowler, J.W. (1981), *Stages of Faith*, San Francisco, California, Harper and Row.

Fowler, J.W. (1987), *Faith Development and Pastoral Care*, Philadelphia, Pennsylvania, Fortress Press.

Henseler, H. (1994), Religiöses Erleben – eine Regression im Dienst des Ich? Überlegungen zur Psychogenese der Religiosität, in G. Klosinski (ed.), *Religion als Chance oder Risiko*, pp 169-178, Bern, Hans Huber.

Hunsberger, B., Alisat, S. Pancer, S.M. and Pratt, M. (1996), Religious fundamentalism and religious doubts: content, connections, and complexity of thinking, *International Journal for the Psychology of Religion*, 6, 201-220.

Hunsberger, B., Pratt, M. and Pancer, S.M. (1994), Religious fundamentalism and integrative complexity of thought: a relationship for existential content only? *Journal for the Scientific Study of Religion*, 33, 335-346.

Kegan, R. (1982), *The Evolving Self: problem and process in human development*, Cambridge, Massachusetts, Harvard University Press.

Kilbourne, B. and Richardson, J.T. (1985), Social experimentation: self process or social role? *International Journal of Social Psychiatry*, 31, 13-22.

Küenzlen, G. (1994), Fundamentalismus: Moderner Anti-modernismus. Kultursoziologische Überlegungen. *Praktische Theologie*, 29, 43-56.

Küenzlen, G. (1996), Religiöser Fundamentalismus - Aufstand gegen die Moderne. in H.-J. Höhn (ed.), *Krise der Immanenz. Religion an den Grenzen der Moderne*, pp. 50-71, Frankfurt/M., Fischer.

Lyotard, J.F. (1984), *The Postmodern Condition: a report on knowledge*, Minneapolis, Minnesota, University of Minnesota Press.

Lyotard, J.F. (1988), *The Difference: phrases in dispute*, Minneapolis, Minnesota, University of Minnesota Press.

Lyotard, J.F. (1993), *Toward the Postmodern*, Atlantic Highlands, New Jersey, Humanities Press.

Marty, M.E. and Appleby, R.S. (1993a), *Fundamentalisms and Society: reclaiming the sciences, the family, and education*, Chicago, Illinois, University of Chicago Press.

Marty, M.E. and Appleby, R.S. (1993b), *Fundamentalisms and the State: remaking polities, economies, and militance*, Chicago, Illinois, University of Chicago Press.

Marty, M.E. and Appleby, R.S. (1994a), *Accounting for Fundamentalisms: the dynamic character of movements*, Chicago, Illinois, University of Chicago Press.

Marty, M.E. and Appleby, R.S. (1994b), *Fundamentalisms Observed*, Chicago, Illinois, University of Chicago Press.

Marty, M.E. and Appleby, R.S. (1995), *Fundamentalisms Comprehended*, Chicago, Illinois, University of Chicago Press.

Merleau-Ponty, M. (1988), *Merleau-Ponty à la Sorbonne. Résumé de cours 1949-1952*, Paris, Edition Cynara.

Noam, G.G. (1985), Stage, phase, and style: the developmental dynamics of the self, in M. Berkowitz and F. Oser. (eds), *Moral Education: theory and application*, pp 321-346, Hillsdale, New Jersey, Lawrence Erlbaum Associates.

Noam, G.G. (1990), Beyond Freud and Piaget: biographical worlds - interpersonal self, in T. Wren (ed.), *The Moral Domain: essays in the ongoing discussion between philosophy and the social sciences,* pp. 360-399, Cambridge, Massachusetts, MIT Press.

Noam, G.G., Powers, S.I., Kilkenny, R. and Beedy, J. (1991), The Interpersonal Self in Life-Span Developmental Perspective: Theory, Measurement, and Longitudinal Analyses, in P.B. Baltes, D.L. Featherman and R.M. Lerner (eds), *Life-Span Development and Behavior,* 10, pp 59-104, Hillsdale, New Jersey, Erlbaum.

Oser, F. and Gmünder, P. (1991), *Judgement: a developmental perspective,* Birmingham, Alabama, Religious Education Press.

Ricoeur, P. (1992), *Oneself as Another,* Chicago, Illinois, University of Chicago Press.

Streib, H. (1991), *Hermeneutics of Metaphor, Symbol and Narrative in Faith Development Theory,* Frankfurt/M., Peter Lang.

Streib, H. (1997), Religion als Stilfrage. Zur Revision struktureller Differenzierung von Religion im Blick auf die Analyse der pluralistisch-religiösen Lage der Gegenwart, *Archiv für Religionspsychologie,* 22, 48-69.

Streib, H. (1998a), Milieus und Organisationen christlich-fundamentalistischer Prägung. Aussteiger, Konvertierte und Überzeugte. Kontrastive Analysen zu Einmündung, Karriere, Verbleib und Ausstieg in bzw. aus neureligiösen und weltanschaulichen Milieus oder Gruppen sowie radikalen christlichen Gruppen der ersten Generation, Teilprojekt 2, in Deutscher Bundestag, Enquête-Kommission, Sogenannte Sekten und Psychogruppen" (ed.), *Neue religiöse und ideologische Gemeinschaften und Psychogruppen,* pp. 108-157, Hamm, Hoheneck .

Streib, H. (1998b), The religious educator as story-teller: suggestions from Paul Ricoeur's work, *Religious Education,* 93, 314-331.

Streib, H. (1999a), Off-road religion? A narrative approach to fundamentalist and occult orientations of adolescents, *Journal of Adolescence,* 22, 255-267.

Streib, H. (1999b), Sub-project on 'Biographies in Christian Fundamentalist Milieus and Organizations' (The research project on 'Drop-outs, Converts and Believers: Contrasting Biographical Analyses of Why Individuals Join, Have a Career and Stay in, or Leave Religious/Ideological Contexts or Groups,' Part III), in Deutscher Bundestag, Referat Öffentlichkeit, (ed.) , *Final Report of the Enquête Commission on 'So-called Sects and Psychogroups'. New Religious and Ideological Communities and Psychogroups in the Federal Republic of Germany*, pp. 402-414,. Bonn, Deutscher Bundestag.

Streib, H. (2000a), Biographical and religious development in Christian-fundamentalist converts and deconverts: a narrative approach, *Journal for the Scientific Study of Religion*, (under review).

Streib, H. (2000b), *Biographies in Christian Fundamentalist Milieus and Organizations. Report to the Enquête Commission of the 13th German Parliament on 'So-called Sects and Psychogroups' (Results of the Research Project on 'Drop-outs, Converts and Believers: Contrasting Biographical Analyses of Why Individuals Join, Have a Career and Stay in, or Leave Religious/Ideological Contexts or Groups')*, Bielefeld, University of Bielefeld, Evangelische Theologie.

Streib, H. (2000c). Seelsorge im Kontext fundamentalistisch-neureligiöser Gruppierungen, in C. Schneider-Harpprecht (ed.), *Zukunftsperspektiven für Seelsorge und Beratung*, Neukrichen-Vluyn, Neukirchener Verlag.

Streib, H. (2001), Faith development theory revisited: the religious styles perspective, *International Journal for the Psychology of Religion*, 11 (in press).

Streib, H. and Schöll, A. (2000), *Wege der Entzauberung. Jugendliche Sinnsuche und Okkultfaszination - Kontexte und Analysen*, Münster, Lit-Verlag.

Tillich, P. (1929), Der Protestantismus als kritisches und gestaltendes Prinzip, in *Main Works/Hauptwerke*, Bd.6, pp. 127-149, Berlin; deGruyter; Evang. Verlagswerk 1992.

Tillich, P. (1931), Zum Problem des evangelischen Religionsunterrichts, in *Gesammelte Werke IX,* pp. 233-235, Stuttgart, Evang. Verlagswerk 1967.

Tillich, P. (1957), Theologie der Erziehung, in *Gesammelte Werke IX,* pp. 236-245, Stuttgart, Evang. Verlagswerk 1967.

Zilleßen, D. (1994), Dialog mit dem Fremden. Vorüberlegungen zum interreligiösen Lernen, *Eangelischer Erzieher,* 46, 338-347.

Zilleßen, D. (1995), Lachen und Weinen. Warum wir Gott nicht so eng sehen, *Evangelischer Erzieher,* 47, 365-370.

9

RELIGIOUS LITERACY
AND DEMOCRATIC CITIZENSHIP

Andrew Wright

Introduction

Traditionally religious education was owned by faith communities committed to the transmission of their own particular religious worldviews. However, the modern era has seen the emergence of liberal forms of religious education committed to teaching about a plurality of religious traditions in a public context divorced from the interests of any specific faith community. Attempts to develop a viable rationale for this new approach to religious teaching are still at an embryonic stage. In an ideal world religious education would be justified on the grounds of the intrinsic importance of religious literacy. However, the subject frequently claims a more pragmatic grounding in its ability to serve the immediate needs of its host communities. The concern of this chapter is to explore the contribution of liberal religious education to the well-being of liberal society as a whole.

The argument that follows is rooted in a number of core claims: first, that liberalism entails the four key principles of freedom of belief, respect for others, democratic consensus on the basis of reasoned argument, and opposition to intolerance; second, that liberal religious education seeks to develop public religious literacy and enhance liberal values; third, that though liberal religious education is effective in supporting the liberal values of freedom of belief and respect for others, its commitment to the principle of reasoned argument is often overshadowed by its censorial attempts to combat religious intolerance; fourth, that the resulting failure to achieve a genuinely liberal religious education is related to a tendency to approach liberalism as a worldview in need of protection, rather than as an interim ethic designed to enhance reasonable human discourse; fifth, that religious education can best serve liberal democracy by developing a religiously literate society in which the value of rational dialogue takes priority over any repressive opposition to religious intolerance.

The contours of liberalism

A comprehensive analysis of the nature of liberal democracy lies beyond the scope of this chapter. Acknowledging the danger of superficiality, I have elected to work with a fairly standard working definition of liberalism. Mark Halstead (1995) identifies three core liberal values: individual liberty, equality of respect and consistent rationality. Liberalism affirms the human right to personal liberty and freedom of belief without coercion, constraint or censorship. This right carries with it the responsibility to tolerate and respect the beliefs of others. The inevitable tension that arises between private freedom and public tolerance forms an essential dynamic within liberalism. Liberal democracy may be said to embrace an ongoing oscillation between the right-wing instinct for individual liberty and the left-wing instinct for equality of respect. It is through Halstead's third core liberal value, that of consistent rationality, that disputes within liberal democracy must be resolved. Only by using reason to adjudicate disputes between defenders of personal freedom and advocates of public tolerance can liberalism hope to retain its integrity. The effective oil for the mechanism of liberalism is reasoned persuasion, ultimately administered through the ballot box. There can be no place here for the use of force, intimidation or violence.

However, a fourth core value is normally added to Halstead's three: the one thing that liberalism can never tolerate is intolerance itself. This value comes into play at that paradoxical point *in extremis* when the principle of tolerance must be suspended in order to protect it from the forces of intolerance. 'It may easily turn out that they [the intolerant] are not prepared to meet us on the level of rational argument . . . we should therefore claim, in the name of tolerance, the right not to tolerate the intolerant' (Popper, 1966: 265). All that is inherently sectarian, totalitarian, fascist or fundamentalist must be actively resisted because it constitutes a core challenge to the very foundations of liberalism itself. In effect, liberalism invokes its own version of the Christian 'just-war' theory: when liberalism finds itself under threat, then extra-liberal methods of defence such as censorship and repression (even on occasions violence and armed conflict) become justifiable. Whenever the values of open democratic society are threatened by the possibility of a descent into anarchy, then the principle of intolerance-of-intolerance must be invoked as a key liberal value.

These four principles of liberalism enjoy an impressive lineage. Beginning from John Rawls (1972, 1993), perhaps the most articulate contemporary defender of the liberal tradition, it is possible to trace back a family tree that includes such progenitors as Karl Popper (1966) and John Stuart Mill (1972a, 1972b), and that has its ancestral roots in the great liberal patriarch and founding father, John Locke.

Locke's liberalism flows equally from his philosophical theory and his political practice. Its philosophical roots are grounded in his empirical epistemology. The *Essay Concerning Human Understanding* acknowledges both the range and limitations of human knowledge (Locke, 1975). For Locke, the source of all knowledge is sense experience. However, though such empirical knowledge provides us with a good understanding of the physical universe, it is less than helpful when it comes to addressing the immediate personal, social and political challenges of ordinary life. Here, empirical fact must inevitably be supplemented with non-empirical beliefs and values, but such beliefs are merely matters of opinion that cannot be justified with any certainly. Locke's epistemology thus raises a crucial question: 'How can a society built upon such uncertain foundations ever hope to survive, let alone flourish?'

The answer to this question is to be found in Locke's political practice. As a diplomat and politician he found himself confronted with a society in crisis, divided by a plurality of conflicting religious and political beliefs. Tensions between monarchists and parliamentarians, and between Protestants and Catholics, threatened to plunge seventeenth-century England into a dark age of violence and depravity. During a diplomatic mission to Brandenberg in 1665 he encountered Protestants and Catholics living together in apparent harmony. This initial experience of liberalism in operation was further nurtured through his political alliance with the Earl of Shaftesbury, an enigmatic defender of religious tolerance in an increasingly intolerant society. Locke was thus drawn towards a liberal pragmatism that sought to establish social order despite the rich diversity of conflicting belief systems.

Locke's *Essay Concerning Toleration* (1993a) and *Letter Concerning Toleration* (1993b), published in 1667 and 1685 respectively, constitute the founding texts of the liberal tradition. Here he develops a fundamental distinction between the realms of private religious belief and public civic polity: 'I esteem it above all things necessary to distinguish exactly the business of civil government from that of religion, and to settle the just bounds that lie between the one and the other' (Locke, 1993b: 393). The role of the public magistrate is limited to that of defender of public order, thereby establishing the conditions in which private freedom can flourish. 'The commonwealth seems to me to be a society of men constituted only for the procuring, preserving, and advancing of their own civil interests' (Locke, 1993b: 393). Optional beliefs and speculative opinions, which for Locke include such issues as the Trinity, purgatory and transubstantiation, may be held freely and stand beyond the concern and competency of the makers of public policy. 'In speculations and religious worship every man hath a perfect, uncontrollable liberty which he may freely use, without, or contrary to the magistrate's command, without any guilt or sin at all' (Locke, 1993a: 109f).

Thus, the core liberal principles of private freedom of belief, made possible through public tolerance of pluralism, established by rational democratic consensus, and protected by the public magistrate's rightful intolerance-of-intolerance are all clearly in evidence in Locke's thinking. These four basic principles have come to form the bedrock of modern liberal society. How, then, does religious education fare within this context?

The experiment of liberal religious education

The rise of western liberal democracy brought with it the advent and rapid expansion of state-sponsored schooling. Inevitably, such schooling proved itself largely conservative in nature, tending to support the political, social and cultural *status quo*. As the commitment of liberalism to the four core principles outlined above gradually became embedded in the western mind-set, so state-sponsored systems of schooling naturally began to utilise religious education as a means of supporting, upholding and reinforcing the prevailing social order. Religion was taught not only because of its intrinsic value, but also because of its ability to support the emergence of democratic citizenship.

The forms taken by religious education are as diverse as liberal democracy itself (Gates, 1991). In France and the United States of America, for example, religious teaching has (at least formally) no place in the system of public education. This reflects the liberal value of freedom of belief, since to teach religion (it is supposed) is to use a public office to impose what are, in liberal terms, essentially private values. However, the potential cost of this strategy is high, since it threatens to undermine the liberal commitment to reasoned debate. The lack of formal religious education in public schools opens up the possibility of widespread religious illiteracy. For some, such an outcome is acceptable as the lesser of two evils: the repression of explicit religious education in the sphere of public education is an unfortunate but necessary strategy if pupils are to be guarded against indoctrination. This position rests on the assumption that religious teaching will inevitably tend towards a confessional advocacy of a particular belief system. It follows that the principle of reasoned debate must take second place to the principle of intolerance-of-intolerance (in the form of the exclusion of religious education from the curriculum) if liberal values are to be upheld.

An alternative approach currently flourishes in, among other places, England and Wales. Here the experiment of liberal religious education takes the form of a commitment to state-sponsored public religious education for all. The danger of confessional advocacy of any particular faith system in this context is dissipated through the adoption of a specifically liberal understanding of the nature and function of religious teaching. The task of the religious educator is not to advocate and nurture religious faith, but to support the emergence of an informed and intelligent understanding of religion independent of the actual faith commitments of both teacher and pupil.

This was achieved in England and Wales through a shift in the early 1970s from a pre-liberal Christian confessionalism to a liberal, open and pluralistic form of public religious education (Copley, 1997; Wright, 1993). Here the task of the teacher was not to advocate any specific religious position, but to present the plurality of religious beliefs in as open, balanced and value-free a manner as possible. The slightest hint of such neutrality collapsing into special pleading, indoctrination or confessionalism was to be firmly resisted. Presenting religion in such a way enabled the liberal religious educator to hold fast to the core principles of freedom and tolerance, while simultaneously opening up the possibility of a public religious literacy rooted in reasoned debate.

Parallel with the neutral presentation of religion was to be found a concern to avoid the reduction of religious education to a mere extension of the history, geography or sociology lesson. It was acknowledged that the essence of religious belief ran far deeper than merely its cultural expression. It was necessary to pass beyond the outer cultural manifestation of religion into the inner experiential core of faith. Though it was certainly not the task of public religious education to instruct pupils as to what they should and should not believe, it was accepted that the teacher did have a positive role to play in maximising children's freedom of belief. Such freedom was perceived to be under threat from a crass secular materialism responsible for eroding our natural capacity for spiritual experience (Hay, 1985). As a result, it was seen to be entirely consistent with the liberal principle of freedom of belief that religious educators should seek to cultivate in children an openness to spiritual experience, provided of course that such cultivation avoided advocating any single belief system.

This dualism between the external objectivity of religious cultural expression and the internal subjectivity of spiritual experience parallels the liberal principles of tolerance and freedom. The objective representation of religious culture in the classroom served to enhance public toleration of religious pluralism, while the subjective exploration of spiritual experience served to maximise the child's personal religious options. Religious education in England and Wales thus sought to gain through inclusion what was achieved in France and the United States of America through exclusion. Both, in their different ways, sought to uphold liberal values. However, the English and Welsh system could claim one distinct advantage: the strategy of the positive inclusion of religious education within the public school curriculum supported the liberal commitment to reason through the development of public religious literacy in a way denied children brought up within the public education systems of France and the United States of America.

Liberal religious education: flaws in the fabric

I have suggested that the English and Welsh system of public religious education opens up far greater opportunities for the enhancement of liberal values than its counterparts in France and the United States of America. However, significant flaws still remain in its fabric. Lacking any secure sense of its own identify, it has instinctively adopted a range of defensive measures that have lead to the repression of open debate. Consequently, it is not yet sufficiently liberal enough to guarantee the emergence of public religious literacy.

Liberal religious education established itself, at least in part, on the back of the development within higher education of Departments of Religious Studies, which developed as an alternative to traditional Faculties of Theology (Hinnells, 1970; Smart, 1966, 1995). As a result, a process of 'understanding-seeking-faith' came to rival the traditional path of 'faith-seeking-understanding' as a starting point for the investigation of religion. This new approach tended to view religion from an immanent rather than transcendent vantage point: as a dimension of human culture rather than as a response to divine revelation. Its secular scientific methods could lay greater claim to neutrality and objectivity than theological investigation dependent upon a prior faith commitment. However, this emergent methodology brought with it a negation of the question of realistic truth that is central to the major religious traditions of the world.

It is simply a brute fact that many religious traditions are non-liberal both in their outlook on the world and in their historical origins. There is, for example, in Islam no notion of the liberal distinction between the spheres of the private and public. Islam makes universal truth claims that embrace the whole of reality and cannot simply be relegated to the domain of private piety. The veracity of the revelation embodied in the Qur'an touches every aspect of human existence, including literature, politics, ethics, economics, aesthetics and religious piety. Consequently, an understanding of this tradition cannot be achieved simply by analysing Muslim culture and religious sensibility. It must also engage with the question of the realistic truth of Islam.

In its concern to remain neutral towards the diversity of religious truth claims, liberal religious education tends to misrepresent the self-understanding of specific religious traditions (Hardy, 1975, 1976, 1979). The process of bracketing out truth claims in the classroom carries with it the implication that realistic truth is not central to the concerns of religious believers. This undermines the integrity of most religious traditions. Indeed, it has been argued that by imposing a working neutrality on religious traditions, liberal religious education advocates by default a universal unitarian theology (Cooling, 1994).

Attempts to recover a place for issues of religious truth within religious education have themselves been subject to a powerful backlash. A significant influence here has been the fashion for non-realistic theology, with its claim that questions of objective truth miss the heart of human religiosity (Kaufman, 1995). Though avoiding a commitment to non-realism, Jackson has suggested that the notion of religion as a systematic belief system is itself a product of modern western academic thought. The traditional concept of *religio* corresponded with a concern for inner piety (*spirituality* is probably the best modern equivalent) whose fundamental focus was on the cultivation of the inner life rather than with external creed and dogma (Jackson, 1997). Religious education's failure to place questions of truth and dogma at centre stage is, on this reading, entirely justifiable.

This tendency to side-step questions of theological truth is also related to a liberal suspicion of forms of religious belief grounded in the 'official' creeds of religious traditions. This is so especially when such dogma is promulgated by those in positions of authority within the religious community. Such exclusive and authoritarian truth claims appear to threaten the principles of freedom and tolerance. Two major strategies have been developed by liberal religious educators in response to this. On the one hand, the distinctive truth claims of individual traditions are undermined by invoking a universal generic notion of religion, thereby forcing specific truth claims to be viewed as parts of a greater whole (Hull, 1991). On the other hand, such specific truth claims are, under the influence of postmodern paradigms of thought, deconstructed in favour of an affirmation of the uniqueness of each individual person's spiritual worldview (Erricker and Erricker, 1994). Both strategies, namely a universalism that dissolves exclusivity into a greater whole and a nominalism that reduces exclusivity to its component parts, serve to undermine the distinctive (and hence potentially totalitarian and sectarian) truth claims made by specific religious traditions.

Liberalism, I am suggesting, struggles to acknowledge the exclusive non-liberal truth claims of specific religious traditions and has developed a range of strategies for bypassing them. This view is confirmed when we consider the place of secular atheism in the liberal religious education curriculum. Secular humanists and Christians originally worked together in establishing programmes of liberal religious education (Smith, 1969). There is no doubt, however, that the secular influence has declined sharply following the 1988 Education Reform Act. This is not due simply to the resurgence of a conservative Christian lobby concerned to influence public policy. David Hay's insistence that religious education must positively challenge secular materialism's undermining of children's natural capacity for religious experience represents a mainstream rejection of atheism that does not flow from any conservative Christian camp. Though some have advocated secular forms of spiritual education (Newby, 1996), the stark reality is that liberal religious education does not generally allow pupils any generous, sympathetic and systematic engagement with those traditions of secular humanism sharply opposed to religion.

The liberal repression of exclusive non-liberal truth claims, whether they be religious or secular, is at its most transparent when the moral dimension of religious education is considered. Liberal religious education was quick to discard the traditional confessional notion that religious education should contribute to the well-being of society by inculcating Christian values drawn from the Ten Commandments and the Sermon on the Mount. In its place it introduced a morality grounded on the liberal principles of understanding and tolerance of religious difference. Exclusive truth claims are believed to threaten this process by invoking images of conflict rather than mutual respect. John Hull has sought to defend the liberal programme by introducing a distinction between authentic and inauthentic manifestations of religious belief. He warns of the dangers of 'religionism': a closed, sectarian, racist, dehumanising and morally objectionable form of religious belief (Hull, 1991, 1992). 'Religionism' embraces an impulse towards religious apartheid and sectarian purity. For Hull, such manifestations of religion are fundamentally anti-liberal and totalitarian, and as such must be actively resisted through the censorship of school textbooks and other teaching resources.

There are, however, major problems with Hull's liberal position. It is impossible to deny the fact that religion is a complex, multifaceted and ambiguous entity. There is currently no public consensus regarding the most appropriate way of representing it. Increasingly, we can make sense of religion only be recognising the existence of a plurality of perspectives, by invoking a diversity of possible meta-narratives. It follows that the demarcation line between authentic religion and inauthentic 'religionism', insisted upon by Hull, is by no means an easy one to draw. It is at this point that liberal religious education is at its most vulnerable and inconsistent: rather than following the standard liberal route of seeking to enable children to engage intelligently with the problem of what constitutes authentic and inauthentic religion, liberal religious educators instead opt for the emergency strategy of protecting liberalism from the perceived threat of anti-liberal religionism. In doing so, it fails to attend to the diversity of possible religious representations and in particular does not allow non-liberal representations a fair hearing. This defence of liberal values paradoxically ignores the liberal commitment to reasoned debate and instead moves prematurely towards a process of repression and censorship.

Despite the enormous strides forward taken by liberal religious education in its task of enhancing the quality of public religious literacy, the experiment still tends to slip into forms of intellectual and cultural imperialism that undermine the very foundations of liberalism itself. This is certainly not a new problem. As Peter Gay

(1973) observes, in his monumental history of the Enlightenment, liberal education has always been faced with a decision between the ideal of freedom established through education, reason and literacy, and the urgent political necessity of imposing social reform. Ultimately, Gay suggests, the impulse for reform tends to takes precedence over the impulse for freedom. As a result, liberal educators found themselves:

> led through the devious and embarrassing detours of repression and manipulation that were a denial and mockery of the world they hoped to bring into being: the very methods used to distribute the fruits of enlightenment seemed to be calculated to frustrate the Enlightenment itself (Gay, 1973: 497).

This is precisely the trap into which liberal religious education has fallen: in France and the United States of America, fear of indoctrination denies pupils formal access to appropriate levels of religious literacy; in England and Wales, the instinct to repress exclusive truth claims, be they religious or secular in origin, rather than encourage open debate between alternative traditions, leads to a similar outcome. Both approaches ultimately undermine the liberal commitment to rational dialogue.

Liberalism: from worldview to interim ethic

Liberal religious education is thus faced with a fundamental dilemma. Though it is in favour, at least in principle, of reasoned debate, it finds itself unable to ignore the fact that many of the world's religious traditions are not particularly liberal in their understanding of the world. The paternalistic representation of such traditions within a liberal interpretative framework serves to stifle reasoned debate and undermines the very foundations of liberalism itself. Yet the alternative of an authentic representation of non-liberal religious traditions runs the risk of allowing pupils access to potentially anti-liberal sentiments, which may potentially threaten the very fabric of liberal society.

The liberal instinct to protect human freedom from anti-liberal repression is set on a collision course with the concern to affirm the value of rational debate. Should the liberal educator bring Salman

Rushdie's *Satanic Verses* into the classroom? To do so may undermine the liberal commitment to respect Islamic sensibilities. Not to do so may contradict the liberal commitment to freedom of expression. It is to the principle of reasoned debate that liberalism normally turns as the appropriate means of resolving such dilemmas, yet it is precisely at this point that liberalism is found wanting. The instinct to censor, which in traditional liberalism was always the last resort, has become the norm. How might this dilemma be resolved? Is liberal religious education's current tendency to prefer the option of censorship over that of open debate an inevitable response to the failure of reason to establish a public consensus? Is liberal education capable of moving beyond an instinctive preference for the *in extremis* measures of censorship in its concern to defend liberal values?

One possible path forward has recently been suggested by Graham Haydon (1997). He proposes that liberal education should discard a hard notion of liberalism as a comprehensive worldview, one committed to its own distinctive beliefs and morality, in favour of a soft notion of liberalism as an interim political ethic. Haydon here implies that aspects of liberalism have become, or at least are in danger of becoming, fossilised into a dogmatic worldview. If he is correct, then this undermines Popper's characterisation of liberal society as being one that is 'open' rather than 'closed'. For Popper (1996: 57), a closed society 'lives in a charmed circle of unchanging taboos, of laws and customs that are felt to be as inevitable as the rising of the sun, or the cycle of the seasons'. In its hard form, liberalism becomes just such a closed society. In an aggressive and politically correct liberalism 'the facts of disagreement themselves frequently go unacknowledged, disguised by a rhetoric of consensus' (MacIntyre, 1988: 2). Liberal religious education, with its preference for censorship over debate, is guilty of adopting just such a rhetorical strategy. Haydon (1997: 127f) argues that if:

> education seems to be preaching toleration as one of the highest of virtues in its own right, it could well be charged with being, politically and religiously, sectarian . . . a society which tried to exclude anyone who was not a liberal in their moral outlook would be a markedly *illiberal* society.

Haydon's (1997: 127f) advocacy of a soft pragmatic version of liberalism allows him to 'distinguish between encouraging people to show tolerance towards diversity and persuading people that tolerance is an ideal in itself'. He suggests that 'the liberal educator has to promote the values that are necessary to living in a liberal society, but [should] stop short of promoting a liberal set of moral beliefs or lifestyle'. Liberal education ought not to act paternalistically by imposing a liberal worldview, but rather find ways of protecting a pluralistic society in which non-liberals and liberals can co-exist. He argues that:

> Liberal educators need to distinguish between the liberal values that are necessary to maintaining a plural society (not because a plural society is necessarily the ideal, but because it is inescapably the kind of society we have) and the values that are themselves marks of a specifically liberal response to moral issues.

Wolterstorff (1996) has argued that this notion of liberalism as a soft interim ethic rather than as a hard worldview is consistent with Locke's original liberal vision. Central to Locke's position is an appreciation of both the necessity and the provisionality of our belief systems. His particular brand of Enlightenment-thinking contrasts with that of Descartes, who in his search for certainty (driven by what Bernstein (1976) characterises as 'Cartesian anxiety') was concerned to draw a clear line of demarcation between clear, unassailable knowledge and mere superstitious opinion. Locke saw his task as a pragmatic, political one, concerned with the effective management of a society in which a plurality of beliefs was becoming the norm. 'How are we to pick our way when we find ourselves forced, as we all are, to leave the small clearing of knowledge and enter the twilight of belief and disbelief?' (Wolterstorff, 1996: x).

Locke's project, Wolterstoff suggests, was not to create a unified worldview, but rather to develop a 'doxastic practice' (from the Greek *doxa* meaning belief, expectation, judgement, opinion) in which communication between alternative and competing belief systems could be maximised. Locke did not propose a worldview, but instead sought to create the conditions most likely to support the journey of humanity from ignorance to enlightenment. For Wolterstorff (1996: 246) 'it is to politics and not to epistemology that we have to look for an answer as to how to do that'. He seeks to rehabilitate the original pragmatic roots of liberalism by recovering 'its animating vision of a society in which persons of diverse traditions live together in justice and friendship, conversing with each other and slowly altering their traditions in response to their conversation' (p. 246).

Liberalism in its hard form sets itself up as a totalitarian regime that requires aggressive policing and protection in the face of the threats posed by anti-liberal forces. Liberalism in its soft form seeks to nurture the human quest for knowledge, wisdom and truth across contrasting and often conflicting worldviews. The former places the liberal value of intolerance-of-the-intolerant centre stage; the latter highlights the principle of rational debate, turning to the repression of intolerance only as a final resort. A shift in the balance of power within religious education from hard to soft forms of liberalism represents both a viable option and an urgent necessity.

Religious literacy for democratic citizenship

At the heart of liberal democracy stands the notion of autonomous, responsible citizenship. This can only be achieved through education. Ignorance does not breed wise citizenship, and the failure of education leaves individuals open to manipulation by repressive social, cultural and economic forces. What then is the role of religious education? How can it best uphold and enhance the health and well-being of liberal democracy?

Wherever liberalism perceives itself to be vulnerable and under threat, it will (like most cultures) inevitably seek to protect itself. It frequently does so by turning to a hard sectarian form of liberalism in which its identity as a coherent worldview is affirmed over against non-liberal alternatives. Both by denying religious education access to the public curriculum, and by censoring anti-liberal religious perspectives, liberal education effectively indoctrinates pupils into just such a hard liberal worldview. The liberal commitment to rational debate is replaced with an anti-liberal policy of repression, censorship and manipulation. The enormous success in the West of establishing the liberal values of freedom of belief and tolerance in the public sphere means that such repression is often disguised and hidden.

At the heart of the matter lies an ongoing failure to distinguish between closed and open forms of education. It has been difficult for many liberal educators to shrug off a restrictive and paternalistic legacy of education-as-advocacy. If to teach something is also to advocate it, then it follows that what is positively taught must conform to the norms of a liberal worldview. Consequently, those aspects of religion that are clearly anti-liberal must be censored and repressed. Curriculum development tends to start from this set of implied assumptions. Religion is to be moulded and pre-packaged into an acceptable liberal form, and anti-liberal religiosity must be censored before it is able to contaminate. The decisions on where exactly the lines of censorship are to be drawn come, in the main at least, from the liberal ascendancy within the religious education profession.

But what if religious education were to understand its role as being that of supporting a soft pragmatic version of liberalism? Its task then will be to uphold and nurture intelligent conversation between religious and secular traditions of all persuasions and tendencies. Here education will never be a process of advocacy, but rather a search for intelligence, wisdom, insight and literacy. The task will be that of enabling children to begin to develop for themselves the ability to make their own way through the maze of what are frequently diverse, messy and contradictory religious options.

In terms of curriculum development, the task will not be one of discrimination and censorship, but of finding ways of enabling pupils to: gain access to an appropriate range of religious and secular worldviews; learn to become intelligent about the pathological dimension of religion; locate themselves within the spectrum of the theological affirmation and secular rejection of religion; develop the levels of religious literacy required of citizens in a healthy democratic society.

Such a religious education for religious literacy will not be an immersion into a hard form of 'liberalism-as-closed-worldview', but into a soft form of 'liberalism-as-open-interim-ethic'. The liberal commitment to freedom, tolerance and wisdom will thus be supported and enhanced by religious education. Its task will be to enable children, and hence the next generation of adults, to become responsible, open and literate in the way they approach, resolve and embrace the ambiguity of religion, in both its liberal and non-liberal manifestations.

Summary and conclusions

Liberalism is untrue to its historical origins and inner integrity if it allows itself to function as a closed dogmatic worldview, established to protect the status quo of liberal democratic society. The desire to uphold the principles of freedom and tolerance must not lead to a premature implementation of the *in extremis* value of intolerance-of-intolerance. This must only ever be a last resort, used only when the liberal commitment to reasoned debate and argument has clearly and unambiguously failed. Premature censorship in the classroom will not enhance the kind of public religious literacy capable of supporting a healthy liberal society.

Liberalism is most true to its inner integrity when it functions as a provisional interim ethic enhancing the human potential for wisdom and insight. Here the values of freedom, tolerance and reasoned debate take absolute priority, and the liberal value of intolerance-of-intolerance is invoked only ever as a last resort. This opens the path towards the cultivation of religious literacy, which is the fundamental contribution liberal religious education has to make to the well-being of liberal society.

References

Bernstein, R.J. (1976), *Beyond Objectivism and Relativism: science, hermeneutics and praxis,* Oxford, Basil Blackwell.

Cooling, T. (1994), *A Christian Vision for State Education,* London, SPCK.

Copley, T. (1997), *Teaching Religion: fifty years of religious education in England and Wales,* Exeter, University of Exeter Press.

Erricker, C. and Erricker, J. (1994), Metaphorical awareness and the methodology of religious education, *British Journal of Religious Education,* 16, 174-184.

Gates, B. (ed.) (1991), *Freedom and Authority in Religions and Religious Education,* London, Cassell.

Gay, P. (1973), *The Enlightenment: an interpretation. Volume Two: the science of freedom,* London, Wildwood House.

Halstead, J.M. (1995), Liberal values and liberal education, in J.M. Halstead and M.J. Taylor (eds), *Values in Education and Education in Values,* pp 17-32, London, Falmer Press.

Hardy, D.W. (1975), Teaching religion: a theological critique, *Learning for Living,* 15 (1), 10-16.

Hardy, D.W. (1976), The implications of pluralism for religious education, *Learning for Living,* 16 (2), 55-62.

Hardy, D.W. (1979), Truth in religious education: further reflections on the implications of pluralism, *British Journal of Religious Education,* 1, 102-119.

Hay, D. (1985), Suspicion of the spiritual: teaching religion in a world of secular experience, *British Journal of Religious Education,* 7, 140-147.

Haydon, G. (1997), *Teaching About Values: a new approach,* London, Cassell.

Hinnells, J. (ed.) (1970), *Comparative Religion in Education*, Newcastle-upon-Tyne, Oriel Press.

Hull, J.M. (1991), *Mishmash: religious education in multi-cultural Britain - a study in metaphor*, Derby, Christian Education Movement.

Hull, J.M. (1992), Editorial: the transmission of religious prejudice, *British Journal of Religious Education*, 14, 69-72.

Jackson, R. (1997), *Religious Education: an interpretative approach*, London, Hodder and Stoughton.

Kaufman, G.D. (1995), *In Face of Mystery: a constructive theology*, London, Harvard University Press.

Locke, J. (1975), *An Essay Concerning Human Understanding*, Oxford, Clarendon Press.

Locke, J. (1993a), An essay concerning toleration, in D. Wootton (ed.), *John Locke: political writings*, pp 186-209, Harmondsworth, Penguin Books.

Locke, J. (1993b), A letter concerning toleration, in D. Wootton (ed.), *John Locke: political writings*, pp 309-435, Harmondsworth, Penguin Books.

MacIntyre, A. (1988), *Whose Justice? Which Rationality?* London, Duckworth.

Mill, J.S. (1972a), *On Liberty*, London, Dent.

Mill, J.S. (1972b), *Utilitarianism*, London, Dent.

Newby, M. (1996), Towards a secular concept of spiritual maturity, in R. Best (ed.), *Education, Spirituality and the Whole Child*, pp 93-107, London, Cassell.

Popper, K.R. (1966), *The Open Society and its Enemies. Volume One: Plato*, London, Routledge and Kegan Paul.

Rawls, J. (1972), *A Theory of Justice*, Oxford, Oxford University Press.

Rawls, J. (1993), *Political Liberalism*, New York, Columbia University Press.

Smart, N. (1966), *Secular Education and the Logic of Religion*, London, Faber and Faber.

Smart, N. (1995), The values of religious studies, *The Journal of Beliefs and Values*, 16 (2), 7-10.

Smith, J.W.D. (1969), *Religious Education in a Secular Setting*, London, SCM.

Wolterstorff, N. (1996), *John Locke and the Ethics of Belief*, Cambridge, Cambridge University Press.

Wright, A. (1993), *Religious Education in the Secondary School: prospects for religious literacy*, London, David Fulton.

10

INTERCULTURAL LEARNING IN A NEW MILLENNIUM: BETWEEN FUNDAMENTALISM AND RELATIVISM

Hans-Georg Ziebertz

Introduction

Article 29 of the United Nations Convention on the Rights of the Child requires that education aims at 'respect for the language and values of the child's own country as well as for those of other cultures'. Children are to be prepared for life in a free society in the spirit of peace, friendship and understanding between peoples and between ethnic, national and religious groups. This may sound obvious, but it is not obvious in every country in Europe and certainly not worldwide. Just because it is not obvious that upbringing and schooling make this their aim, pedagogic theory is required to prepare pupils for a life where cultural egoism is reduced and cultural diversity seen as an opportunity. We ought next to take a closer look at a number of aspects of Intercultural Learning in the 'postmodern' context. The theory pointed out in this chapter is that Intercultural Learning ought to pave the way for permanent co-existence in a multicultural society and must, therefore, avoid two extremes: cultural fundamentalism on the one hand and cultural relativism on the other hand. For this we need an adequate discourse model, and Intercultural Learning (and interreligious, too) must help pupils to practise new ways of changing their perspectives. These reflections have their origins in the German situation; but their consequences have far wider applicability.

From Education for Foreigners to Intercultural Learning

The question of how people of different nationalities, different religions, different skin-colours can live together was recognised as an educational challenge in countries like the United Kingdom and the United States of America very much earlier than in Germany (although German history in particular would have provided enough reasons to address the problem earlier). Society in the United States of America has always been characterised by a high ethnic mix, while in the United Kingdom there was easy access from the Commonwealth. In this way the so-called 'melting pots' grew. Other European countries experienced a strong migrant influx as, for example, Algerians and Moroccans went to France, and Surinamese and Indonesians went to the Netherlands. The colonial past was an important factor; quite often, generous immigration policies compensated indirectly for colonial guilt. If we take the concept of Intercultural Learning and review the stages of its development in Germany, we shall see clearly how it has grown and the impact it has had (Auernheimer, 1990; Jäggle, 1995; Nieke, 1995).

Foreign-language teaching theory
After 1960 the economic miracle attracted a flood of immigrants looking for work in Germany. Pedagogics was in a difficult position: the influx of foreigners was economically desirable, but there was disagreement about its political significance and no certainty about future developments. It could be argued that foreign workers would replace each other so that each group would remain in the country for only a limited time and only some would send for their families. On this supposition, limited measures would be enough and would ensure that the children's basic educational needs were met. This was the background to the so-called first phase of 'Education for Foreigners', which simply amounted to foreign-language teaching. Children were to be instructed in the German language in the shortest possible time, giving them the opportunity to benefit from the German school system. Over and above educational measures, the aim was damage-limitation on two fronts: first, as it was assumed that the foreign children would be returning to their own countries, they were to be kept in touch with their own roots for the transition period; second, the new situation should not be allowed to undermine the school system and current curricula.

As we all know, some of these assumptions were not realistic. Above all, the idea that immigrants were willing to go back home proved mistaken. So when they expected to stay, the question became: how to respond with appropriate educational measures. The politics of the 1970s were marked by the wish to see Education for Foreigners as education for *assimilation* and, later, for *integration*. Assimilation means adjustment and expects those who are to be assimilated to give up the traditions they have brought with them. If foreigners wish to remain in our country, it is argued, they should accept our language, values and culture. The integration concept was a little less drastic. It allowed the notion that what was culturally foreign could at least be integrated in limited segments into the dominant culture.

All these concepts are linked by the dualism of a culture of visitors on the one hand and strangers on the other hand. It is foreigners who are the 'problem', for they give rise to particular practical and theoretical considerations (Nieke, 1995: 76). As for their children, their deficits are conspicuous when compared with normality as represented by German children. What could have been more appropriate than to charge pedagogics with the task of removing deficits quickly and bringing foreign children up to the level of 'German normality'? This area was seen particularly as a special aspect of social pedagogics.

Multicultural education

In the course of criticism of these developments, the 1970s proposed the concept of 'multicultural education'. This was a counter-movement to the idea of assimilating and integrating foreign children into German normality, and required that all minorities should be allowed the possibility of a permanent and unimpeded development of their way of life without being absorbed into the majority. There was increasing recognition that migration would not simply be a temporary phenomenon and that the social and cultural changes provoked by (but not only by) immigrants seeking work were irreversible. Concepts of multicultural education are now showing that it is not enough to project the problems of coexistence onto foreigners but that we are all concerned with the problem of how we are to live together (Bukow and Llaryora, 1993). Looking to the future, a number of very different ideas have been formulated: we cannot deal with them here (cf. Auernheimer, 1990: 26ff, 196ff).

Proponents of multicultural education are united in a threefold criticism. First, they criticise the sanitised concept of deportation, which consists of removing the problem by offering well-intentioned assistance to foreigners to return home. The economic slump of 1973 (oil-crisis) was grist to the mill of advocates of this concept. Second, they criticise the assimilation concept, which aims at merging what is different and strange with one's own culture, thus extinguishing the distinctive differences. Third, they criticise the integration concept, which allows certain foreign traditions, but shows its tolerance above all when these are practised in certain ghettos and do not threaten the existence of one's own culture (cf. Nieke, 1995: 76ff). This threefold criticism relates to the monocultural perspective of Education for Foreigners, which treats what is different and strange as something opposed, as something that cannot be reckoned to belong to one's own reality.

Reacting to what is 'foreign'

In recent years much more wide-ranging thought has been given to this subject. No longer is the perception of processes of cultural differentiation linked exclusively with the presence in Germany of foreign fellow citizens. In the field of educational studies the awareness has grown that a many-sided problem is emerging in Education for Foreigners. Certainly, there is a contrast between what is foreign and what we are used to, but our interest ought to be directed not only at those who are perceived to be foreign, but also at ourselves and the way we look at foreignness (Schäffter, 1991: 11-42). Foreignness as a problem also lies within ourselves. If foreignness is labelled 'foreign', then it is not due only to the particular characteristics of certain groups of people but also to a distorted vision that makes us stigmatise certain distinguishing marks. To put it more bluntly, foreignness is not a personal characteristic, but it is imposed. When we realise that we ourselves produce foreignness, then we scrutinise our perception more closely (cf. Ziebertz, 1994a: 18f).

There is a further factor: when we realise the way in which we experience phenomena as 'foreign', there is a blurring of the clear dividing line between what is foreign and what is our own, and the narrowness of our own perspective becomes evident. We are able to see that there is much that is foreign in our own culture (Miksch, 1991). Around us we see and recognise other values, norms and worldviews. For instance, the otherness of certain forms of sexual orientation raises questions regarding our attitude to homosexuals in a world where heterosexuality is the norm. In other words, when we understand the limitations of our perspectives, we are inevitably confronted with the question of what is actually meant by individual and collective identity.

Even this short sketch allows us to see that there have been significant changes in the development of concepts, ranging from the early Education for Foreigners to our contemporary understanding of Intercultural Learning. Though we must continue to seek particular solutions to particular problems (for example, the encouragement of multilingualism), our perspectives are now focusing on one fundamental pedagogical question, namely, how do upbringing and education relate to what is different and foreign? The classical questions (for example, relations between indigenous and non-indigenous populations, and racism) are now part of current intercultural pedagogics, but intercultural pedagogics goes beyond them. The perception is growing that all thinking about educational processes ought to concern itself with multiplicity and cultural diversity.

Cultural diversity as the norm

'Cultural diversity' is not a problem extraneous to pedagogics. In fact, it provides an inherent, central challenge to Intercultural Learning. We are becoming increasingly aware that children and young people have to be equipped for a life of multiplicity. This means that the shaping of a possible identity is not simply culturally predetermined; nor can it be. I prefer the concept of 'pluralism' to the noun 'multiculture'. What then are the relevant indicators for Intercultural Learning in our pluralist culture?

In his well-received book, *Unsere postmoderne Moderne (Our Postmodern Modern Age)*, the German philosopher Wolfgang Welsch (1993) examines the genesis of the postmodern state of pluralism. For him 'postmodern' does not mean a new era but the modern age become reflective. The use of the concept 'postmodern' is based on a predisposition towards the analytical, not the normative.

Using the concept of culture, Welsch is able to demonstrate pedagogically relevant changes. The classic concept of culture was still tied to the notion that any particular culture coincided with the closed, unitary culture of the nation state. This is an idea that still attracts votes, even today; but it is a grossly inadequate description that does not do justice to either the inner complexity of a culture or the mingling of cultures. Consequently, another idea that is behind all this also collapses: this is the idea of culture as a 'sphere', with a closed external surface and a central core, which may be touched by other spheres. The idea requires a compulsion towards unity within and, at the same time, a sealing-off of externals, which could neither succeed nor be credible today. What is foreign in other cultures does belong, in part at least, to the inner content of one's own. In other words, talk of 'own' and 'foreign' can no longer presuppose that each is homogeneous in itself. The development of postmodernism is thoroughly undermining the foundations of thinking in terms of spheres and pillars. It is obscuring boundaries within the multiplicity of received traditions, as well as the many levels of intermingling with other traditions. Moreover, religion, as part of the essential content of culture, is no exception to this. In evidence, we need only ask what the link is between a Polish Catholic and a member of the Dutch Church in terms of their concepts of religious symbolism.

It follows that we have to question critically the term 'inter'. The idea of 'intercultural' is often understood as a concept positing an encounter between two (or more) entities, closed off in themselves, which use dialogue to pursue mutual understanding and co-operation. Radical pluralism as constituted in the postmodern age seems to require a differentiation of this concept. Pluralism does not only extend to the relationship of cultures to each other, but also to every received culture, that is to say, to the variety of ways of life and social backgrounds within a classically defined cultural area and to the multiple interpretative patterns and unquestioned certainties valid within it. These are no longer marked by being coterminous with the borders of Bavaria, Germany or Europe; no longer does their homogeneity distinguish them from other regions.

What is significant for pedagogic considerations is that pluralism has become altogether more radical and more charged with conflict, that it has expanded extensively and intensively, that it now reaches down to the grass-roots (Welsch, 1993: 4ff). For Welsch (1993: 320) the decisive, qualitative change of the postmodern age is the fact that:

> all descriptions, all strategies, all solutions . . . will in future [have to] grow from the ground of multiplicity. . . . Within this framework, not against it, we [must] conceive of unity.

We are, therefore, not only concerned with the relationship between a minority and a majority culture, but with diversity in both. In a multicultural society we can scarcely assume that there are any longer any common convictions or common roots, with or without foreigners. Religion, too, no longer offers an agreed position. Religion itself seems to be pluralist (Knitter, 1985). On a very abstract level there may perhaps be consensus, but then the devil is in the detail: for what sense does it make to be agreed about the value of justice when this provides a way of advocating both capital punishment and the right to life?

The more closely we look, the more varied diversity becomes, and the more difficult it becomes to answer the question: how we are to deal with the divergent phenomena within our culture on the educational plane? I should now like to touch on two possible reactions to cultural pluralism that lead to different consequences for Intercultural Learning, namely, the danger of fundamentalism and the problem of relativism.

Monocultural perspectives and the danger of fundamentalism

In Germany until well into the 1980s, public debate of right-wing nationalist views was held on the other side of a kind of social threshold. Public denunciation of such positions might have been expected in view of past events. For some years now, this threshold seems to have been removed, or at least lowered noticeably. Youths who subjected young foreigners to a bloody beating-up in the East German city of Magdeburg in May 1994 bore on their jackets the slogan, 'I am proud to be German'. When an asylum-seekers' hostel was set on fire in the city of Rostock, the cheering mob expressed a mindless contempt for human beings that could only recall the darkest days of German history.

But we are living in the third millenium. The media constantly report greater or lesser attacks on businesses, residential properties and places of worship. The result is that not a few accept this as a normal state of affairs. The growing attitude that one's own culture should be emphasised and what is foreign rejected is, however, not only a German phenomenon, as is clear from a look at neighbouring countries. This is not to relativise the problem but to show its dimensions. Enquiries have shown very exactly that ethnocentrism has not been overcome in Europe (cf. Silbermann and Hüsers, 1995). Ethnocentrism means valuing one's own ethnic group positively and another (or others) negatively. Whatever the reasons, amongst them is the feeling that one's own identity is being submerged by foreigners and foreign things. If we look for the identity-model that is at the root of this thinking, we encounter predominantly negative determinants: identity is what distinguishes me or my own group, country and people from others. We are dealing here with cultural exclusivity, and any pluralist phenomena found within it are evaluated negatively and an ideal of unity opposed to them. The ideal derives from one's own tradition or from something that is projected as ideal onto it. Often enough, it is an ideal of managed reality and not reality itself. We know from empirical enquiries among school students in Germany and Holland that there is a correlation between cultural and religious exclusivity. In other words, cultural and religious exclusivity seem to show up comparable awareness structures (cf. Ziebertz and van der Ven, 1996).

In the world as a whole, religious exclusivity has held its own well into the latest phase of the history of religion. We meet it in all religions. Its public face is particularly evident when it expresses itself in fundamentalist movements. Even though Islamic fundamentalism is referred to particularly frequently in the headlines, we must not ignore corresponding tendencies in Judaism or Christianity, and even in the Asian religions. To take but one example bearing on the Christian religion, it was less than two decades ago that Christian theologians presented apartheid (the rule of Whites over other races in South Africa) as the will of God, thereby theologically legitimating a deeply racist position. If we go back further into history, we encounter a great number of bloody campaigns, destructive of life and spirit, deriving their legitimation from a certainty seemingly sanctioned by a religio-cultural exclusivity. Alongside explicit forms of ethnocentric thinking there is a less explicit grey zone, which must not be underestimated, as it is a breeding ground for hostility towards foreigners.

It is an unavoidable conclusion that cultural exclusivity, like religious exclusivity, is not neutral. It is all too often the ground on which physical and mental violence is prepared. For this reason we are right to criticise those concepts of identity linked with it that separate or exclude (cf. Jäggle, 1995: 245). At the same time, we have to recognise that up to a point a sense of identity always requires distinguishing features in comparison with others (Krewer and Eckensberger, 1991: 591). That individuals can only define themselves in relation to others is a fundamental insight of the idea and process of interaction. The conclusion that we define ourselves in relation to others, however, does not necessarily lead to the exclusion of what is different. It does not necessarily lead to the assumption of a power-orientated attitude of dominance or superiority. And it is at this point that the educational process intervenes.

Multicultural perspectives and the problem of relativism

The extensive loss of normative authorities, which give direction to individual and collective life, is an experience that has led to a problem for many people. It is not just that lack of direction and the sense of being burdened or pressurised lead to the reduction of pluralism to the monoculturalism that I have outlined (Jäggle, 1995: 248; Ziebertz, 1993); over and above this we are experiencing the reaction to the view that it really does not matter which road we travel. Convictions other than our own are the concern of others. We expect to be left in peace with our own convictions. Disputes about their desirability and validity fade away before the generous 'permissiveness' to travel any road. As long as our own choice is not affected, 'anything goes'. This relativism simply underlines how self-evident pluralism has become and how it is considered unlikely that fundamental agreement is possible in all things (cf. Welsch, 1993: 322). At the same time, this relativism can be rooted in the best of motives: to support the convictions of a small group countering a majority view; to see diversity as an enriching 'colourful multiplicity'; to grant everyone the right to realise his or her own potential, and much more besides. A multicultural view can claim to seek to avoid the dangers associated with monocultural thinking.

But there are critics of the way a multicultural approach is turned into educational policy. These critics stress that the approach depends on a harmony of cultural elements that does not really exist. As a result, the majority elements could dominate, on the Darwinian pattern. The core of harmony inherent in the multicultural approach cannot contend against this. Nor can one see what dynamic formative forces are released by this approach, apart from the practice of tolerance. To put it more abstractly, relativism is problematical because it cannot be a matter of indifference what content we ascribe to concepts of 'human dignity' and 'human rights', what the objection to 'racism' is, whether 'peace and justice' are attainable or how 'humankind and nature are to be reconciled'. Seen pragmatically, humankind's way of life on this planet follows different paths. People must get on with each other, and future generations will have to bear the consequences of their decisions. We need agreement if we are to develop ways of life jointly. Then everything cannot be equally valid. To define which aspects of life are worth upholding is to make a normative statement which ill-accords with relativism. If we adopt the approach logically and argue that diversity is the highest value of all, we find ourselves in a dubious educational situation where, for instance, we would have to teach children to let contrary views on racism stand because they are equally valid.

Neither the relativism of the multicultural approach nor the latent exclusivity of the monocultural approach convinces. That being so, we need a third way.

Diversity, an issue in Intercultural Learning
Let us return to the question of how we can justify the approach posited by Intercultural Learning if we wish to avoid the weaknesses of both the monocultural and the multicultural approaches. A decisive

question is whether it is still permissible to assume unity in difference or how it may be brought about. Without some kind of unity in the sense of normative perspectives we can no more conceive of upbringing and education than of sensible living together (Otten and Treuheit, 1994). At first sight pluralism seems to embody the opposite of unity (Heelas, 1998; Parker, 1997). It seems so because frequently it is supposed that the presence of diversity is itself the aim, or, to put it another way, because there is diversity as it is, we must desire it as it is. But why should we draw this conclusion? Would it not be more sensible to develop educational concepts that do pluralism justice? Such concepts ought neither to dismiss nor avoid diversity; on the contrary, they must treat it as an issue, and in this connection four aspects deserve particular consideration in my view.

First, in a pluralist, multicultural society, unity is not something given but something to be worked for. Unity must be found in diversity. This finding occurs much more readily where learning aims at a process rather than a stock of things learnt. Finding unity means adopting the way of dialogue, with oneself and with others. In this, interactive and communicative aspects are more important than the accumulation of knowledge (Schlüter, 1994).

Second, one cannot have or produce unity in a pluralist, multicultural society without considering others. The road to cultural diversity is via others. Here a major part can be played by an anthropological perspective that is orientated towards the essential character of its subject, that is, the stranger or strangers: it is a matter of understanding these and allowing them to be different without our assuming attitudes of power. Young people must be able to recognise the limitations of their thinking. The move from what is central to oneself is the first step towards a change of perspective, towards the attempt to learn from what is foreign and to see as strangers see, to understand and learn to live with contrasts. Our perspective does not then require us to make what is different the same as what is our own or to incorporate it, but to recognise the dimensions of diversity and to understand them, so that we may ask what value we attach to their being generally desirable. The extension of our view may well imply that there is more truth in all perspectives taken together than in any one perspective alone (Ziebertz and van der Ven, 1996).

Third, assuming an attitude of power results particularly frequently from the experience of difference. Difference, competition and conflict are characteristic features of modern pluralism. One could use educational policy to take the sting out of these and follow a harmony model, concentrating on common elements which would all too easily neutralise contrasts; but it is the very acceptance of difference that is the critical test for the ability to practise tolerance and the basis for educational policies teaching us to live with difference (cf. Nicke, 1995: 242ff). Conflict is the problem, not consensus, and that is why diversity is definitely an issue that must be faced. Children and young people do not need to be protected from their everyday experiences. They must be equipped not to flounder when they meet them.

Fourth, for this we need an adequate discourse model (cf. Schlüter, 1994). An appropriate form of discourse would free communication from the compulsion to attain universal consensus or endure total heterogeneity and would, in my opinion, express a great sense of reality. Increasingly, agreement will be limited to issues that are partial and temporary, because the dynamics of change permit of no freezing of points of view. It is communicative action that helps to bring about cohesion. In this respect, communicative action is the final norm that we cannot ignore.

Learning to change and evaluate perspectives

To take the multicultural situation seriously and to help it to develop constructively means, therefore, that Intercultural Learning must seek out contact between conflicting claims and, indeed, face the duty and challenge of forcing the pace of cultural pluralism (Heytink and Tenorth, 1994).

The chief task of Intercultural Learning will have to be the preparation of students for life in diversity by addressing such diversity, and by helping them to develop appropriate strategies to look critically at diversity. In this way we recognise that we are all strangers and aliens to each other, more or less. At the same time, we have to be able to coexist, and so we need ways of coming to an understanding about the aims of our actions.

Intercultural Learning (and interreligious, too) must help pupils to practise new ways of changing their perspectives. This is not primarily a matter of defining what is one's 'own' and what is 'foreign', but above all of recognising how we perceive our 'own' and the 'foreign'. We therefore do not simply ask, 'what are other religious perceptions like?', but also, 'how do we wish to approach other cultural traditions and religions, and how do we let them approach us?' This theory of learning, which does not at this stage touch on the question of suitability of age or development, aims at practising decentralised and reciprocal exchange of perspectives. With reference to 'Hermeneutics of the Foreign/Strange' (Schäfer, 1991), we are able to describe four modes of encountering other cultures and religions. They show how 'faithfulness to one's own' and 'openness towards the foreign' can be seen together.

The first mode sees the foreign as *counter-image*. This relationship-mode is rooted in the feeling of being threatened. Anyone studying the European press will repeatedly encounter concrete examples of the counter-image model, for example Islamic and Jewish fundamentalism. Islam and Judaism are identified with fundamentalist movements, which are seen as threatening. This threat is countered by taking up position behind barriers. This can culminate in 'hatred of Turks' for instance.

The second mode sees the foreign as a *sounding-board* for one's own tradition. What may still be discovered of this tradition is seen as the result of a process of emancipation; by contrast, the foreign has retained a certain naturalness and is imbued with symbols of a lost unity. One example is western instrumental thinking about nature, emancipation from the wholeness of the creation, followed by the rediscovery of wholeness, particularly through eastern, African and native American religiosity.

The third mode sees the foreign as an *amplification* of one's own tradition. This makes the 'blind spots' of one's own world visible and asks what possibilities of enrichment the foreign tradition may offer. Examples of this are the renaissance of myths, forms of eastern wisdom and meditation, the richness of other rites (dramatic staging, dance, movement) compared, for example, with the Christian liturgy, which, in its Roman-Catholic form, seems to practise kneeling and standing as its only physical movements.

The fourth mode sees the foreign as something *complementary*. What is foreign cannot simply be absorbed into one's own tradition; instead, there are reciprocating autonomies, which can also allow nonintegrability as a component. Implicit in this model is the important notion that one's own tradition cannot tolerate a limitless assimilation of foreign ideas, nor that the 'foreign' can be understood and assimilated without reservation.

It cannot be the case that we should prefer only *one way* of experiencing the foreign and reject others. All four modes of encounter are to be seen as ways of human experience.

The model of the 'counter-image' seeks to set limits to the foreign. If this were the *only* perspective it would undermine intercultural and interreligious learning, There may, however, be circumstances that require limits to be set. If all religions are not to be valued equally and deemed to be equally good, it must be possible to find criteria for the determination of values. For instance, we need in a western context to determine what place the individual has in a religion. This first perspective is *relative* compared with the other three modes of encounter.

The 'sounding-board' and 'amplification' models harness the foreign for their own purposes. Thus, they revive their own nearly-lost traditions, or they draw attention to problem areas that are not to be found in their own cultural and religious tradition but that can enrich it. At the same time the bounds of their own tradition predominate. They are less concerned with understanding the foreign than with its interpretation within their own culture and religion. These perspectives, too, may be legitimate and useful; in connection with the *other* three modes they are *relative*.

Finally, the 'complementarity' model embraces the foreign and the native as complementary notional structures. Differences on one side or the other are recognised. Differences are not 'relative'; nor can they be accommodated in a unitary 'super-structure'. The possibility of mutual understanding is to be found in the penetration of complementarity. At the same time complementary thinking takes us to the bounds of understanding itself. This way of thinking seems to offer us the most fruitful model in our approach to cultural and religious pluralism. However, on developmental and psychological grounds it can only show its worth when applied to older pupils.

As these four modes represent what is actually experienced, it is important that all four are expounded in schools. Pupils should be able to recognise that they express the reality of all four in different situations. But they should also learn how great the scope is of the different modes. This extension of perspectives makes clear that there are problems behind an either/or attitude. It demonstrates the weakness of the attitude that rejects the validity of one particular point of view and instead declares every point of view acceptable and exchangeable. It also shows that there are limits to encounter, that reciprocal autonomy must be respected and that this must not lead back to the erection of mental barriers.

If we are to concern ourselves with other cultural traditions and religions it must be a concrete aim to understand the importance of becoming aware of the encounter modes. At the same time, the fourth mode of complementarity seems decisive to me, if we are to develop it as a didactic framework of perceptions for a dialogue-orientated religious education system. Within this, native and foreign are equally respected. With this we arrive at the dual conclusion that foreign traditions are not available for unlimited adaptation and that the native area must be protected against inflationary expansion. And yet native and foreign must not be consigned to a failure of communication. If we can throw light on the contexts of intercultural and interreligious learning, we shall also see clearly that in the last resort we are concerned with our own cultural and religious understanding and with the following questions: where do we stand, what do we adhere to, what do we believe in? Our dialogue with the foreign must not divert us from our own religious identity, but can lead us to it.

Conclusion

We may conclude that Intercultural Learning is, therefore, not only a cultural comparison but the pursuit of mutual obligations within diversity. Its method is not to let things be, but friction. The attitude it expresses is not a sense of regret for lost unity, not fear of diversity, but readiness to develop stuctures. Where there are divergent claims there must be no forced decisions, nor can they be simply avoided. Knowing that because of human limitations there is no perfect solution to what the true, genuine and good life is, we are charged under the conditions of pluralism to look for orientation norms and discuss their validity. Every point of view is a question addressed to all others. Validity has to be struggled for again and again, not outside diversity, but within it. The Christian religion can no longer produce this unity (in Europe) for all. Nonetheless, religion remains a central factor in the culture of certain populations, and is, therefore, already a part of intercultural learning processes. However, we need to speak about religion in the plural. Often enough religions have themselves been involved in a deplorable way in processes of monocultural polarisation. Of course, increasing attention is also being paid to the signs of the times within and between the religions and to the search for those possibilities of encounter that aim at understanding, mutual respect and tolerance. Because the idea of permanent and effective Intercultural Learning is unthinkable if interreligious learning processes are excluded (Heimbrock, 1993; Schlüter, 1995; Ziebertz, 1994b), we are here concerned with joint tasks in educational theory and theology or in religious education. In this field it could be a particular task for religious education to bring to light the potential for understanding that is implicit in the religions, namely, the inviolability of the dignity of men and women, peace, justice and the preservation of the creation.

References

Auernheimer, G. (1990), *Einführung in die interkulturelle Erziehung,* Darmstadt, Wissenschaftliche Buchgesellschaft.

Bukow, W.D. and Llaryora, R. (1993), *Mitbürger aus der Fremde,* Opladen, Westdeutscher Verlag.

Heimbrock, H.-G. (1993), Interreligiöses lernen. religionsunterricht in Deutschland zwischen singularismus und multikulturalität, *Evangelischer Erzieher,* 45, 573-586.

Heelas, P. (ed.) (1998), *Religion, Modernity and Postmodernity,* Oxford, Blackwell.

Heytink, F. and Tenorth, H.-E. (eds) (1994), *Pädagogik und Pluralismus,* Weinheim, Deutscher Studien Verlag.

Jäggle, M. (1995), Religionspädagogik im Kontext interkulturellen Lernens, in H.-G. Ziebertz and W. Simon (eds), *Bilanz der Religionspädagogik,* pp 243-258, Düsseldorf, Patmos.

Knitter, P.F. (1985), *No Other Name? A critical survey of Christian attitudes toward the world religions,* Maryknoll, New York, Orbis Books.

Krewer, B. and Eckensberger, L. (1991), Selbstentwicklung und kulturelle Identität, in K. Hurrelmann and D. Ulich (eds), *Handbuch der Sozialisationsforschung,* pp 573-594, Weinheim and Basel, Beltz.

Miksch, J. (ed.) (1991), *Deutschland: Einheit in kultureller Vielfalt,* Frankfurt, Otto Lembeck.

Nieke, W. (1995), *Interkulturelle Erziehung und Bildung,* Opladen, Leske and Budrich.

Otten, H. and Treuheit, W. (eds) (1994), *Interkulturelles Lernen in Theorie und Praxis,* Opladen, Leske and Budrich.

Parker, S. (1997), *Reflective Teaching in the Postmodern World,* Buckingham, Open University Press.

Schäffter, O. (ed.) (1991), *Das Fremde,* Opladen, Westdeutscher Verlag.

Schlüter, R. (1994), *Ökumenisches Lernen und interkulturelles Lernen: eine theologische und pädagogische Herausforderung*, pp 27-53, Lembeck, Bonifazius.

Schlüter, R. (1995), Religionspädagogik im Kontext ökumenischen Lernens, in H.-G. Ziebertz and W. Simon (eds), *Bilanz der Religionspädagogik*, pp 176-192, Düsseldorf, Patmos.

Silbermann, A. and Hüsers, F. (1995), *Der 'normale' Haß auf die Fremden*, München, Beck

Welsch, W. (1993), *Unsere postmoderne Moderne*, Berlin, Akademie Verlag.

Ziebertz, H.-G. (1993), Religious pluralism and religious education, *Journal of Empirical Theology*, 6 (2), 78-98

Ziebertz, H.-G. (1994a), Theologischer kontext der religionendidaktik, *Christlich Pädagogische Blätter*, 107 (2), 13-19.

Ziebertz, H.-G. (1994b), *Religionspädagogik als empirische Wissenschaft*, pp 105-194, Weinheim, Deutscher Studien Verlag.

Ziebertz, H.-G. and Ven, J.A v.d., (1996), Religion in religious education: an empirical study in the Netherlands and Germany, *Panorama: international journal of comparative religious education and values*, 8, 135-145.

CONTRIBUTORS

The Revd Professor Jeff Astley is Director of the North of England Institute for Christian Education and Honorary Professorial Fellow in Practical Theology and Christian Education in the University of Durham. His recent publications include *Learning in the Way: research and reflection on adult Christian education* (2000) and *God's World* (2000).

The Revd Professor Leslie J. Francis is Director of the Welsh National Centre for Religious Education and Professor of Practical Theology at the University of Wales, Bangor. His recent publications include *Joining and Leaving Religion: research perspectives* (2000, co-edited with Yaacov J. Katz); *Religion in Education 3* (2000, co-edited with William K. Kay) and *The Values Debate: a voice from the pupils* (2001).

Dr J. Mark Halstead is Reader in Moral Education at the University of Plymouth and Director of the RIMSCUE Centre. His recent publications include *Education in Morality* (1999, co-edited with Terence H. McLaughlin), *The Development of Values, Attitudes and Personal Qualities: a review of recent research* (2000, co-authored with Monica J. Taylor), and 'Philosophy and Moral Education: the contribution of John Wilson', a special issue of the *Journal of Moral Education* (2000, co-edited with Terence H. McLaughlin).

Professor Brian V. Hill enters the new millennium as Emeritus Professor of Education, Murdoch University, Western Australia. His recent publications include *Beyond the Transfer of Knowledge: spirituality in theological education* (1998) and articles on 'The search for meaning in the academy: a personal reflection' (1999), 'Education and the planet in crisis: old wine for a new millennium?' (2000) and 'Seeking a value consensus for education' (2000).

Professor Mary Elizabeth Mullino Moore is Professor of Religion and Education, and Director of the Program for Women in Theology and Ministry, Candler School of Theology, Emory University, Atlanta, Georgia. Her recent publications include *Teaching from the Heart:*

theology and educational method (1998), *Ministering with the Earth* (1998), and articles on 'Teaching for justice and reconciliation in a conflicted world' (1999) and 'Sacramental teaching: mediating the holy' (2000).

Dr Eleanor Nesbitt is Senior Lecturer in Religions and Education in the Institute of Education, University of Warwick. Her recent publications include *The Religious Lives of Sikh Children* (2000) and *Guru Nanak* (1999, with Gopinder Kaur).

Mandy Robbins is Teaching and Research Fellow in the Centre for Ministry Studies, University of Wales, Bangor. Her recent publications include *The Long Diaconate 1987-1994: women deacons and the delayed journey to priesthood* (1999) and 'Leaving before adolescence: profiling the child no longer in the church' (2000).

Professor Friedrich Schweitzer is Professor of Religious Education and Practical Theology at the Tübingen Protestant Faculty of Theology. He is co-editor of the *German Yearbook of Religious Studies* and of the German journal of *Education and Theology*. His recent publications include *The Child's Right to Religion (Das Recht des Kindes auf Religion*, Guetersloh, 2000).

Professor Heinz Streib is Professor for Religious Education and Ecumenical Theology at the University of Bielefeld, Germany. His recent publications include *Biographies in Christian Fundamentalist Milieus and Organizations* (2000), *Wege der Entzauberung. Jugendliche Sinnsuche und Okkultfaszination* (2000, co-authored with Albrecht Schöll) and *Faith Development Theory Revisited: the religious styles perspective* (2001).

Dr Andrew Wright is Lecturer in Religious and Theological Education at King's College London, where he is Programme Director of the MA in Religious Education and responsible for doctoral research students in the Centre for Theology, Religion and Culture. His recent publications include *Learning to Teach Religious Education in the Secondary School* (2000, with Ann-Marie Brandom) and *Spirituality and Education* (2000).

Professor Hans-Georg Ziebertz is Professor of Religious Education at the Faculty of Theology at the University of Wuerzburg (Germany). He is head of the empirical theological research programme *Religious Education in Plurality*. His recent publications include *Religion, Christentum und Moderne* (1999).

Name Index

A

Albrow, M., 159, 160, 174
Alisat, S., 190, 195
Andersen, S., 45
Appleby, R.S., 163, 175, 177, 196
Armstrong, F., 117, 133
Arnst, C., 118, 133
Arora, R., 140, 153
Astley, J., 6, 9, 10, 17, 22, 26, 27, 29, 31, 33, 34, 37, 38, 40, 41, 239
Attfield, D., 88, 93
Auernheimer, G., 222, 224, 237
Augustine, D.S., 117, 133
Austin, W.H., 33, 38

B

Bains, T.S., 152, 153
Balding, J., 47, 76
Ballard, R., 147, 153
Baltes, P.B., 197
Banner, M.C., 28, 38
Barbour, I.G., 17, 25, 27, 28, 30, 32, 33, 38, 39
Barker, M., 47, 78
Barnes, C., 146, 154
Barot, R., 155
Barrier, N.G., 153, 154, 156
Barrow, J., 151, 153
Barton, L., 117, 133
Batson, C.D., 48, 76
Baudrillard, J., 11, 79, 81-86, 91, 93, 95
Bauman, Z., 83-85, 91, 93
Baumann, G., 141, 153
Beauboeuf-Lafontant, T., 117, 133
Beaudoin, T., 186, 195
Beck, U., 159, 174, 175
Beckford, J.A., 175

Beedy, J., 188, 197
Benjamin, H., 98, 112
Berger, P.L., 49, 76, 105, 112, 165, 176, 185, 195
Berkhof, H., 17, 38
Berkowitz, M., 196
Bernal, J.D., 34, 38
Bernstein, R.J., 213, 217
Bertens, H., 81, 93
Beyer, P., 162-165, 174
Bhaskar, R., 37, 38
Bibby, R.W., 49, 50, 76
Blos, P., 192, 195
Bouma, G.D., 48, 49, 76
Bouma-Prediger, S., 25, 38
Bowers, C.A., 130, 131, 133
Bowman, M., 153
Brackley, P., 118, 134
Bromley, D.G., 176
Brook, L., 78
Brooke, J.H., 17, 38
Bruce, S., 50, 78
Bukow, W.D., 223, 237
Bultmann, R., 22, 38
Bushnell, H., 143, 153
Butler, R., 140, 144, 152, 153
Butterfield, H., 17, 38
Butterwegge, C., 174

C

Campbell, W.S., 40, 94
Campbell, G., 54, 76
Carey, J., 118, 133
Casanova, J., 164, 174
Cashmore, E., 59, 76
Chalmers, A.F., 37, 38
Clark, S.R.L., 25, 39, 41, 42
Clifford, J., 137, 154

General Index